RAIDERS
THE WORLD'S
ÉLITE STRIKE FORCES

BATTLE STANDARDS MILITARY PAPERBACKS FROM DAVID & CHARLES

BATTLE STANDARDS

THE RAIDERS

THE WORLD'S ÉLITE STRIKE FORCES

RICHARD GARRETT

A DAVID & CHARLES MILITARY BOOK

British Library Cataloguing in Publication Data

Garrett, Richard.
    The raiders: the elite strike forces that
    altered the course of war and history.
    1. Commando troops—History
    I. Title
    355.4'22   U262

    ISBN 0-7153-9203-4

First published 1980 in hardback
by David & Charles Publishers plc
This paperback edition published 1988
by David & Charles Publishers plc
and printed in Great Britain
by Redwood Burn Limited, Trowbridge, Wiltshire
for David & Charles Publishers plc
Brunel House   Newton Abbot   Devon

Distributed in the United States by Sterling Publishing Co Inc
2 Park Avenue, New York, NY 10016

Cover photographs
Front: U.S Marine Corps (Force Recom) on excercise.
Back: U.S. soldiers in Vietnam.
        Both pictures courtesy of the U.S. Department of Defence.
        Transparencies from Aerospace Publishing

Contents

Introduction

In 1940, when Britain was very close to defeat, the Commandos came into being. So far as the British Army was concerned, they were a novelty. Before that date the idea of small units fighting independently against much greater formations had never been considered by the British; nor had attacking an enemy coastline by stealth, or using methods that seemed to owe more to gangsterism than to the honourable profession of soldiering. Significantly, the chief sponsor of these irregular forces was a civilian (Winston Churchill), though certain regular officers were quick to see their value.

On a somewhat wider basis, however, raiding is as old as history itself; indeed, it might be argued that this was how warfare began. But when large armies are on the march, or when the tide of affairs turns (as it had done by 1944), so do the raiders' assignments change. They lose much of their independence, and tend to become the spearhead of a very much larger formation. The North African landings of 1942—and, indeed, D-Day itself—are examples of this.

Similarly, in the Korean War, US Rangers fought as an integral part of army divisions. During the final months, they were disbanded completely, and the men scattered among ordinary battalions.

But there is another reason for raiding—a psychological one. When British troops burned Washington in 1814, nobody could have imagined that it would directly affect the war's outcome. But it must have seemed impressive. Similarly, the Franco-British landing on the island of Aland in 1854 had no great strategic purpose. It did, however, convince tax-payers that all these soldiers and sailors were not wasting their time (and the nation's money) enjoying the summer weather of the Baltic, and doing little to advance the Allied fortunes.

In this respect, raiding comes under the heading of 'public relations'—a form of verbal warfare much practised by commerce. In the future, this may very well be its chief purpose, for the rattle of a commando's knife makes less noise than that of a sabre; the advance of an army will probably cause a war, whilst the quick arrival and departure of raiders may produce more moderate reactions. The battle-ground will not be some shell-battered stretch of land, but the tolerably comfortable quarters of the UN's Security Council.

The raid on Entebbe airport demonstrates my meaning. The sudden snatch of a plane-load of hostages certainly attracted the world's notice—and even, in most cases, its admiration. But that was as far as it went. The invasion of Uganda by large forces might possibly have sparked off World War III.

In this book, I have attempted to write a history of raiders, and to illustrate it by a dozen such operations. In view of the richness of World War II material, it has been difficulty to decide what to omit. In many, though by no means all, instances, the techniques employed were similar. Surprise, speed, and expertise in the use of weapons and ground, are qualities without which nobody engaged in this kind of operation can hope to survive for long. But, in each case, the purpose has been different, and my work may, perhaps, provide a small catalogue of raiding's applications—especially when it involves the arrival of such forces from another element (the sea or, sometimes, the sky).

A great many people have helped me with the research for this book. I should like to thank especially, the librarians of the London Library, the Imperial War Museum, the National Maritime Museum, the National Army Museum and officials at the Public Record Office. I have also had reason to be grateful to Colonel J. E. Greenwood, of the US Marine Corps— Deputy Director for Marine Corps History, Colonel Lowell Bulger of the United States Marine Raider Association, Robert L. Brown—also of the United States Marine Raider Association, who did me the honour of making me an 'Honorary Raider', to my cousin—Lieutenant Colonel Bliss Croft, US

Army (Retired), and to far too many other former raiders to be listed here. Without their assistance, this work would have been impossible.

Richard Garrett

Prologue

During the 15th century BC on an unnamed day between the years 1475 and 1449, the Egyptian King Thutmosis III decided to attack the port of Jaffa. He entrusted the operation to a Captain Thute—a man who had already distinguished himself in the sovereign's precociously efficient secret service. Thute had a fine sense of the economics of warfare. The perfect operation, he believed, was one in which the gains were out of all proportion to the numbers of men and materials used.

If he besieged Jaffa, the proceedings would be long and expensive. How much better to adopt a more subtle approach. Instead of pitting his men against the port's substantial defences, he decided to take it from within.

He selected 200 crack troops. On the voyage, from Alexandria, each was baled up in a flour sack. Other soldiers, disguised as civilian labourers, carried them from the dock to a point well within the walls. The parcelled warriors—none the worse from an uncomfortable experience—cut themselves loose and took the garrison by surprise. Jaffa fell at a very moderate cost. Captain Thute can fairly be described as the world's first commando officer.

Whether the Greeks really employed a wooden horse for the reduction of Troy is a matter for speculation. If they did, it achieved what nearly ten years of conventional warfare had failed to accomplish. According to legend, the idea was conceived by a general named Epeius. He was obviously a soldier of rare imagination.

While carpenters were busy building this giant semblance of an animal, Epeius withdrew the greater part of the army to a neighbouring island. He correctly assumed that the Trojan king, Priam, would take this as a sign that the campaign was coming to an end. After all, there had been disputes within the Greeks' high command; many troops had died of plague; several heroic warriors had been killed; and the walls of Troy were still intact. To abandon the struggle might be sensible.

Once the horse had been completed, a small force of shock troops was concealed inside it. The Trojans were invited to accept this elegant, if rather cumbersome, masterpiece on behalf of the goddess Athena. Priam, despite the misgivings of his daughter Cassandra, agreed, The city gates were opened, and the counterfeit gift was wheeled in.

That night, the Greek warriors returned from the island. By dawn, there were about 100,000 deployed at the city's approaches. Their comrades inside the horse suddenly emerged. They rushed the main gates and opened them. Within an hour or two, Troy had been transformed into a place of fire and death.

In Northern Europe, Britain's shores have been the scene of many attacks by raiders—and, indeed, by invaders. The first of which there is any documentary evidence is Caesar's excursion in 55 BC. Designed as a punitive expedition, it could not be accounted a success.

Caesar's plan was to employ a force of 10,200 infantry supported by a strong formation of cavalry. The infantry, squeezed together in eighty transports escorted across the Strait of Dover by war galleys, made the trip successfully. At 10.00 on an August morning, they fought their way ashore at a point on the coast of Kent between Deal and Walmer. The horsemen, unfortunately, did not turn up. The naval officer in charge miscalculated the tides and the wind. The vessels never moved far from their point of departure near Boulogne.

But, even if they had arrived, it seems doubtful whether they could have accomplished a great deal. Later in the day, the weather deteriorated. With the prospect of a storm hurling the ships on to an unkind shore, the legions were hurriedly re-embarked and returned to their bases in France.

Next year, profiting no doubt by the mistakes, the cavalry arrived according to plan, and the expeditionary force penetrated inland as far as Wheathampstead in what is now

Hertfordshire.

The Roman expeditions were the work of tolerably large formations. The Viking pirates, perhaps, came closer to the concept of latter-day commandos. Between 786 and 802 AD, they carried out an incalculable number of raids on the coasts of Scotland, England and Ireland. They came in small numbers, arriving unexpectedly and moving quickly. On foot, they marched in single file—though they usually rounded up all the horses in the vicinity of the beach-head. Mounted on these extempore chargers, they galloped inland, burning and looting. Presently, rich with plunder, they returned to the ship and departed on the next tide. Surprise, speed, mobility—the Vikings had all the essentials of irregular warfare. They also had a shrewd awareness of the best targets to select. Religious communities figured high on their lists of priorities. For one thing, many of them possessed considerable wealth; for another, the landings were unlikely to be opposed.

Holy Island at Lindisfarne off the Northumbrian coast was one favourite objective. By all accounts, the monks were warned of an impending raid by the appearances of lightning and dragons in the sky, and by blood dripping from the roof of St Peter's church in York. But such omens were not very specific and could not be relied upon. Nor, indeed, could a small flock of devout and peaceful men have done much against these tough warriors.

The Norman invasion of England in 1066 was an impressive feat of organisation. A force of about 8,000 soldiers was transported from France to Pevensey on the Sussex coast—using 600 transports screened by twenty-eight war galleys. The weather was perfect; and, since Harold and his Saxons were busy fighting an army of Norwegians up in Yorkshire, the landing was unopposed.

But, even if Harold's men had been on the shore, it seems unlikely that the outcome would have been affected. William had archers in his army; the Saxon king had none. With these bowmen supplying a barrage of covering fire, the Norman troops would have been able to struggle ashore. The site of the battle would have been nearer the sea; but William, one suspects, would still have earned the title of 'Conqueror'.

The Romans and the Normans provide good examples of combined operations using conventional forces in a standard military setting. But the essence of raiding (a description that cannot be applied to the Norman invasion) is its versatility. On at least one occasion, it achieved the effects of a successful naval battle and at a much more moderate cost.

After the defeat of the Armada in 1588, the Spaniards rebuilt their fleet. Less than ten years later, it was larger and better equipped than its ill-fated predecessor. With squadrons based at Cadiz and Ferrol, it seemed uncomfortably likely that England might be once more in jeopardy.

English sailors accumulated a good deal of experience of raiding during expeditions against Spanish colonies in the West Indies and Central America. As the Earl of Essex and Lord Howard of Effingham saw matters, this technique could be used for more strategic purposes. Rather than wait for the men-of-war to emerge from harbour, they could be destroyed while riding at their anchors.

A force, led by Essex and Howard, set sail from England in 1596. A great deal depended upon surprise. It was announced that the vessels were heading for Brittany. Inevitably, the news reached the ears of the Spanish naval authorities, who seem to have believed it.

On passage, the English ships were screened by smaller units—which kept at a distance any inquisitive eyes likely to be interested in them. The result was that the raid took the defences at Cadiz completely unawares. The English penetrated into the harbour; soldiers were put ashore, whilst others swarmed aboard men-of-war at the anchorage. Within a short space of time, forty warships and merchantmen were destroyed, and a considerable amount of stores went up in smoke. The damage was estimated at 12 million ducats—a very considerable sum.

During the 18th century, a new breed of soldier was born in North America. Known as 'Rangers', these men belonged to levies that ranged the forests to protect settlers against the depredations of the Indians. They were not products of the drill sergeant's art, but farmers and hunters—men who were crack shots and had an instinctive understanding of how to use ground to the best advantage. Lightly armed, and not burdened by the heavy trappings of an elegant though not very practical

uniform, they could travel much more quickly than conventional troops. Amateurs they may have been, but for this kind
of work they were much more effective than their professional
counterparts.

When the Seven Years' War broke out in 1756, it became
very clear that the North American Indians would side with
the French against the British colonists. Much of the trouble
would be likely to come from the region around Crown Point—
at the southern end of Lake Champlain and on the edge of the
Adirondack Mountains. Crown Point, clearly, would have to
be taken and a garrison installed there.

The men best equipped to handle Indian warfare were the
Rangers, whose own methods were not dissimilar to those of
the Indians. The task of assembling a unit and carrying out
the operations was given to a man named Robert Rogers, the
son of an Irish immigrant. Rogers Senior was a farmer and
hunter who had met his death some years earlier at the hands
of a friend—who (or so the story goes) shot him in mistake for
a bear. Rogers himself had grown up with a sound understanding of conditions in the forests and mountains and and on
the water. He had travelled over many miles of wild country,
where there were no roads and a man had to be self-reliant.
He understood—and was,indeed, sympathetic towards—the
Indians. Nevertheless, he was ruthless enough when it came to
fighting.

Rogers' Rangers, which included regulars in their ranks,
were given the task of a reconnaissance force. Although irregulars, they had to conform to what he called his 'Plan of
Discipline'. This meant that, just as any other soldiers, they
were subject to the articles of war. They had to be present at
roll call, and ready to go into action at very short notice. When
on patrol, they moved in single file to present a smaller target.
At night, half the formation remained on guard while the
others slept.

The principles governing their deployment have served as an
inspiration for such operations ever since. First of all, they had
to maintain their objective—to win by taking the offensive.
They had to exploit the virtue of surprise (which depended on
faultless security), and each company had to be economic in
terms of men and materials. Speed and mobility counted for a

great deal. What was more, while armies of regular soldiers ceased campaigning during the cold months and moved into winter quarters, the Rangers remained in action. They fought wearing snowshoes; they fought from boats; they even fought on skates. Rogers demanded toughness and endurance from his men, but he set them a good example. He could, according to his biographers, out-march, out-row, and out-fight any one of them.

By supplying the army commander with information, this paragon of campaigning virtue and his rough-living warriors became popular with the military authorities. They also demonstrated their talents by mounting effective ambushes, and by destroying French settlements suspected of helping the enemy. More units were formed; Rogers, now a major, was given command of all such forces.

When, in 1758, an opposed landing was made at Louisburg, four companies of Rangers (600 men) fought beside grenadiers and light infantry units. Their performance was so good that when, in the following year, Wolfe was planning his assault on Quebec, he was encouraged by George II to include these troops in his advance guard. He asked for the assistance of Rogers himself, but the commander-in-chief, General Jeffrey Amherst, insisted on his presence at army headquarters.

The taking of Quebec was a major military operation. Nevertheless, broken down into its components, it had several characteristics of a successful commando raid: the putting ashore of a force by stealth on an enemy-held coast, the inclusion of troops such as the Rangers and the Light Infantry (whose marksmanship and mobility gave them a strong affinity with the less regular soldiers), and the intelligent judgement of the tide's effect on the landing craft. Indeed, Wolfe excelled in combined operations—possibly because, in the disastrous expedition to destroy the French base at Rochefort in 1757, he had experienced a classic example of how such things should *not* be done.

Nearly two centuries and a good many wars lay between the careers of William Pitt and Winston Churchill. The two men, however, had several things in common. One of them was the conviction that, if an hostile army occupied the coast of France, it should be harassed unceasingly.

In 1757, Pitt was anxious to ease the pressure on the Prussian and Hanoverian armies by creating a diversion. Intelligence reports suggested that the Channel and Biscay coast were lightly guarded. A raid in force was likely to meet with only moderate opposition. If it were successful, it might compel the French to withdraw forces from their operations in the East.

The most promising target seemed to be Rochefort where, according to a British Officer who had passed through the town shortly before war broke out, a massive arsenal was guarded by a comparatively small garrison. Indeed, if this man was to be believed, there were no more than 10,000 French troops strung out along the coasts of the English Channel and the Bay of Biscay. The destruction of Rochefort and its store of ammunition should be easy enough.

A force consisting of ten regiments of infantry, fifty light horse and a contingent of gunners was assembled. To convey it to Rochefort, there was a fleet of transports equipped with barges for putting the troops ashore, sixteen ships-of-the-line and an assortment of frigates, fireships and bomb-ketches. The only thing the expedition (of which Wolfe was Quartermaster-General) lacked was an adequate commander-in-chief. For want of anyone better, a prematurely senile general named Sir John Mordaunt was given the appointment. In his youth, he had been a brave and thrusting officer. Now, at sixty, he was prone to spasms of nervous irritability. But, what was more pertinent to this present assignment, he was almost incapable of making a decision.

The force sailed towards its objective; and, presently, it returned. All that it had accomplished was the destruction of one small fort on an island at the approaches to Rochefort. A venture that cost at least £1 million had accounted for the lives of perhaps thirty-five Frenchmen. That was all. Mordaunt had dithered, ignored the advice of the navy, and then—convinced that two days of useless discussions had taken away the precious element of surprise (which it had, though this was unimportant; there were no available French reinforcements in the vicinity)—pronounced the mission too dangerous. It was an excellent example of how to bungle a good idea.

In 1809, the ineptitude of Mordaunt was matched by a military expedition to the island of Walcheren. The main objective was to destroy French naval power in Flanders by wiping out the base at Flushing, demolishing the dockyard at Antwerp, and by either sinking or capturing ships in the lower Scheldt. Two years had passed since the operation had been conceived; and, even on the point of departure, there were unnecessary delays.

Strategically, the idea was sound; indeed, if it had succeeded, it might also have eased the strain on the Prussians who were again under pressure. But, once there, the commander-in-chief (ironically, Pitt's eldest son—the second Earl of Chatham) showed himself incapable of taking any decisive action. The army, instead of making a rapid advance, was kept hanging about in the vicinity of Flushing. The French withdrew their ships to an anchorage higher up the Scheldt and reinforced their garrisons. Then the weather turned nasty. An epidemic of fever broke out, and the troops died at the rate of 200 to 300 a week. Eventually, the operation was called off with nothing accomplished.

Rogers had understood; Wolfe had understood; the Viking raiders, and the men who set fire to the Spanish fleet at Cadiz realised it; even Thutmosis III seems to have been aware of it; the essence of such operations is a sharp awareness of the objective, a decisiveness, a determination to press matters forward—and, then, surprise and speed. In the early part of the 19th century, there was one naval officer who had demonstrated what could be done. His name was Lord Thomas Cochrane. Unfortunately few people took Cochrane's exploits seriously, and he received no rewards for his initiative. Napoleon, who dubbed him 'Le loup des mers' (sea wolf), had more respect for him than the British powers in Whitehall; and yet, in 1808, this brilliant seaman—with no more than the crew of one frigate, its complement of Marines, and a few not very able-bodied Spaniards—delayed the advance of an entire French army.

1 The Fort

On 16 February, 5 1808, Napoleon's forces, already in Spain as the result of a Franco-Spanish attack on Portugal, marched into Madrid and occupied it. Two weeks later, they took over Barcelona. On 2 May, a furious populace rose up against the French in Madrid. In June, when the Spanish monarch was replaced by Bonaparte's brother Joseph, the revolution spread across the country. The days when the two nations had fought side by side were over. The Peninsular War had begun.

In the late autumn of that year, an army commanded by General St Cyr set off from southern France. Its objects were to reinforce the Barcelona garrison, and to wipe out the Spanish forces in Catalonia. It was composed of 6,000 French troops augmented by Italians and Swiss. The one obstacle in its eighty-or-so mile path was a coastal town of normally small importance, Rosas.

Once this huddle of houses—guarded by a citadel within, and by the battered hulk of a castle named Fort Trinidad on the nearby cliff-edge—had been taken, the way to the west would be clear. Beyond that, the prospect for independently minded Spaniards was bleak.

The British commander-in-chief in the Mediterranean was Admiral Lord Cuthbert Collingwood. Collingwood had served under Nelson. He was an officer who applauded dash; who appreciated personal initiative—even when it took an unorthodox turn. He had been particularly impressed by the captain of the frigate HMS *Imperieuse*: a tall, lanky Scotsman with a mop of red hair named Lord Thomas Cochrane, heir to the earldom of Dundonald.

So far as Their Lordships at the Admiralty were concerned, Cochrane was a problem. Outspoken, daring and with small regard for conventional methods, his record was impressive. On several occasions, he had engaged in actions that more cautious commanders might have avoided. He was considered impetuous, even foolhardy, but his rashness had paid off in the shape of a handsome number of captured ships. In each case, and often against more powerful opponents, the vessels had been taken at the cost of only small casualties.

This was important, for Cochrane was a commanding officer who showed concern for his men. He seemed to regard each death in action as though it were a personal tragedy. But even this did not please his masters. On one occasion, the irrascible First Lord, Earl St Vincent, refused one of Cochrane's officers promotion on the grounds that too few of the ship's company had been killed. Without death, it seemed, there could be no glory.

Whether Cochrane made his superiors uncomfortably aware of their own shortcomings, or whether his somewhat original handling of situations made them uneasy, this ebulliently clever officer was heartily disliked in Whitehall. It was, perhaps, to Collingwood's credit that he openly displayed so much faith in him.

At an earlier meeting in Gibraltar during the late spring of 1808, the Admiral had given Cochrane orders to assist the Spaniards by every means in his power. It may not have been very specific, but it gave *Imperieuse's* captain ample scope for his initiative. In early November, the frigate and her intrepid commanding officer were sailing off Barcelona, lobbing rockets onto the French, and generally making a nuisance of themselves to the occupying power. Through his telescope, Cochrane was able to watch the operations on shore, in which ill-equipped Spanish troops were ranged against wretchedly unequal odds.

He received a more detailed view of the situation when a party of Spanish officers rowed out to the ship. Everything, they stressed, depended on time. The revolutionary council at Gerona, about thirty miles inland, had promised substantial reinforcements. Once they arrived, the French would be hurled back in disorder. They might even be prised out of Barcelona.

Cochrane may have believed them, though the situation seemed to be deteriorating rapidly. Then, on 19 November, he was told that St Cyr's units had reached the outskirts of Rosas, and he decided that the time had come to intervene on land. The *Imperieuse* turned away from Barcelona, and set off on a north-easterly course towards the beleaguered town. The sea was calm, the visibility, good; but the wind was dropping. On the following day, it died out completely. Ten miles from her objective, the frigate lay becalmed. Cochrane gave orders to drop anchor.

The impatient officer was not to be put off by an indolent wind. Although there was another frigate, HMS *Fame*, on station in Rosas Bay, he may have suspected that the situation required his personal intervention. As events of the next day or so made clear, he was correct.

That afternoon, the spasmodic sounds of gunfire to the north-east suggested that a heavy exchange of shells was taking place between *Fame* and the French batteries on the heights above the town. Shortly after nightfall, he was rowed ashore in the ship's gig. By 9.00 pm, he was conferring with the Spaniards. The state of affairs was even worse than he had expected. Ten days before, on the 9th, the French artillery had pounded a breach in the citadel. The reinforcements from Gerona had not arrived; unless some sort of miracle occurred, these men were proposing to surrender.

Cochrane ordered the crew of the gig back to the ship. The coxswain was to present his compliments to the second-in-command, and ask him to get under way with all possible speed. By dawn, he ought to be in a position to rake the French positions with gunshot.

But the wind refused to stir itself, and *Imperieuse* languished at anchor. Urgent though it was, the bombardment of the enemy would have to wait.

Cochrane's decision to remain on shore had two reasons behind it. He felt that his presence might deter these tired and battle-stained Spanish officers from giving in. It would also allow him the opportunity to make a thorough reconnaissance. He summoned up all his skill acquired over several years as a naval officer and a Member of Parliament, and argued, explained and asked questions. There was something about his sincerity and his obvious capability that impressed the weary Spaniards.

The idea that one frigate, with its small resources of manpower, could hold up an entire army might have seemed ridiculous. Nevertheless, he managed to convince them that something could be done. He did not promise a victory; that would have been too much. But he made them believe that he and his men could delay the enemy's advance until the reinforcements arrived.

On the following day, there was a light breeze—sufficient to waft *Imperieuse* into Rosas Bay. North of the town, Cape Creux, the final flourish of the Pyrenees, jutted out into the sea like an enormous breakwater. Inland, scrub-covered hills were ranged in ranks towards the horizon. The air was clear; the scene lit by a brilliant sun mirrored in the quiet waters of the bay. A few hundred yards offshore, HMS *Fame* lay at anchor, occasionally sending a broadside towards the French forces.

When Cochrane returned—tired after a night spent talking, covering long distances and exploring—his first action was to visit *Fame's* commanding officer, Captain Bennett. Bennett explained that a detachment of his Marines was up in Fort Trinidad, assisting the Spanish defenders. But, in his opinion, the position had become untenable, and he proposed to withdraw them. Cochrane could do as he pleased.

Although Bennett was senior to him, Collingwood's discretionary orders gave the Scotsman what amounted to an independent command. He was not required to take instructions from *Fame's* captain; nor did he receive any. It was just as well, for he had already decided upon what to do.

The key to the matter, he believed, was Fort Trinidad. Supported by gunfire from the frigates in the bay, and supplied by a ferry service of boats, it could remain in business almost indefinitely—and certainly long enough to allow reinforcements to arrive from Gerona. In any case, it seemed unlikely that the French would continue the advance towards Barcelona as long as this potentially troublesome strongpoint remained occupied.

Before dawn on 23 November, boats crowded with fifty seamen put off from *Imperieuse* on passage to the fort. Thirty Marines were due to follow later in the day. Among the officers Cochrane decided to take with him were Mr Guthrie (the ship's

senior surgeon), the master gunner and a midshipman named
Frederick Marryat (the future Captain Marryat, author of *Mr
Midshipman Easy* and a good many other works). This young
man was to serve as his adjutant.

Fort Trinidad was situated half-way up the cliff. It was
overlooked by a range of hills inland; to seaward, a sheer drop
lay between it and the beach. Since all supplies would have to
be brought in from the frigates, this precipitous approach might
have been considered a disadvantage. But its new occupants
were sailors; men who were used to shinning up rigging, and
who could make the ascent easily by using rope ladders. It also
promised the *Imperieuse* gunners good shooting at the French
batteries stationed on the hilltops above the site.

Cochrane likened the fortress to a church. It had three
prominent features; one, 110 feet high, resembled the tower;
another, 90 feet high, the nave; and the third, 50 feet high, the
chancel. It was solidly built and, although much had already
been hurled against it, the structure was still sound. As an
added advantage, the proximity of the high ground afforded
the enemy only a limited field of fire.

As an expert in gunnery, Cochrane was able to foresee the
French commander's intentions. It followed the method used
by most of Napoleon's artillerymen under such circumstances.
The shells would be directed at one point—battering it again
and again until they had effected a big enough breach to admit
infantry.

From this point of view, Fort Trinidad's location was a
decided advantage. Owing to the close proximity of the hills,
the enemy gunners would be compelled to concentrate their
fire on the tallest tower, for it was impossible to range on the
others and they could not depress their barrels sufficiently to
fire at the base. The most they could hope to achieve would be
to penetrate this lofty edifice at a point about fifty feet above
the ground. There could be no question of the foot soldiers
making their assault without difficult and dangerous use of
scaling ladders.

Cochrane was quick to notice these advantages. To the less
experienced and zealous eyes of Midshipman Marryat, however,
Fort Trinidad had little to commend it. He saw only the filth
and the dust created by shattered masonry, and the tired,

frightened and unkempt figures of the Spanish soldiers who manned it. Captain Bennett, he felt, had 'shown more than a sound discretion' when he pronounced the fort untenable.

As he afterwards recorded, much of the building seemed to be in ruins. There were heaps of fallen stones, a great deal of rubbish; the useless remains of broken gun-carriages and the split barrels of guns. To make matters worse, Marryat noted, a detachment of Swiss sharpshooters had dug in on a mound no more than fifty yards away. 'If', he wrote, 'a head was seen above the walls, twenty rifle bullets whizzed at it in a moment, and the same unremitting attention was paid to our boats as they landed'.

Nor was this all. The French gunners had established a battery of six 24-pounders on another crest—some distance away to the north. Whilst it could do little to assist the artillerymen closer to hand in their efforts to effect a breach, it made life on the ramparts an extremely hazardous business.

In Whitehall, Cochrane was dismissed as unorthodox. This may have been; but 'inventive' or 'ingenious' would have been better adjectives. He had no guns, and his replenishments of ammunition would depend on the ability of *Imperieuse's* boat crews to pass unscathed through the curtain of small arms' fire from the Swiss detachment on the hill. Since he might well find himself cut off from all assistance, he could not allow his men to be profligate in their rate of fire. The geography of Fort Trinidad would have to work on his behalf.

Again and again, his thoughts returned to the tower, and the probable point at which it would be breached. The layout in this quarter, he decided, would serve very well. Within the tower, close to the wall, there was a supposedly bomb-proof arch, fifty feet high. When the crown of it was removed, it opened up a deep chasm into which any invader would be likely to fall. Of course, the probability had to be considered that, once discovered, the French advance guard would bring up planks to create a rough-and-ready bridge. Cochrane decided to save them the trouble.

Ordering forage parties to collect all the timber they could find, he caused a platform to be constructed. It was carefully placed across the now missing top of the arch. He then sent out to the frigate for a large supply of so-called 'cooks' slush'—

in other words, grease. This, Cochrane decided, should do the
trick. Treated to a lavish application, the apparently inviting
approach would become extremely slippery. 'With the slightest
pressure from behind', he noted, 'the storming party must have
fallen to a depth of fifty feet, and all they could have done, if
not killed, would have been to remain prisoners at the bottom'.

In addition to his own men, Cochrane now had under his
command a motley collection of Spanish troops and a company
of Irish mercenaries. The Spaniards had been given the task of
building this booby trap, and they seemed to enjoy it. Indeed,
it appeared to improve their morale. But Cochrane was not yet
done. He now ordered the *Imperieuse* to be stripped of top
chains, which were ferried ashore. By a happy chance, the
frigate had a large number of fish hooks on board. Once the
chains had been festooned about the place—mainly in the area
of the breach—they were adorned with these objects. They
were so securely fastened, Cochrane remembered afterwards,
'that there was little danger of those who were caught, getting
away before they were shot'.

Perhaps it was against the vaguely chivalrous rules of combat,
but such niceties no longer mattered. As Marryat wrote, 'at
that time I thought just as little of killing a Frenchman as I
did of destroying a filthy little night predator' (the fleas in
which Ford Trinidad abounded).

After a while, life settled down into a routine. Every night,
men were put to work filling sandbags, gathering debris from
the shell-blasted walls and attempting to fill the growing hole
in the big tower. It was a thankless task, for every day their
efforts were demolished by the guns on the hilltop, which
maintained a constant and alarmingly accurate fire. The Swiss
snipers made trips to the shore by *Imperieuse's* boats extremely
difficult. Food became scarce—though Cochrane, believing that
regularity was the secret of all manner of things ranging from
discipline to good health, insisted that the hands should still be
piped to dinner. The fact that it sometimes amounted to little
more than ship's biscuits and water did not seem to matter.

Another French battery of 24-pounders was installed on the
hilltop, and the fire intensified. There was hardly a moment
between dawn and dusk when a shell did not hurl itself at the
fort. The gunners seemed to relax their efforts only to give their

overworked field pieces a chance to cool off. The giant granite
blocks from which the fort had been constructed were at once
a source of strength and danger. They stood up well under
bombardment, but the impact of a shell, or even a musket ball,
caused chips to fly off. Performing in much the manner of
shrapnel, these accounted for several of the wounded. Cochrane
himself fell victim to one of them. He was peering round a
corner, watching one of the artillery batteries. No sooner had
his head appeared, than a shell crashed into the masonry
nearby and a splinter struck him in the face. The splinter, he
wrote 'caused me intolerable agony... [it] flattening my nose
and then penetrating my mouth. By the skill of our excellent
doctor, Mr Guthrie, my nose after a time was rendered service-
able'.

Marryat had little good to say of their situation. 'Never', he
recorded, 'were troops worse paid and fed, or better fired at.
We all pigged in together, dirty straw and fleas for our beds;
our food on the same scale of luxury; from the captain
downwards, there was no distinction. Fighting is sometimes a
very agreeable pastime, but excess palls on the senses; and here
we had enough of it, without what I always thought an
indispensable accompaniment, a good bellyful.'

Nevertheless, the interior of the fort was looking better. The
rubbish had been cleared away; the mounds of stones were
diligently being plugged into the breach; and the booby trap
had been reinforced by barriers of sandbags, masonry and the
iniquitous chains from which the fish-hooks dangled. Two mines
had also been prepared. One was located at the base of the big
tower. The other, some yards away, contained sufficient explosive to send the rest of the premises skyhigh. The idea was that
they should be detonated if it became necessary to evacuate
the fort. Cochrane decided that a ten-minute fuse would suffice
for the tower; for the rest, it would be enough if the crumpled
remains of Fort Trinidad were demolished by the time he and
his men had returned to the frigate.

There was still no sign of the promised reinforcements. At
midnight on 26 November, the French made a more substantial
assault on the town of Rosas, and occupied the whole of it
apart from the now seriously breached citadel. The guns on
board *Imperieuse* and *Fame* did their best to intervene, but it

was no use. Despite heavy casualties, the French were able to consolidate their gains.

At about this time, Cochrane seems to have experienced an uncharacteristic moment of doubt. Two of the Marines had been killed by shot and a third put out of action by a stone splinter. 'I began to doubt', he observed, 'the propriety of sacrificing men to the preservation of a place which could no longer be tenable'.

Two days later, the enemy fire slackened. At about noon, a small party of Frenchmen approached the fort, carrying a white flag of truce. Cochrane asked what they wanted. They had come, the officer in charge shouted, to offer terms for honourable surrender. The answer was brief, 'No!' The visitors seemed in no hurry to depart. Now it became obvious that they were using the occasion to make a detailed scrutiny of the defences. This, white flag or no white flag, was not to be permitted. To hurry them on their way, a few hand grenades were tossed in their direction. The party moved off with unmilitary haste. Next day, five batteries opened up from the neighbouring hills. The citadel in Rosas became totally isolated, and the one bright episode on an otherwise gloomy day was when the two frigates fired on the French with remarkably good effect.

But worse was to come. Having the run of Rosas, the French now established gun positions on the sea front with the idea of stopping all traffic between *Imperieuse* and *Fame* and the beach at the foot of the cliff. The badly embattled men in Fort Trinidad were completely cut off from all sources of supply. Unless the soldiers from Gerona arrived within a few days, Cochrane and his men might be starved into submission.

Cochrane normally slept soundly. On the early morning of the 30th, however, he woke early. Perhaps it was the result of a dream; but, he recalled, he had 'an impression that the enemy were in possession of the castle'. It was, he knew, illogical. Nevertheless, the idea refused to go away. He lay, restless, for a while—trying to go back to sleep. But the idea would not budge. Presently, he clambered to his feet and wandered out on to the ramparts.

Everything was quiet. Some stars remained in the fading night sky; a veil of mist was slowly lifting from the valleys and dissolving above the dark hills. He chided himself for giving way to such fantasies. 'I felt half ashamed', he noted.

A few feet away, a loaded mortar was trained in the direction he expected the enemy to use for an assault. 'Without other object than that of diverting my mind from the unpleasant feeling', he lit a taper and fired it. The early morning silence was shattered by the explosion—echoed a few seconds later as the bomb burst behind a nearby brow.

It was as if he had switched on an elaborate arrangement of stage effects. The scene, so placid in the moments before the sun came up, erupted into action. There was a sudden volley of musket fire, the bullets slapping themselves against the stone walls. Down below, the previously unpopulated landscape became filled with soldiers. Marryat, who had been on watch, noticed that 'the black column of the enemy was (now) distinctly visible, curling along the valley like a giant centipede'. The instant they had been waiting for—dreading, perhaps—had arrived. The elaborate defences of Fort Trinidad were to be put to the test.

Cochrane shouted, 'To arms—they are coming!' Within three minutes, according to Midshipman Marryat's timing, every man was at his post.

The French had already shown the quality of their fieldcraft. They had come within a few yards of the fort without the slightest sound to betray their intentions. The possibilities appalled Cochrane. 'The dawn of the 30th', he wrote, 'might have been our last, but for the interposition of what some persons may call presentiment... To the purposeless discharge of that piece of ordnance we owed our safety, for otherwise they would have been upon us before we even expected their presence; and so exasperated were they by our obstinate defence that very little attention would have been paid to any demand for quarter.'

Everything now became clear: the officer who, under a flag of truce, had tried to make a more detailed reconnaissance; the barrage from the five batteries on the previous day—every shot aimed at the growing hole in the tower's walls; it all added up to preparations for an assault.

There had been a few moments when the enemy had seemed to hesitate as if dismayed at the immensity of the undertaking.

But, before very long, they had erected scaling ladders and a detachment of grenadiers was swarming upwards towards the breach. It was now light enough to make out details, and Cochrane himself was able to count forty men who had penetrated the great granite bastion and were now poised in front of the wooden platform which was thick with cooks' slush. More were coming up the ladders and, at the bottom, the ground was crowded with men in blue uniforms, each awaiting his turn.

But now Cochrane's plan, so carefully rehearsed, was put into action. A beautifully timed volley shattered the cluster of grenadiers in the breach. Some fell backwards on to the heads of their comrades below; others rushed forward, slipped on the grease, and tumbled into the chasm. For the moment, the fort was clear of intruders. To make sure that there were no more, something had to be done about the soldiers waiting at the tower's base.

A supply of hand grenades had been prepared for just this. They were thrown from the ramparts; and, to add to the carnage, shells were lowered on ropes—their fuses timed to explode when they were about half-way down. Simultaneously, the sailors, the Marines, the Spaniards and the Irish mercenaries opened fire at the now chaotic enemy force. Suddenly, it was all over. The survivors of the assault party were in full retreat. The officers, their swords drawn, tried to prod them back into action, but it was useless. Some, it seemed, preferred to die from a sabre-cut in the back—rather than return to the hell beneath Fort Trinidad's tower.

The colonel in charge of the advance guard had died within minutes of the action beginning. Marryat had noticed him, 'cool and composed as if he were at breakfast'. He lobbed down a grenade, which fell between the Frenchmen's feet. The officer calmly picked it up, and threw it some distance before it exploded. Marryat tried again. This time, it was disdainfully kicked to one side without doing any damage. This, it seemed, was a game that could continue until Marryat ran out of grenades. But now Cochrane was standing beside him, watching the grim comedy. 'Nothing', he said 'will cure that fellow but an ounce of lead on an empty stomach—it is a pity, too, to kill so fine a fellow—but there is no help for it'.

He then relieved Marryat of his musket; took careful aim and hit the colonel in the breast. The French officer staggered a matter of about ten yards in the direction of a small bush. Then he collapsed. He died, Marryat noticed, with 'his sword, which he still grasped in his right hand, rested on the boughs and pointed upwards to the sky'.

But Cochrane could be compassionate. The last man to leave the walls of the fort was a more junior officer. Cochrane came across him, alone and defiant—his sword ready for action. The captain slowly raised his rifle; the French lieutenant looked at him calmly, making no plea for mercy. 'He stood like a hero to receive the bullet', Cochrane observed, 'without conde- scending to lower his sword in token of surrender. I never saw a braver or prouder man. Lowering my musket, I paid him the compliment of remarking that so fine a fellow was not born to be shot down like a dog'. The Frenchman was, he said, at liberty to escape down the ladder. 'Upon which intimation he bowed as politely as though on parade, and retired just as leisurely'.

Prisoners later reported that the assault party had been composed of one company of grenadiers, two of carabineers, and four of men from the 1st Light Regiment of Italy. In all, there had been about 1,200 troops. The action had cost them fifty men known to be killed—though, taking into account the wounded who were dragged to safety, the total casualty list probably amounted to nearly 100. Cochrane's losses had been extremely moderate—two Spaniards and one Marine.

The French assault force had been repulsed, but news of this did not apparently reach the main body. The silence that followed the attack presumably gave the impression that it had been successful. At all events, within minutes, a sizeable force appeared over the crest plodding towards the fort. When they were well into the open, Cochrane gave orders to fire. Two volleys were sufficient to blast holes in the ranks. Then, aware at last that the strongpoint was still occupied, they turned and fled. The humiliation of the retreat was made more bitter by jeers from Fort Trinidad's now very elated occupants.

A pile of dead bodies and a jumble of broken scaling ladders were all that marked the events of a few short hours on 30 November. The French had managed to take away most of

their wounded with them; a few remained as prisoners, to be
treated by the capable Mr Guthrie. But something, clearly,
had to be done about the corpses. It would not be easy. The
French could not be expected to return for a task that might
add to the grim pile. If anything were accomplished in the way
of burial, it would have to be carried out by the men in the
fort. But for them, too, it was dangerous, for the area was
covered by the 300 trigger-happy Swiss in their entrenchments
fifty yards away.

By the following afternoon, the daytime heat had blackened
the mortal remains, and peasants living in the vicinity had
picked over the dead men's possessions. Cochrane was far from
happy about the situation, and he ordered Marryat to do
something about it. He might, the captain suggested, try flying
a white handkerchief from a pikestaff. That, surely, would be
interpreted as flag of truce.

Not without misgivings, the young midshipman assembled a
detail, armed the men with spades, and set about what appeared
to be a hazardous task. One of the sharpshooters fired a random
shot, which wounded one of the burial party. But then, presumably seeing the white handkerchief, the marksmen held their
fire.

After a while, Cochrane came out and joined the squad. The
appearance of the tall captain in his braided uniform seemed
to reawaken the Swiss. The chance of killing Fort Trinidad's
commanding officer, was perhaps, too good to ignore. There
was spasmodic firing at first, and Cochrane signalled the men
to run for cover. Marryat supposed he should remain behind.

Supervising the birual of the dead had not been Cochrane's
sole intention. He wanted to take a closer look at the Swiss
positions. Walking at what Marryat described as a 'funeral
pace', he studied the scene, now and then making a remark.
The Swiss sharpshooters were in no doubt about his intention.
They increased their rate of fire until the air seemed to be thick
with bullets. This was too much for young Marryat. His
commanding officer might be prepared to risk his neck on what
seemed to be an unnecessary errand; he, personally, was not.
He edged up to the captain. 'Sir', he said, 'as I am only a
midshipman, I don't care so much about honour as you do;
and therefore, if it makes no difference to you, I'll take the

liberty of getting under your lee'.

Cochrane laughed. 'I did not know you were here', he said. 'I meant you to go back with the others. But since you are out of your station, I will make that use of you that you so ingeniously proposed to make of me. My life may be of some importance here, but yours if of very little. Another midshipman can be had from the ship only for the asking. So just drop astern, if you please, and do duty as a breastwork for me'.

By what seemed to be a miracle, the two men returned to the fort safely.

After the attack, the French seemed to lose interest in Fort Trinidad. In any case, the citadel in Rosas had not yet fallen, and this was a more promising target. The next few days were comparatively quiet. So far as the men from *Imperieuse* were concerned, the enemy appeared to be mostly preoccupied in directing its fire on to the frigates' boats and frustrating their attempts to reach the shore. It was a sound enough idea. As the French must have realised, Cochrane and his men were now very short of food—and, no doubt, of ammunition as well.

To fill in the time, the master gunner and one or two men tried to put together a new 24-pounder from the litter of damaged guns that cluttered up a corner of the fort. The attempt was unfortunate. Enough parts were salvaged to construct a weapon that appeared sound enough. When a French detachment began work on throwing up an entrenchment nearby, it seemed a good opportunity to test it. Five men were employed on loading the hybrid piece of ordnance. As they were ramming home the cartridge, it suddenly blew up. A Marine had his arms torn off and died soon afterwards. One of the seamen was thrown over the wall and fell fifty feet. Surprisingly, he survived. Although badly injured, he was taken off to the frigate, where he underwent surgery. Eventually, he recovered and was sent home.

After nearly six weeks, Fort Trinidad was still in business, and its original complement had suffered amazingly few casualties. Nor were the French able to resume their drive to Barcelona. On the face of it, the situation was satisfactory. There were, however, two flaws. Down at the citadel, the breach in the walls had become so large that the Spanish troops were no longer making any attempt to repair it. The French artillery were directing eleven guns on it, and it could not be long before they delivered the final blow.

Closer to hand, the weather, which had been mostly calm, now seemed to be building up into something more violent. By 4 December, a gale was blowing. Out in the bay, *Imperieuse* was dragging at her anchors. If this went on she would have to put to sea to ride out the storm. The alternative was to be blown on to the beach.

The rising wind seemed to be a signal for a general worsening of the situation. The troops in the citadel made a sortie, but they were repelled with heavy losses. Up near Fort Trinidad, the enemy had completed a new battery, and were, as Cochrane recalled, 'trying its effect on us somewhat unpleasantly, every shot knocking down great quantities of stone'.

On the following day (the 5th), the French gunners treated the citadel in Rosas to another severe pounding. By 8.00 that morning, the breach was big enough for an assault, and a body of troops stood in readiness to force its way in. And then, suddenly, everything became quiet. Watching the scene through his telescope, Cochrane noticed that the shock force was now 'lounging about'. The attack, obviously, had been called off. He could draw only one conclusion: the Spanish commanding officer must be discussing terms for capitulation.

'Under these circumstances', he wrote, 'it became my duty not to sacrifice our marines and seamen to the mere excitement of fighting a whole army which could now pay us undivided attention'. The time had come to quit. He signalled *Imperieuse* to prepare the boats to evacuate his force. Then he applied himself to setting the fuses in readiness for blowing up the fort. At 11.00 am, he sent a further signal. The ship's boats were to come inshore.

Cochrane's men departed in the manner they had arrived: down rope ladders. At the same time, the frigates put down a heavy barrage on the French positions. It was just as well, for the work of leaving the fort took time. In addition to the British, the Spaniards and the Irish were also taken off, and it was not until 1.00 pm that Cochrane and the master gunner, now alone, were able to ignite the fuses and make their departure.

As the boats set off from the shore, the Swiss sharp-shooters made their final gesture by unleashing a few brisk volleys of musket fire. But the luck of the men of Fort Trinidad continued to hold. All the shots went wide of their marks. What was more, the wind had turned in the sailors' favour, enabling *Imperieuse* to close in on the beach and narrow the distance.

The first charge exploded when they were still in the boats. The great 110-feet high tower, that had endured so much punishment, erupted in smoke and dust and a cascade of falling stones. The second was due to go off once they were on board the frigate and, ideally, when she was under way. But nothing happened. Something, it seemed, had gone wrong with the fuse. It may have been jerked out of place by the fury that toppled the tower. In any case, it didn't much matter. The French could resume their march on Barcelona. The reinforcements from Gerona would never arrive now; the drama was over.

Events at Fort Trinidad had been more than a raid—and less, perhaps, than a siege. Statistically, eighty men, assisted by others of dubious courage and value, had held up an army of more than 6,000 for six weeks. If the citadel had held out, and if the weather had remained calm, it could have been for very much longer. The only serious difficulty was that of getting ashore supplies from the ships.

Above all things, it was a splendid example of warfare at its most economic; of the power of an unorthodox commander against an enemy that fought according to the manual. But, despite much praise in the press and from Collingwood, Their Lordships at the Admiralty could offer Cochrane nothing better than censure for 'excessive use of powder and shot'. In terms of British lives, the affair had accounted for only four dead. Perhaps it might have pleased the Whitehall pundits if there had been more. How, they may have asked themselves, can there be heroism without greater death?

Or was it the traditional senior officer's mistrust of the unconventional? Irregular troops, fighting irregular actions, have always been slightly suspect. Management, whether of armed forces or industrial undertakings, prefers men who go by the book of rules.

———

The Anglo-American war that broke out in 1812 was a direct

result of the conflict with France, which had been raging across
Europe on and off since 1793. One of its causes was that United
States merchant ships were trading with Europe. Others were
the British harassment of United States merchant ships; the
Royal Navy's tendency to board them and impress into service
members of their crews; and, inevitably, incidents on the United
States-Canada frontier.

Most of the United States' forces were concentrated on the
Canadian border, for this was the most likely direction from
which any invasion would come. It was a sensible idea—with
the threat from France apparently over after Napoleon's
abdication in 1814, Britain had forces to spare for North
America. Sure enough, regiments of veterans from Europe were
transported across the Atlantic during the early summer of that
year.

But by concentrating her best troops on the Canadian
frontier, the United States left her eastern seaboard dangerously
unprotected. The Royal Navy took advantage of this. Acting
in something of the manner of World War II Commandos,
sailors and Marines carried out hit-and-run raids on the coasts
of Connecticut, Massachusetts and Maine. On one occasion,
the raiders penetrated inland for the better part of sixty miles,
wreaking havoc in the Maine town of Bangor.

The purpose of these operations was usually to provide a
diversion, or else to act as a reprisal for what was considered
ungentlemanly conduct on the part of the Americans such as
the incident in April 1813, when troops entered Toronto (then
named York and serving as the capital of Upper Canada); they
burned down the parliament buildings and destroyed the
archives. Such depredations clearly could not be allowed to go
unpunished. On 2 June, 1814, three transports carrying soldiers,
accompanied by the 74-gun HMS *Royal Oak*, three frigates,
three sloops, two bomb-vessels and five smaller warships set sail
from Bordeaux in France. Three weeks later, the convoy
dropped anchor at Bermuda, where other men-of-war and a
further 2,500 troops were added to its strength. The job of
avenging Toronto had begun. For the burning of one capital
city, another was about to be put to the torch. The target was
Washington.

2 The President's Lodgings

The plan that led to the burning of Washington's public buildings was conceived by a naval officer named George Cockburn—the same officer who in August 1815, achieved the further distinction of conducting Napoleon into exile at St Helena. It might be unfair to attribute a personal motive to the undertaking, but there was one office block that Rear Admiral Cockburn was eager to see go up in smoke. This was the headquarters of the *National Intelligencer*—a daily newspaper that had published some harsh editorials about the Royal Navy's raids on the eastern seaboard of America—and, especially, about his own part in them.

In the early summer of 1814, Cockburn and his fleet were stationed in Chesapeake Bay, the huge tongue of water that provides the maritime approaches to Washington and Baltimore. Occasionally, a force of United States militia would survey the ships from between the trees that adorned the shore—and then make itself scarce. The weather was fine. For their part, some of the natives actually seemed to be friendly, and Cockburn took long walks on shore. During the expeditions, he was accompanied by a force of Marines. The men were spread out, and each was issued with a bugle. The idea was to blow it if you got lost, or if you encountered the enemy. Since the going was not difficult and the militiamen seemed to have no stomach for a fight, the musical instruments remained silent.

Cockburn enjoyed these outings into the country. More to the point, however, he used them to study conditions on shore, and to pick up information. There was, he soon discovered, a force of US gunboats stationed in the Petuxent—a river that enters Chesapeake Bay north of the Potomac. These ships, he gathered, were commanded by a Commodore Joshua Barney. He was, by all accounts, a man who deserved respect. The gallant Joshua Barney had enjoyed a long career as captain of deep-sea ships; and earlier in the war, had served with considerable effect as a privateer.

After a good deal of deliberation, Cockburn completed his plan and set it before his commander-in-chief, Admiral Alexander Cochrane (a relative of Lord Thomas Cochrane, of the *Imperieuse*). There should, he suggested, be three phases: the defeat of Barney and his gunboats; the burning of Washington; and then a forced march to Baltimore, which would share the capital's fate.

Cochrane conceded that the proposal was a good one, but he insisted that all Barney's ships be put out of action before any thought of raiding Washington was entertained. As for Baltimore, he was more cautious: they would see how things stood after the attack on the capital.

While Cockburn was making his excursions along the shores of Chesapeake Bay, a convoy was heading across the Atlantic from Bordeaux, bringing 2,500 British troops under the command of Major General Robert Ross. These men were all regulars: veterans of campaigns in Europe who could be relied upon to give a good account of themselves, and who should be more than a match for the half-trained, unseasoned militia.

The troops at the Americans' disposal may have been less than adequate, but matters were not helped by the situation inside Washington. The President, James Madison, was continuously at odds with his Secretary of War, John Armstrong. The defence of the area had been entrusted to a general named William H. Winder. Winder had been captured by the British in a relatively unimportant engagement on the shore of Lake Ontario. He had spent a comfortable period of captivity in Canada, during which he had tried to arrange a truce for the exchange of prisoners. He himself had been released earlier in the year, and he now found himself in charge of 15,000 unmobilised militiamen and a pitifully small force of regulars. When he complained to Secretary Armstrong that this was inadequate, he received no satisfaction. Indeed, the Secretary seemed to suggest that, if he continued to complain, Winder could step aside, and he, John Armstrong, would do the job himself.

Nor were Winder's problems confined to the inadequacy of his men in the field. Since the establishment did not run to the provision of a headquarters staff, he had to carry out all reconnaissances by himself. As a result, he was in a state of almost continuous exhaustion—without, it had to be admitted, accomplishing very much.

The fleet bringing General Ross and his regiments westwards dropped anchor at Bermuda on 24 June, and Ross transferred himself to Admiral Cochrane's flagship, the 80-gun HMS *Tonnaut*. He and Cochrane left for Chesapeake Bay on 2 July, with *Tonnaut* accompanied by the 36-gun frigate HMS *Euryalus*. By the 14th, they were holding discussions on board Cockburn's flagship, HMS *Albion*, near the mouth of the River Potomac. A month later, the troopships arrived. Augmented by a further 2,500 men who had been serving in Bermuda, the army's total strength was now about 5,000.

President Madison was not taken by surprise. In the Belgian town of Ghent, statesmen were meeting to discuss whether anything might be done to end the 'Napoleonic War'. Inevitably, news of the expedition's sailing from Bordeaux reached their ears; and, no less certainly, they passed the information on to Washington. These reports were confirmed by messages sent from the French port. By 26 June, Madison was in possession of a good many of the facts. A week later, the first British ships were sighted off the American coast. The president called a meeting of his heads of department for the following day.

The outcome of the meeting was that the area around Washington was put on a war footing by the creation of the so-called Military District. In theory, about 12,000 militiamen from Pennsylvania. Maryland and Virginia were to be mobilised, but held in reserve, ready to move off at a moment's notice. The District of Columbia was to supply 3,000 troops,

though these men were only half-trained. In the event, the
neighbouring States' contribution was small. Anyone who
studied the mass of correspondence, the orders and rescinded
orders that accumulated during the next few days could have
come to only one conclusion. During the coming crisis,
Washington would largely have to fend for itself. Pennsylvania,
Maryland and Virginia were concerned with their own affairs.

Since the plan was Madison's, it followed almost automatically that Armstrong would disagree with it. When Winder
pointed out that the response was nothing like sufficient, and
that he must have more men at once, Armstrong turned his
request down. Considering that the expected invasion force was
thought to contain between 8,000 and 9,000 regular infantry
and about 400 cavalry, the president might well have doubted
his colleague's grasp of the situation. But, as so often in the
uneasy working relationship, his notion of firing the Secretary
of War fizzled out.

Winder set up his headquarters in the small town of Bladensburg about five miles from the outskirts of Washington. For the
next few days, he occupied himself in making reconnaissances;
tiring himself out and learning little. In the end, he decided to
deploy his troops in two lines on the high ground overlooking
the town. His artillery (seven guns manned by regulars) ought
to be able to command the road leading to the capital—which
passed through their positions—and a bridge across the Potomac
at the edge of Bladensburg. It was little enough in the way of
defence for the United State's foremost city. To do justice to
Winder, however, he estimated correctly the route that the
British must take.

Cockburn's plan was that the fleet should move out of
Chesapeake Bay, and travel some distance up the Petuxent
River to Benedict—a village on the right bank. At this point,
the troops would disembark. According to the American idea,
the entrance to this river would be blocked by Barney and his
gunboats. But what could these small vessels, each armed with
no more than two guns, accomplish against the fire power of a
ship-of-the-line? What match would they be for 36-gun
frigates—or, indeed, for the lesser vessels in this display of
British sea power? If the Petuxent had been less navigable,
Barney might have hoped that the invading warships would

run aground. But the river was broad and deep, and its placid waters concealed few hazards. Barney was a brave man, but he was not a fool. As Cockburn's giants edged into the Petuxent, he withdrew—creeping upstream mile by mile, escaping beyond range of those deadly guns. Eventually, he came to a stop a mile or so above Benedict.

On 19 August, General Ross's soldiers came ashore without any opposition. Washington was about fifty miles away, and the prospect was not entirely without blemish. That August, there was a heat wave. The sun burned down fiercely from a sky clear of all clouds. The air was heavy with dust, and the long march ahead would have been hard going even for men in the cream of condition. But many of these soldiers had been confined to troopships for the better part of three months. During the next few days, the would have to cover long distances. It was, perhaps, asking a good deal of them.

But first, Commodore Barney and his gunboats had to be dealt with. At daybreak on the 20th, Rear Admiral Cockburn assembled a small armada composed of the ships' armed boats and tenders. Marines under the command of a Major Robyns were packed into them—including a detail of artillery. As the force set off up river, the frigates *Severn* and *Hebrus*, and the brig-sloop *Manly*, brought up the rear.

Joshua Barney's flagship was a sloop named *Scorpion*, armed with eight cannon. The rest of his small fleet was made up of sixteen gunboats—each with a gun in the bows and another at the stern. The larger boats mounted 32-pounders and carried a crew of sixty men; the smaller, 18-pounders (with a complement of forty). The vessels were now lying at anchor. *Scorpion* was in front; the rest moored in line behind her.

Like all the days that summer, it was brutally hot. The British seamen shone with perspiration as they toiled at the oars; the frigates and the brig-sloop had fallen some way behind for want of a wind to fill their sails. As the distance between the British and Americans closed, Barney's vessels should have opened fire. Admittedly, the gunboats in their line-astern positions were not at that moment able to do much about it, but *Scorpion* should have made some attempt at an engagement. It was almost as if Robyns and his Marines had come across a ghost fleet.

Then, suddenly, it happened. A sheet of flame shot into the air from *Scorpion's* forecastle. Seconds later, there was a violent explosion. When the smoke cleared, the sloop was little more than a smouldering hulk. Not long afterwards, it sank. It was as if this had been a signal. The sixteen gunboats had been similarly prepared with demolition charges. Now, one by one, they were torn apart by exploding gunpowder. Soon there was not one of them left. As for Barney and his sailors, they were well on their way to the Navy Yard in Washington, taking five naval guns with them.

Major Robyns' time had not been entirely wasted, however. Moored in the vicinity of the flotilla were thirteen schooners. Some of them were too old and dilapidated to be worth removing. The others were commandeered and taken back to the fleet's anchorage. As an added bonus, their holds turned out to be full of tobacco, which was distributed among the men.

As it later transpired, the decision to destroy the gunboats had been dictated by the Navy Secretary in Washington. If the decision had been left to Commodore Barney, Robyns and his Marines might have met with substantial opposition.

With the gunboat flotilla destroyed, Admiral Cochrane considered it safe to proceed with the second part of the plan. The column marched out of Benedict on the same day with the 85th Light Infantry in the lead, followed by the 4th Foot, with the 44th Foot bringing up the rear. Also present were Deacon's Rocket Brigade, members of the Marine Rocket Corps and a detachment of sailors hauling three small cannons. The advance guard was commanded by a Colonel Thornton.

The road was rough; the dust was choking; and the sun blazed down. For men who had been confined so long to the close quarters of ships, everything added up to a nightmare march. But encouraged by the steady beat of the drummers, they made a brave show. The local inhabitants seemed to be keeping indoors. As for the militiamen, their hitherto low profile had now vanished completely. By the end of the first day's march, the British had covered fifteen miles and reached the village of Nottingham. Twenty-four hours later, they arrived in Upper Marlborough. The names were nostalgic. It was almost as if they were taking part in a civil war at home.

By now, the troops were tired out, and Ross ordered a rest period of twenty-four hours. Washington was less than twenty miles away. There must, surely, be some opposition between here and the objective. It would not do to send these men into action without taking sufficient precautions. They had, he believed, everything that was needed except energy. It was nothing that relaxation could not remedy. Early on the 24th, the column formed up again. If everything went according to Cockburn's schedule, there would be fires blazing in the capital that night.

Within minutes of the British troops leaving Benedict on the 20th an American horseman rode out of the village with a report for Washington. The president received the news calmly and summoned Winder. The general, he now decided, should take command of 2,000 troops—most of them militia, though with a stiffening of regulars—and put his plan into effect at once. Winder demurred. Such things take time. He could not hope to have the men in position before the 22nd. Madison agreed. It would be time enough.

The events of the next day were confusing and no one was more confused than those taking part in them. Winder seemed to spend most of his time riding to and fro' between Bladensburg and the capital. None of the rank and file and few of their officers knew what was actually happening. When they reached the high ground above Bladensburg, there was little attempt to co-ordinate their deployment.

By this time, Barney and his now shipless mariners had arrived in Washington, and been assigned to guard the Navy Yard. With the prospect of action some miles down the road, the commodore was disgruntled. If there was to be fighting, he was determined to have a part in it. He protested to Secretary of War Armstrong, who told him to remain where he was. The president, on the other hand, seemed to take a more reasonable view (in Barney's opinion). After a good deal of argument, Barney's naval force took to the road.

At it happened it was all to the good. Winder believed that his troops would be severely outnumbered; Tobias Stansbury, who was commanding a militia brigade from Maryland, supported by gunners from Baltimore, took a similar view. As always on such occasions, there were promised of reinforcements, but nobody took them very seriously. The prevailing mood was one of defeat, and a train of waggons was already making its way out of Washington, transporting the official records to a place of safety. The presence of a man such as Joshua Barney—who was disinclined to accept the prospect of losing, and was still angry at the order to destroy his gunboats— might well improve morale. Winder, certainly, could not be described as an inspiring figure and seemed to be on the verge of a breakdown.

By the time they assumed their final positions, the militiamen and their regular comrades had been moved hither and thither about the various defence stations for the better part of thirty hours. Throughout this period, they had gone without sleep. They were now footsore, very tired, and somewhat dispirited. Nor, had anyone cared to think about it, was their deployment calculated to restore confidence.

Admittedly, the bridge across the river was covered, and so was the road to Washington. But this was the best that could be said of a not very good job. General Winder had made no attempt to make sure that one unit could support another, and he had paid little attention to his flanks. The result was that, in the coming engagement, the British would be able to deal with each unit individually without fear of harassment from the others.

Roughly, the formation was strung out in two lines, one behind the other and separated by a field and some orchards. There was nothing basically wrong about this—except that the fruit trees made certain that units in the rear could not see what was happening to those in front. In the event of the front line crumbling, the situation was liable to become chaotic. Nor was the situation helped very much by visitors from Washington. Secretary Armstrong was one of the first arrivals. He found little to praise in Winder's plan, and he made a number of alterations to it. Then, losing patience, he decided to dismiss the general and replace him by a brigadier named Monroe. Fortunately common sense eventually prevailed, and Winder remained in command. It was, after all, rather late in the day to make drastic changes.

Doubtless in an attempt to improve morale, President Madison and his cabinet also put in an appearance. The president inspected the troops and then decided to have a good look round. His questing mind almost landed him in trouble. Anxious to see the ground on the far side of Bladensburg, he nearly ran into the British advance guard. To have run such a risk suggested carelessness, for the approaching soldiers were easily detected by the clouds of dust that marked their progress along the highway. At 1.00 pm in the afternoon of 24 August, 1814, the leading troops of Thornton's light brigade entered Bladensburg.

It was a pretty little town, and the surrounding orchards and gentle hills set it off beautifully. But the men of the 85th Light Infantry had not come to admire the view. After this long march, their feet were hurting. Washington was still some distance away, and they now had to cross the Potomac. There was, they had heard, one bridge and a couple of fords some distance away on either side of it. If the Americans intended to deny them entry into their capital, this would be the place to do it. The bridge could well become a death trap, for this was the point on which they would train their guns. The next hour or so were liable to be very dangerous indeed.

The first shell exploded before they reached the bridge. It killed some men and wounded others. Thornton seemed undismayed. The bridge had to be crossed at no matter what price. He halted the column; ordered two units to move off to the fords up and downstream, and detailed a party to storm the crossing. Meanwhile a detachment from one of the rocket regiments was moving into the town and preparing to set off its bombardment from behind the shelter of a warehouse. A few minutes later, the air seemed to vibrate with the sound of the missiles taking off.

A Congreve rocket—or the version used by the army—was not a very efficient instrument of war. It could not be aimed with any precision, and its explosion achieved relatively little destruction. However, a whole battery of them made a great deal of noise and, with their tails of fire streaking behind them, they provided an awe-inspiring spectacle. What they lacked in lethal qualities, they made up for by their effect on morale.

To the militiamen from Maryland, the rockets were terrifying. They had never until then encountered anything like them. Before very long, they were in a state of near-panic, and

a major named William Pinkney (a lawyer and diplomat in
civilian life) gave the order to withdraw. At about the same
time, a house in which one of the American guns had been
sited was destroyed. The leading troops of the 85th ran towards
the bridge.

The light infantry was among the élite of the British army.
Its troops were not intended to stand firm in rigid squares, or
in unbreakable lines. As their description implied, they travelled
light. They were used for scouting, skirmishing—anything that
combined a need for quick mobility, skilful use of ground and
accurate shooting. As a result, they were subjected to less severe
discipline than ordinary foot soldiers. In a crisis, each man had
to be able to look after himself.

With surprisingly few casualties, they gained the far side of
the river. Using the trees in one of the orchards as cover, they
presently rejoined the road to Washington. The Maryland
men, who had been pushed back in disarray by the rockets,
rallied when they reached the second line; but soon the real
flaw in Winder's plan revealed itself. He had not paid enough
attention to the highway. The flanks of the units on either side
were completely out of touch with each other. Now, with the
British light infantry moving briskly up the road, they were
completely separated.

And the 4th Regiment of Foot was crossing the bridge.

The Marylanders, restored to rather better fettle, counter-
attacked on Winder's orders, and some of the light infantry
were repelled as far as the river. But the respite for the seriously
worried Americans did not last for long. Streams of British
soldiers, who had crossed the fords, were converging on either
flank. From behind the warehouse in Bladensburg, the rockets
were soaring into the air at an increasing rate. All this was too
much. Winder ordered his gunners and the 5th Maryland
Militia to retreat. Colonel Stansbury was taking similar action
on the far side of the road. The first line of defence was
shattered.

Meanwhile, Thornton regrouped his men and told them to
take things easy for a few minutes. It had all been too simple;
the men were almost euphoric with their success. What they
did not realise was that the greatest obstacle was yet to come.
On a hilltop some way down the road, Commodore Barney

had mustered his sailors, five guns and a force of about 3,000 militia that he had picked up on his way from Washington. The naval officer had watched with scorn the ill-favoured antics of Winder, Stansbury and their men. This was no way to fight a war. He intended to demonstrate how it should be done.

Half an hour later, he was given the opportunity to do so. The light-infantry men were running towards him, charging his position. Barney's five guns fired in splendid unison; and for their part, although the militia may not have discharged a perfectly judged volley, they and the gunners did sufficient damage to stem the attack. The 85th was compelled to go back and try again—and with appreciably fewer men.

Twice more, the light infantry charged the position, and twice more they were driven back. Colonel Thornton was wounded and casualties generally were high. But all the Americans seemed to be making mistakes that day. Barney's error was not to be content with sitting tight. If he had remained in this position, the road to Washington might have been long and attended by much death. But, flushed with his successes, he now decided to counter-attack. He did not, perhaps, pay sufficient heed to the 44th Foot, which was now working its way round the left flank.

Barney's counter-attack was unintentionally sabotaged. Seeing the 44th advancing and unaware that the light infantry had already been driven back three times, Winder suddenly gave an order to retreat along the entire front. At first, the withdrawal was controlled, but it needs only a small spark to unleash panic. The militiamen were now blundering backwards whilst Barney's men were trying to press forward. As if this were not problem enough, the hill that had proved such a tough obstacle to the British was now attacked from three different directions.

Everything had happened very quickly. The tide of the retreat had swept over the hill, dragging some of the defenders with it. Now the commodore and the rest of his men were isolated, menaced by the approaching redcoats of the 44th and by the light infantrymen. The militiamen took a quick look at the situation, and decided that Winder had the right idea. They retreated swiftly, but without Commodore Joshua Barney. In any case, he seemed to be seriously wounded. They presumably hoped the British had a surgeon who would patch him up.

The British, as it happened, did have medical assistance to offer the commodore. They had admired his courage, and they treated him very well. A prisoner he may have been, but they handled him as though he were an honoured guest.

Everything now seemed to be strangely silent. The rocket launchers were packing up their gear; a long line of red-coated foot soldiers was crossing over the bridge; in front, the columns were forming up for the last leg of the march to Washington. Before very long, the citizens of Bladensburg would be left in peace once more—able to enjoy what was left of a sunny afternoon. From start to finish, the destruction of Winder's plan had taken less than two hours.

At 8.00 pm that evening, General Ross and Rear Admiral Cockburn, at the head of about 1,000 troops, paused at a point two miles from Washington. The soldiers were drawn up in line; seeing no signs of any opposition, Ross and Cockburn decided to go on into the city, accompanied by only a small escort. Before long, their horses were clattering along the main street—heading for the Capitol. Suddenly, from two houses nearby, a volley of musket fire punctured the evening stillness. One of the bullets killed Ross's horse. Three of the soldiers were wounded.

Perhaps the first city of America was not as free from hazards as it had appeared to be. Cockburn rode back and presently returned with a company of light infantry. The houses concealing the sharpshooters were surrounded and set on fire. Fanned by the gentle evening breeze, the flames happily devoured them—and then spread to the Capitol. Washington's ordeal by fire had begun.

In other parts of the city, the sounds of explosions signalled that the work of demolition was not confined to the British. The Americans too, were in the business—blowing up anything that appeared likely to benefit the enemy. Among the victims were two of the bridges across the Potomac. Farther westwards, long processions of refugees were moving out into the country. Among them were President and Mrs James Madison.

By 10.30 pm all the troops had arrived from Bladensburg. Ross and Cockburn, now leading 200 soldiers, rode in triumph to the White House. The premises were completely deserted.

There had once been a guard armed with two pieces of cannon at the approaches, but it had been withdrawn. Ross nodded to one of his officers, 'Burn it,' he said. The act was carried out by the spreading of gunpowder and the application of a torch. It worked very well.

Cockburn had promised himself a treat. Still smarting from what he regarded as unjust attacks by the *National Intelligencer*, he was determined that he, personally, should send the newspaper office up in flames. He was about to ignite the gunpowder, when somebody pointed out that the fire would spread to neighbouring houses. Was this what the admiral wanted? Cockburn held his hand, fighting his private battle with temptation. He had, after all, no quarrel with these harmless residents. With a shrug of his shoulders, he put down the torch. Regretfully, the *National Intelligencer* would live to insult him another day.

But the capital's important public buildings were less fortunate. The Senate House, the House of Representatives, the Treasury, the War Office—one by one they went up in smoke. At the arsenal situated at Greenleaf, the incendiarists were unlucky. The buildings caught alight quickly. Unfortunately, the soldiers had overlooked a well in which a large supply of gunpowder was concealed. When the flames reached it, it erupted in a fearful explosion. Twelve men were killed; thirty officers and other ranks were wounded.

The Navy Yard was put to the torch—and, with it, went a 1,600-ton frigate that was ready for launching and a sloop-of-war named *Argus*. Next morning, the Secretary of State's office was added to the toll. When the cost was counted, it was estimated that public property valued at $737,163 had been destroyed; plus the White House (estimated value: $234,334); plus $93,613's worth of public offices. Expressed in sterling terms, a contemporary accountant calculated that the bill came to £365,463.

Anyone in the British ranks who was superstitious must have slept uneasily that night. Not long after the work had been completed, a violent thunderstorm broke out. The down-fall undoubtedly checked the spread of the blaze, and must have saved many homes. Nevertheless, it arrived too late to quench the humiliation of Washington. Next morning, accompanied by three of his officers, Ross strolled along the deserted streets, inspecting the damage. The burning of Toronto had been more than adequately avenged.

General Ross was a realist. They had completed parts A and B of Cockburn's plan, and done them very well. The cost had been about 200 casualties—most of them inflicted by Commodore Barney's determined stand. The operation had not taken long; were they now to proceed with part C—to make a forced march to Baltimore and wreak further havoc?

Two of the bridges over the river were in pieces; the troops were now very tired, added to which about 4,000 United States soldiers were massing at Georgetown—which was really no more than a continuation of Washington to the west. The general decided that enough was enough. His men paraded and began the march back to Benedict at 8.00 pm. Four days later, on the 29th, they returned to the anchorage. They embarked in the transports on the following day.

The *National Intelligencer* had the last-but-one word on the raid. The operation had, announced its editorial writer, been accompanied by excessive and manifold atrocities'. To which an English newspaper replied with the accusations of 'the vilest slander by the Federalists against not only the British army, but the entire nation.'

Perhaps Rear Admiral Cockburn had been wise to put down the burning brand. After all, you can always rely on one newspaper to attack another.

With the possible exception of Navarino, when a combined fleet of British, Russian and French ships defeated the Turks and secured the independence of Greece, there was no major naval engagement between Trafalgar and the first World War. Similarly, after Waterloo, the British Army was under-employed until the outbreak of the Crimean War in 1854. In such a state of naval and military stagnation, there was no great call for regular forces, and none for irregulars. Nor, indeed, did the talents of raiders find any opportunity in Crimea. After Balaclava, everything seemed to become bogged down in front of Sevastopol. With its confusion of objectives and its imperfectly understood orders, the Charge of the Light Brigade might have served as an example of how not to carry out this kind of warfare—though it was not a raid, and those taking part were certainly not commandos. However, if the Crimean campaign was the big picture, a 'B' feature was being enacted in the Baltic. It did not attract much notice, though it included one action that is very relevant to this narrative. The event took place on the island of Aland, at the entrance to the Gulf of Bothnia.

3 The Island

On 5 August, 1854, readers of the *Illustrated London News* were informed that the Russian fortress at Bombarsund, situated on an obscure island at the eastern end of the Baltic, had been taken by British and French forces 'with great loss on both sides'. The magazine admitted that the news was culled from telegraphic dispatches sent from Copenhagen and Stockholm, and that its accuracy could not be relied upon. Since the attack had not yet taken place, it might also have added that the announcement was, indeed, a little premature.

The drama of suspense continued. Three weeks later, the *Illustrated London News*'s man on the spot was explaining that, contrary to the magazine's earlier account, the stronghold had not yet fallen. 'Our people will succeed,' he assured his readers, 'but at fearful cost of life and limb.' This time, the periodical was behind events. Bombarsund had already been reduced to a few piles of smoking rubble, and the 'cost of life and limb' had been very reasonable. According to the First Sea Lord, Admiral Maurice Berkeley, there was 'not enough blood to please the people of England'. A war, after all, could not be accounted a good one, unless the casualties were high.

Whether the reduction of the defences at Bombarsund did anything to advance the Allied cause is, perhaps, debatable. It did, of course, show the taxpayers of Britain that the fleet stationed in the Baltic was doing something. Whilst this may not be a very good reason for committing thousands of men and a wealth of material to action, it mattered to the politicians. It was of particular concern to the First Lord of the Admiralty, Sir James Graham. Although the Baltic fleet was in the very capable hands of Admiral Sir Charles Napier, Graham did his best to run such campaigning as there was from his desk in Whitehall.

The decision to send the fleet to the Baltic was, it might be argued, a sound one. Events in the Crimea had stripped Britain of military resources. The Russians, on the other hand, had a large army at St Petersburg, and a sizeable collection of ships on station at Kronstadt and at Sveaborg (less than two miles from Helsinki). If this mass of war resources could be slipped through the Baltic and into the North Sea, it might wreak havoc on the English coast. Napier's job was to contain it—or, better still, destroy it.

Sir Charles Napier had been given the assignment on 7 March 1854—three weeks before Britain declared war on Russia. He was sixty-eight, a veteran who had entered the service in 1799. He was popular with the public, and respected as a commander who tempered courage with common sense.

The fleet that Napier took with him to the Baltic was an impressive mixture of steam and sail. Unfortunately, as so frequently happened at the start of the Crimean War, it lacked a number of essentials. The Admiralty charts were woefully inadequate guides to the complex waters of the eastern Baltic. This state of affairs might have been remedied, if the Admiralty had allowed him funds to pay a decent bounty to locally recruited pilots. The Admiralty did not, and the pilots preferred to apply themselves to more profitable activities.

Nor, at first, was there sufficient ammunition. Napier was cautioned to 'hold hard on the expenditure of shells for practice'. These things, after all, cost money. To show a profit, a shell must explode in anger against a hostile person or object. Using live ammunition for training, it was hinted, was a luxury that only the wealthy could afford.

If Napier had been able to bring the Russian fleet to battle, and to destroy it in an engagement reminiscent of Trafalgar, everybody in England would have been delighted. But matters were not so simple. Kronstadt and Sveaborg were defended by substantial artillery emplacements. The entrances to both ports were littered with rocks and shoals—a maze in which a prudent navigator moved very carefully and slowly. To increase the hazards in this respect, the Russians had laid minefields. Each

of these 'infernal machines' (as Napier called them) was filled
with 450 pounds of powder and fired by means of galvanic
batteries. The admiral had a very healthy dislike for them.

Under such circumstances, any idea of attacking the Russian
ships at their bases was madness. If they came out to fight the
British intruders, it would be another matter. But they did not.
The best Napier could hope to do was to keep them riding
harmlessly at their anchors. It was easily done by enforcing a
blockade across the entrance to the Gulf of Finland.

Napier, in his flagship *Duke of Wellington*, and Graham in his
comfortable Whitehall office were both wondering what to do
next. To maintain a fleet ready for action is a costly business.
You cannot allow it to remain unused, waiting for an enemy
that never arrives. To justify the expense, there had to be a
battle.

Graham, ever eager to make suggestions, poured out his
thoughts to the admiral. There were, he believed, three things
that should be done. The ships must 'complete the blockade of
the Gulf of Finland'. Having done so, Napier should find an
anchorage where adequate supplies of water would be available. Finally, he might do well to study a collection of islands
known as Aland (now Ahvenanmaa) to see whether it offered
any opportunity for offensive operations.

The admiral took a similar view. It was, he replied, possible
to spend all summer blockading the gulf—'though this will not
please the people of England'. Any idea of fighting the Russian
fleet off Kronstadt was out of the question, since it refused to
leave port. Aland it had to be. 'If we do not attack the islands,'
he told Graham, 'I do not see what else we can do.'

Aland is an assortment of pieces of land—some of them no
more than rocks—situated so to speak at a crossroads. To the
north, the Gulf of Bothnia separates Sweden from Finland to a
point just short of the Arctic Circle. Eastwards, the Gulf of
Finland is like a finger pointing to Leningrad (then St Petersburg); southwards lies the Baltic. Estimates of the number of
islands vary from 700 to 6,000 (though the latter must obviously
include reefs). The larger units in the archipelago are covered
by lime and birch trees, with the contours rising above them
and culminating in granite peaks. There is little arable land; in
1854, the inhabitants made a precarious living from fishing and

by transporting timber and live fish between Sweden and Finland.

Sweden had ceded this complexity of real estate to Russia in 1809—much to the indignation of the inhabitants. The Tsar had concentrated his fortifications at a place named Bombarsund on the largest island, Aland itself. According to a correspondent from *The Times*, the work had taken twenty-five years and cost £6 million. If this were so, both time and money must have been squandered. In the early summer of 1854, there were only three forts, and all the signs suggested that, whatever design had been conceived, it was not yet complete. More probably, the sums related to a much bigger idea, in which Bombarsund was to be developed as a garrison town, and the strongholds made a good deal more substantial.

For the time being, about 2,500 troops were uncomfortably accommodated—convinced, perhaps, that the best defences of Aland lay in the surrounding sea. The waters abounded in shoals and reefs; the pattern of channels that separated one blob of land from another was sufficient to confuse the most able navigator. During winter, the ocean usually froze over. This, clearly, was a deterrent to the commanders of any ships that might try to lay siege to Bombarsund—though troops had already crossed over the ice from Finland on several occasions. Indeed, the Russians were known to have stationed two battalions of skating infantry at Kronstadt.

With the ice at its maximum thickness (eight feet) cavalry, too, had made the trip from the mainland. Napier was well aware of this, and he had a very understandable dread of his vessels being caught by the cold weather. Whatever had to be done must be accomplished reasonably quickly—at any rate by the beginning of October. For the moment, however, he had to wait. This was to be a combined venture by the French and British. The former had not yet arrived, and there was no knowing when, exactly, they might put in an appearance.

Estimates of the number of troops required to overwhelm Bombarsund varied considerably. From a dusty old file, somebody at the Admiralty had produced statistics suggesting that the wresting of the Aland archipelago from Sweden all those years ago had been accomplished by 40,000 soldiers. This, clearly, was an exaggeration. However, the British and French

governments did not feel inclined to take chances. They decided
that a minimum of 10,000 men would be necessary. Napier
disagreed. He felt that half this number would be sufficient.
But then the admiral, for all his years, was a man in a hurry.
At a dinner to celebrate his appointment as commander-in-
chief, Baltic, he had chided the army on its laborious methods
of conducting a siege. All those approach trenches and elaborate batteries, and one thing and another—were they really
necessary? 'Oh,' he protested with an expressive wave of his
hands, 'I have no time for that at all.'

In the late spring and early summer of the year, this still
quiet corner of the Baltic and its tributaries manifested an odd
mixture of war and peace. Admiral Henry Chads, one of the
squadron commanders, had brought his wife with him. On
several occasions, a sharp-eyed Russian observer at Kronstadt
might have noticed two yachts racing each other offshore. If he
had known about such things, he would have identified one as
the Earl of Lichfield's *Gondola*; the other as *Esmerelda* belonging
to a Mr Campbell. Once, when one or the other of them was
becalmed (the records do not state which), it was taken in tow
by the steam-propelled battleship, HMS *Princess Royal*. And
when, at the end of July, the French men-of-war arrived under
the command of Admiral Perseval-Deschenes, the British officers
were particularly impressed by the hospitality of their
wardrooms. Lavish supper parties, it seems, took pace 'in the
gayest manner possible'.

Amid all this, the Swedish mail steamer plied unmolested
between Sweden and Finland—carrying, as everyone knew,
letters and dispatches destined for St Petersburg. Nobody saw
any reason to detain it. Such an act might upset the Swedes—
whose assistance appeared to be needed. Surely, it was hoped,
they might feel inclined to enlist in the Allied fleet—and to
lease Napier the small steam gunboats he required to negotiate
the archipelago's tortuous channels.

The Swedes declined both invitations. It would suit them
better to remain neutral, and to enjoy the profits that were
rapidly piling up from the sale of inferior merchandise at grossly
inflated prices to these foreign visitors. Even the possibility that
Sweden might be able to repossess Aland and the other islands
failed to produce a change of heart. The country had managed

well enough without them for the past forty-five years; and, once the Allies had departed, what was to prevent Russia from retaking them?

Before the French arrived, however, Napier had virtually sealed off the Gulf of Finland; and a squadron of steamers was on station off Kronstadt, watching out for any signs of activity by the Russian fleet. Nevertheless, Napier was worried. It was nearly the end of June; there was still no sign of the promised ships and soldiers from France. The weather might be well past its prime before an attack on Bombarsund could be mounted. What was more, cholera—the plague of the Crimea—was scarcely less virulent in these more northerly parts. One hundred men had already died from it. In the wardrooms of the fleet, the officers had formed the habit of drinking brandy diluted by warm water. It was, they believed (or professed to), a preventative.

On 22 June, Captain Hall in the steamer *Hecla*, accompanied by *Valorous* and *Odin*, took it upon himself to bombard Bombarsund for eight hours. He used up all his ammunition, and, apart from destroying a few guns near the shore, seemed to have done little damage. The one noteworthy happening was when a Russian shell landed on *Hecla*'s quarterdeck without exploding. Although it was obviously in an extremely dangerous condition, a midshipman named Lucas pitched it over the side before it exploded. Young Mr Lucas was promoted to lieutenant on the spot. When, two years later, the Victoria Cross was introduced for deeds of valour, he became the first member of the Royal Navy to receive it.

Nearly two months would have to pass before Napier could commit himself to the challenge of Aland. But although events seemed to be moving very slowly, in fact a pattern was emerging. In July, the survey ship *Lightning* began to chart the archipelago and its channels using buoys to mark those that might best serve the fleet. Among the men on board was a Mr Biddlecombe, Master of the Fleet, who had rightly decided that something must be done to repair the appalling lack of knowledge about local conditions.

In late July, a letter from Graham informed Napier that the first contingent of French troops had sailed from Calais on the 16th, and that others would soon be following. Ten days later,

when the admiral was making his own survey of Bombarsund
and its approaches, a message informed him that the French
military commander, General Baraguey d'Hilliers, was on his
way. The general, it seemed, was travelling in considerable
comfort: the Emperor Napoleon III had put the royal yacht,
La Reine Hortense, at his disposal for the campaign.

Whatever the high command of this expedition may have
lacked, it was not wanting in experience. Napier had served in
the Royal Navy for fifty-five years. The commander-in-chief of
the French squadron, Admiral Perseval-Deschenes, had fought
against Nelson at Trafalgar; and d'Hilliers had lost one of his
hands from frost-bite during Napoleon's retreat from Moscow.
Indeed, the youngest member was the British general, Harry
Jones, who had been withdrawn from Crimea for the occasion.
Brigadier-General Jones was a mere sixty-three. Among his
previous expeditions had been the disastrous trip to Walcheren
in 1809. The best that could be said of it was that it might
have shown him how these operations should not be conducted.

Such a preponderance of old age might have suggested an
over-cautious approach to the undertaking. Napier was, admittedly, chided by Graham for his 'mania' concerning rocks and
shoals. Since the Admiralty's parsimonious attitude over the
payment of bounties to Swedish pilots compelled him, as he
put it, 'to steer from rock to rock', the approach was excus-
able—even praise-worthy. And, indeed, the First Lord was to
show himself even less willing to take chances. He was continually warning the admiral that: 'Your duty does not extend to
the impossible.'

Like Sir Joseph Porter in HMS *Pinafore* (to whom he can not
unreasonably be compared), Sir James Graham's knowledge of
the sea and ships was limited. But this did not prevent him
from bothering Napier with useless advice. When, for example,
the second contingent of French troops arrived in a convoy of
four British line-of-battle ships, he made it clear that, upon no
account, must these vessels be put at risk. The soldiers should
be transferred to small steamers before they were set ashore.
To anyone on the spot who had studied the surveys made by
the crew of HMS *Lightning*, this was obvious. The large warships
drew too much water to be taken anywhere near the shore.

Napier described his French colleague, Perseval-Deschenes as 'a very gentlemanly man'. While it was doubtless true, he was not always easy to deal with. When Napier asked him to assign ships to the blockade of Kronstadt and Sveaborg, he refused. When he was asked to detach his steamers for other duties, he stubbornly shook his head. The British admiral was determined to leave this north-eastern corner of Europe before October brought the first frosts, but Perseval-Deschenes protested that this was not soon *enough*. Indeed, it soon became clear that neither of the French commanders had any great liking for the campaign.

By 6 August, the forces had assembled. The French had a fleet of nineteen vessels—including eight ships-of-the-line (one of them a steamer), six sailing frigates, one steam frigate and five assorted steamers. The British had twenty-seven ships of which thirteen were screw steamers-of-the-line, six were sailing vessels and five were paddle steamers. One warship, HMS *Belleisle*, had been converted into an hospital ship.

This was a new kind of fleet. Its vessels did not depend upon the whims of barometric pressure to carry them about their duties; an offsea wind was no longer able to confine warships to port. The coming of steam had produced that most priceless of assets: mobility at any time and under almost any conditions.

Many senior naval officers had deplored the innovation. They disliked the clouds of black smoke that poured from the funnels, and the soot that despoiled an immaculately scrubbed quarter deck. They regarded the machinery as unreliable (which, in fact, it sometimes was), and they deplored the entry of a new type of man into the Royal Navy—the engineer. These oafish intruders were, they told themselves, no better than engine drivers, and they were apt to refer to them as such. As a result, relationships between deck and engine room were often under considerable pressure.

Napier had none of these prejudices. In 1819, he had presided over an attempt to introduce the French to the virtues of an iron steamship by arranging a demonstration on the River Seine. Now, he told himself, the introduction of steam warships would be more than justified. To attempt a landing under sail in these treacherous waters would have been impossible.

In terms of military strength, his force was now considerable. General Baraguey d'Hilliers had nearly 10,000 men under his command—plus eighty horses to haul his artillery pieces and 500 engineers to construct what he considered to be the essentials of siege warfare. On the British side, Harry Jones had a mixed bag of sappers and Royal Marines amounting to about 2,000. This may seem a modest contribution, but the sailors would also be taking part, and so would the large 32-pounder guns from the ships. The total force should have been sufficient to reduce two, or even three, strong points of Bombarsund proportions.

Napier had done his best to ensure that no supplies or reinforcements reached Aland from Russian bases in Finland. But in a geographical complexity such as this, a complete blockade was impossible. On 10 August, the steamer HMS *Locust* was on patrol at the north-eastern approaches to the island. Some minutes before noon, one of the look-outs reported a sail on the horizon. Lieutenant Day, *Locust*'s commanding officer, ordered the quarter-master to steer towards it. The Russian ship (for such she obviously was) changed course, and headed for an inlet that was littered with shoals and rocks. With *Locust*'s obviously greater draught, and her inadequate charts, it was impossible to follow the intruder. Some other route would have to be found.

While Day was preoccupied with these thoughts, two more ships suddenly appeared on the scene. They had, it appeared, been lurking in the shelter of a small island, waiting for the moment when Day's attention would be distracted by the sailing ship. Now that they had been spotted, they hoisted the Russian ensign; and ran for one of the creeks that bit into the coast of Aland itself. Their decks were crowded with soldiers.

Locust's gunners opened fire on them at a range of 2,000 yards. As might have been expected, the shells exploded wide of the mark. By the time the 32-pounders had been reloaded, the Russian captains had run their vessels on to the beach. The troops jumped ashore and ran for the cover of a nearby wood.

For the next few minutes, the British steamer's guns pounded the wood—with, it at first seemed, some effect. The soldiers reappeared briefly—now carrying a number of wounded. Moving at the double, they hurried along the edge of the creek,

dashing from one clump of trees to another, until they vanished
into the interior. Day brought his ship to within 700 yards of
the shore. He considered lowering the boats and sending a
party of sailors in pursuit, but such a course might have been
disastrous. Using the ample cover of the woods, the Russians
could have left behind an ambush to cover their forced march
to Bombarsund. Day knew when he was beaten. Forlornly,
Locust turned about and headed for the deeper water. Under
such conditions, what could a man do?

Mr Biddlecombe, Master of the Fleet, had done his best. For
weeks, the survey ship *Lightning* had been engaged in making
elaborate surveys of the archipelago in a brave attempt to fill
in the great gaps of knowledge on the charts. To do it
thoroughly was a task that might have taken years. There was
just too much of it; too many islands, too many shoals, too
many reefs, too many rocks. Without local knowledge, it was
impossible to come to terms with this navigator's nightmare.

Locust was, perhaps, fortunate. At least she remained afloat.
But how much longer would it be before more reinforcements
arrived? Reports suggested that the garrison at Sveaborg had
been increased to 40,000 men—of which 9,000 were said to be
in readiness for some special operations. It was not difficult to
guess what it would be. Perhaps the estimate that 10,000 Allied
troops would be needed to reduce the forts was not so extravagant after all.

On the following day, Napier was informed that 300 Russian
gunboats were standing by—waiting for orders to smash a hole
in the blockade.

The admiral may have been in thrall to 'a mania' concerning
rocks and shoals, but it was understandable. The steam frigate
HMS *Valorous*, had been on her way to join the squadron
guarding the entrances and exits of the Gulf of Bothnia, when
she ran on to a rock. She had been steaming at only 3 1/2
knots. Nevertheless, she remained transfixed for two hours.
When she was freed, her hull was found to be badly damaged.
As she limped away, she ran on to another hazard, where she
remained for four days.

HMS *Leopard* was searching for a passage between a group
of islands, when she ran on to the shore. She was stranded for
nine hours. And so it went on. The Russians, on the other

hand, were accustomed to these waters. As Lieutenant Day's experience had shown, enemy steamers were able to penetrate inlets that were far beyond the Royal Navy's capability. And how was a ship's captain to proceed cautiously, feeling his way over a sea bed in which fathoms suddenly became feet—and feet, inches? In the heat of action, there was little time to spare for prudence.

The month of October haunted Napier. By then, Bombarsund had to be reduced to a harmless wreck of fallen masonry—of dead men and guns that would never fire again. By then, his ships had to be beyond the perils of a frozen sea. But how long would the job take? It was now the first week in August. The operation would have to go forward—regardless of the dangers that lurked beneath the bland surface of this maritime crossroad. At 1.00 pm on 7 August, the soldiers were transferred to the small steamers that would take them ashore.

Bombarsund lay on a peninsula at the south-eastern end of Aland. Apart from a small outpost of seven guns on an island some yards offshore, there were three main elements to the defences: Fort Tzee to the north, Fort Nottich some distance to the south-west, and the so-called Great Fortress on the south-eastern tip. They were laid out in a triangle, with Fort Tzee at the apex. The sides had yet to be filled in—which meant that there was no covered approach from one to another. Forts Tzee and Nottich were circular; the Great Fortress was built in the shape of an arc—roughly following the line of the coast. All had iron roofs. Napier described the Great Fortress as 'a large two-decker of granite'. It contained, he suspected, eighty—or, perhaps, more—guns.

With trails of smoke streaming from their lanky funnels, and their hulls shaking with the hard-labouring machinery, the small steamers headed for the shore at daybreak on the 8th. All told, there were three landings. Two forces of French soldiers established beach heads on the southern end of the peninsula—whilst a British contingent commanded by a Colonel Graham went in at the northern end. There was no opposition; none of the vessels went aground, and the troops reached the beaches 'without', according to one observer, 'so much as a wet foot'.

At the same time, the steam sloops *Amphion* and *Phlegeton* opened fire on the seven-gun battery offshore. Within forty minutes, they had pounded it to pieces, and the enemy troops had made a hurried departure for the security of Bombarsund.

So far, everything seemed to have gone unusually well. Graham had expected heavy opposition to his landing on the north shore; but, unaccountably, the Russians seemed to have overlooked this line of approach. Or had they concentrated their defences inland from the beach—using the cover of the woods to lay a trap? The Colonel felt inclined to move cautiously. His force consisted of an advance guard—made up of 100 Marines and twenty sappers and miners—led by Captain King. This was followed by 400 Marines, seventy sappers and miners, and four field pieces. Finally, 2,000 French Marines under General Jones's command brought up the rear.

Tramping cautiously along a trail between the birch trees, with reconnaissance parties operating out front and to the sides, the advance guard edged its way slowly towards the forts. Everything was suspiciously quiet. At one point, they came across two masked batteries—obviously intended to cover this line of approach, but they had not been completed. There were simply piles of earth, a few boulders, but no signs of any soldiers. It was almost as if the Russians had lost interest in this corner of the island.

Presently, the August sun now well up, the trees came to an end and King's men found themselves on a small plain, walled in at one side by a rock face. Ahead of them, Bombarsund seemed to doze in the late morning light, its guns silent and no movements of troops to break up the calm, strangely inanimate scene.

The French force—four battalions of the 51st Regiment and units from the Chasseurs—had enjoyed an equally uneventful experience. The Russians had allowed them ashore; had not molested their approach; and now appeared content to watch them throw up earthworks without so much as firing a shot. The arrival of reinforcements on the 10th had suggested that they intended to hold on to Aland even if the cost were considerable. But now, with the Allies literally at the gates, they seemed reluctant to do anything about it. Either the garrison commander was playing an extremely subtle game, or else something was seriously wrong inside Bombarsund.

But the preparations to reduce the forts were not yet complete. The French artillery pieces were 16-pounders augmented by four 8-inch mortars, and there were eighty horses to haul them to their destinations. The British naval guns were very much larger, and the only way of getting them into position was by manpower. Captain Hewlett, the commanding officer of HMS *Edinburgh*, had been put in charge of the operation. Under his supervision, Captain Ramsay of HMS *Hogue* had caused a number of large wooden sledges to be built—each big enough to take a gun, its carriage and all its gear. Teams of 150 sailors, each led by a senior lieutenant, were detailed to drag them over what Admiral Chads (who was in charge of the landings) described as 'execrable ground, the greater portion of which was steep rocky hills and ploughed fields'. The distance was four miles.

At 5.00 am on the 10th, the first units in this procession of sweating, swearing tars and their cumbersome charges set off towards the main camp. As if this combination of rough ground and unwieldy burdens were not punishment enough, the sailors had to struggle along without anything on their feet. Some half-wit at the Admiralty had supplied the fleet with an issue of shoes that, without exception, was made up of sizes that were much too small. The footwear had been sent back with an angry note; the official in Whitehall had promised to do better next time.

Sure enough, when the supply ship *Tyne* had arrived on 22 July, there was a large consignment of shoes on board. Out of ninety-eight pairs issued to HMS *Edinburgh*, eighty-five were still too small. Thus, of the entire crew of one of the flagships, only thirteen men were adequately shod. Other vessels had similarly dismal tales to tell.

By 10.00 am, the first batch of guns had arrived in camp. At various places on the route, French soldiers had cheered the straining blue-jackets and, now and again, had come to their assistance. Nevertheless, the men were tired—content to lie on the ground and prepare their lunch.

As ill fortune would have it, they were not allowed to rest for long before being recalled to their ships. A paddlesteamer, HMS *Penelope* had run aground within range of the Great

Fortress's guns. They might have to assist in hauling her off.

Using a short cut, they made the return journey in forty-five minutes. By this time, *Penelope* was in serious trouble. The fortress had suddenly become alive and was pounding her with red hot shot and shells. A French officer, who had gone to her aid, was decapitated; a shot passed through the chest of a midshipman who was in the steering flat, and three other members of her crew had been killed. *Hecla* was trying to get a hawser across when she, too, came under fire. Before long, three of her men were wounded and her hull was badly damaged. The guns of the fleet were ranging on the fortress to some effect; but the paddlesteamer was still lodged stubbornly on the beach. Eventually it became necessary to throw her guns overboard. Now considerably lighter, *Penelope* refloated—albeit badly damaged.

The day that had been 10 August was used up. No more guns could be shifted into position; the next round in the sailors' ordeal by hard labour would have to wait until dawn on the 11th. This time, 200 men were harnessed to each sledge; and, to improve the men's morale, a band of the Royal Marines marched beside them, playing an accompaniment. By 10.30 am, the guns had been delivered.

At about this time, there were signs of activity from the Russians. Small parties ran from the forts and set fire to everything that would catch alight—burning down the scrub and the trees, and assuring that little cover remained to conceal the assault parties. Three of the enemy soldiers took the opportunity to desert. When questioned, they reported that one of the Tsar's ADCs had arrived in the Great Fortress. He had informed the commandant that fifty gunboats had been packed with reinforcements and might be expected to arrive at any minute.

The previously placid appearance of Bombarsund had been misleading. If the gunboats managed to penetrate Napier's screen of steamers; if the garrison managed to hang on for long enough... it was all a question of time. The Russians needed it; the Allies feared it. And, by the time the necessary batteries had been built and the bombardment could begin, it would be the 13th. Finland was—how far away? No more than twenty-five miles. If the deserters had been right, the reinforcements might well arrive too soon for the Allies' comfort.

Hour after hour moved sluggishly by, with the earthworks slowly taking shape and, thankfully, no sign of the gunboats. By the evening of the 13th, the preparations were at last ready. At 4.00 am the following day, just as the first streaks of dawn were seeping into the sky above Finland, four French 16-pounders opened up on Fort Tzee. A battery of mortars presently joined in, lobbing its bombs on to the iron roof and blasting a gap in it.

Under the cover of this barrage, the Chasseurs swarmed forward, zig-zagging their way from the cover of one rock to another, sometimes finding shelter behind a tree that had escaped the incendiarists. Holes began to appear in the fort's walls, but the garrison was responding with heavy gunfire and volley upon volley from the infantry's rifles. Nevertheless, after a few hours, the Russians' enthusiasm seemed to flag. Just as the light was beginning to fade, a white flag of truce appeared in an upper window of the tower.

Baraguey d'Hilliers was quick to respond. A bugler sounded the cease fire and, accompanied by a few foot soldiers, d'Hilliers made his way to the fort. The commandant asked him for a four-hour truce. It did not require very much astuteness to see the reason for this. Far from proposing a curtain raiser to surrender, the Russian officer obviously wanted a breathing space in which to bring up reinforcements and ammunition from the Great Fortress. D'Hilliers brusquely told him that he might have one hour's respite and not a second more. The commandant turned the offer down. Minutes later, Fort Tzee was back in business.

But now the roof had been entirely demolished. Amid the clouds of smoke that poured from the interior were fragments of rafters. When darkness came down, the fire on both sides ceased—though the French troops were not proposing to bed down for the night. They used the occasion to surround the fort; to make sure that the beleaguered Russians could no longer hope for any assistance from their neighbours. By dawn on the 14th, they were all in position, and three of their 16-pounders celebrated the coming of daylight with a trio of perfectly aimed shots. This time, Fort Tzee made no reply.

There seemed little point in prolonging the agony. A company of Chasseurs volunteered to take the fort by storm. As things transpired, no such assault was needed. The door was hanging open, blasted from its hinges; nobody stood in the men's way as they ran down a corridor leading to the commandant's office. As they pushed into the room, that unfortunate officer rushed at the nearest man—only to be prodded firmly in the ribs by a French bayonet. Suddenly, the fury died. With a tired shrug of his shoulders, he handed over his sword. Fort Tzee was finished.

It was, perhaps, surprising that it had caused so much trouble. Only a few members of the garrison were still alive, and nearly all of them were drunk. They had, it now became clear, threatened mutiny after the plea for a four-hour truce had failed. Although they still had plenty of salt fish for food, they were short of ammunition. The interior of the fort was dreadfully damaged; in dark corners, the stench of death betrayed fifty corpses that had been hastily plunged into barrels of quick-lime. Yes, said the commandant, he had hoped for reinforcements during the night. No, they had not arrived. Somebody had let him down.

Later that day, the guns of the Great Fortress were turned upon Fort Tzee. Before long, fires broke out and a spark wafted down to what remained of the gunpowder in the basement. As *The Times* correspondent reported, 'a rumbling sensation was first felt, immediately followed by two tremendous explosions, and the fort was seen to rise in the air as an indescribable mass'.

But Fort Nottich and the Great Fortress were still giving a reasonably good account of themselves. At 8.00 am on the 15th, the 32-pounder naval guns opened up on the former at a range of 750 yards. The Russians returned the fire, and the artillery duel went on for several hours. Among the perils that now faced the British gunners were showers of granite splinters chipped off from the walls by exploding shells. Quite early in the proceedings, a Russian bullet knocked off a piece of iron from one of the navy's gun carriages. It plunged into the side of a young lieutenant named Wrottesley, who was evacuated to the hospital ship *Belleisle*. He died a few hours later.

By this time, the naval guns were blasting gaps in the fort's walls, but the Russian resistance continued. By mid-afternoon, they had only one field piece left in action. Its fire was almost stifled by the heaps of fallen masonry that threatened to bury it. But, time and again, the Russians cleared it away and the gun remained in action. Finally, at 6.30 pm, the debris overwhelmed it.

That evening, 300 Marines marched up to the ruins of Fort Nottich to escort the prisoners (120 of them) down to the Allied camp. The sea between Aland and Finland was empty. There was no collection of distant specks, no tell-tale feathers of smoke, to indicate the approach of those fifty gunboats with their troop-filled decks.

While Fort Nottich was under bombardment, thirteen ships of the fleet turned their 32-pounders on to the Great Fortress. For hour after hour they slammed shells at its thick granite walls, which appeared to have an almost infinite capacity to withstand punishment. Nearer to hand, seamen from HMS *Blenheim* had managed to lower the ship's 10-inch pivot gun (which weighed five tons) into a boat. With *Blenheim*'s commanding officer, Captain the Hon F. T. Pelham, taking personal charge, it was transported to the offshore battery that *Amphion* and *Phlegeton* had smashed on the first day of the operation. Now Captain Pelham had added his contribution to the general mayhem. The Russians seemed to take exception to the enemy using one of their own bases for an attack and thus directed much of their fire towards *Blenheim*'s gunners. It was a lot of fuss to make about very little, and it made the French task of dealing with Fort Nottich much easier.

Miraculously, or so it seemed, Pelham and his men continued firing without incurring a single casualty. General Harry Jones's ADC, Lieutenant Cowell of the Royal Engineers, was not so lucky. He discharged his pistol by accident, and wounded himself in the leg.

Once Fort Nottich had been reduced to a crumble of stone, the entire force, navy and army alike, was able to apply itself to the Great Fortress. Presently the now familiar white flag fluttered from a window. The drama of Aland was over, and 2,255 prisoners were taken into captivity. Estimates of the Allied casualties varied. Baraguey d'Hilliers put the figure at twenty-one (which thereafter earned him the nickname of 'General Vingt-et-Un') whilst Napier believed it to be 120. In fact, a forlorn collection of tombstones found years afterwards on the island added up to 160.

So far as the press in Britain was concerned, it was a glorious victory. One of the first people to congratulate Napier was Lord Thomas Cochrane, now the Earl of Dundonald. Wrote Cochrane, 'Those only who are acquainted with the difficulties you have had to surmount, and the nature of the obstacles assigned you to encounter, can appreciate the perseverance and the moral courage requisite to overcome the one and surmount the other.'

Was he referring to the Russian defenders of Aland, or to the unvanquished warriors of Whitehall? Was, indeed, the titanic raid on Aland anything more than an exercise in public relations? It may have prevented a breakout by the Russian Baltic fleet, and saved the English coast much trouble and suffering. But, as a glance at an atlas shows, another way of doing it would have been to blockade the exit from the Skagerrak. It might have been so much simpler—and, in a world where ships' captains were discouraged from using live ammunition for training purposes, cheaper.

To trace the pedigree of a Commando or a United States Ranger is not an easy task, for it is made up of innumerable strands. The soldiers who took part in the Aland raid were all regulars, conducting themselves in the traditional manner. They needed to take their time—and, if in doubt, to remember the instructions in the drill manual. Commandos, though uniformed soldiers subject to the discipline of the service, have always adopted a less rigid attitude—and there can be no doubt that, had they been available in 1854, the forts at Bombarsund might have been knocked out more quickly and with greater economy of manpower. Whether the cautious politicians in Whitehall would have tolerated such an approach is less certain.

During the American Civil War, the Confederates were often compelled to apply unorthodox, and sometimes very ingenious, measures—simply because they had not the resources of the industrialised North. The classic example is their use of the submarine, which was the epitome of irregular naval warfare. After numerous failures, and at considerable cost of submariners' lives, they succeeded in sinking the USS *Housatonic*, a steam-driven warship that was the pride of the Federal navy. It was a desperate action; but, in the face of the North's much superior navy, there was little alternative.

A search of the annals of the Civil War reveals few examples of combined operations. When Captain David Glasgow Farragut took New Orleans, he elbowed his way up the Mississippi with a smashing display of naval might. The army's only contributions was to land troops afterwards and to create a reign of terror. Similarly, at Mobile, the port was eventually closed by the sheer fire power of Farragut's ships.

Troops were landed at Port Royal in 1861, and at Wilmington, North Carolina, in 1864. The latter was the last Confederate port accessible to blockade runners—the only place where the South, lacking in industry, could make good this deficiency from the world outside. As the final chink in the blockade, it had to be closed.

Major General Benjamin F. Butler made the first attempt on Christmas Day, 1864, with 16,000 troops under his command. He landed 2,500 of them; but when, after two days, his gunners seemed to have made little impact on the defences, and when a storm threatened the ships, he withdrew in panic.

Butler was succeeded by General A. H. Terry, who made his attack on 15 January, 1865. At 2.30 pm, after a heavy and extremely accurate bombardment from the navy, the soldiers were put ashore. The Confederate garrison surrendered at 10.00 pm.

Such operations, however, cannot be described as raids. They were long-term operations, and not the concern of this book. To find better examples, it is necessary to look inland. This was the first war in which railways played an important part. The Northern, Federal, forces depended on them for many of their lines of communication; and, on the whole, they served them well. But they provided an abundance of targets for the Southern, Confederate, raiders.

In this respect, a cavalry general named Nathan Bedford Forrest excelled himself. On 13 July, 1862, leading a regiment of 1,400 horse, he cut the Federal supply line ten miles from Nashville, and took prisoner the 1,700-man garrison at the cost of only eighty troopers. The raid caused operations to be suspended for two weeks while the line was repaired.

December, 1862, saw Forrest in action again. This time, accompanied by 2,500 men, he demolished sections of track and several bridges over which supplies to General Ulysses Grant should have been travelling. For good measure, he inflicted 1,500 casualties on Grant's forces, and tied up 20,000 men who wasted a lot of time trying to intercept him.

During 1864, when Sherman was advancing into Atlanta, fear of Forrest compelled him to assign 80,000 of his 180,000-man army to the task of guarding communications. No stretch of permanent way, it seemed, was safe when this Confederate horseman was in the vicinity.

General Forrest commanded regular cavalry units in a dashing manner. The men who served under the Federal agent J. J. Andrews in 1862 were quite another matter. Although they were all volunteers from the 2nd, 21st and 33rd Ohio Infantry Regiments, they changed into civilian clothes for their new duties. The difference between the honourable profession of a soldier and the nefarious occupation of a spy is a suit of clothes. Once these men joined Andrews, they forfeited their right, in the event of capture, to be treated as prisoners of war. It may seem hard, for their intention was the same as that of the colourful General Forrest—to blow up railway lines.

Andrews had set himself the task of disrupting Confederate rail communications by demolishing bridges at the northern approaches to Chattanooga. He and his men made their way behind the Confederate lines, stole a railway train, and, against most laws of probability, travelled a good distance towards their objective. They might have been more successful if the weather had been better. Unfortunately this was a period of exceptionally heavy rainfall, and their charges failed to explode. Eventually, they were rounded up by Confederate forces; Andrews and several of the men were hanged. Others were saved by the timely arrival of a Federal division under General O. M. Mitchel.

W. C. Quantrill, who was active in Kansas and Missouri, might have protested that he was a legitimate member of the Rangers—though it seems doubtful whether latter-day members of that honourable corps would wish to acknowledge any kinship. Among the personnel of his guerrilla band were Frank and Jesse James and two members of that other notorious outlaw family, the Younger brothers. The Quantrill record is one of theft and murder, and he did the Confederate cause far more harm than good. He and his men seldom selected a target that was able to offer any resistance—the trouble usually began after the raid. But, by then, they had disappeared south (usually into Texas) after the manner of the desperadoes so many of them later became.

For the record, three examples will suffice. There was the time when the Quantrill band sacked Lawrence, Kansas, set fire to 200 buildings, and killed about 150 civilians; the occasion when they attacked a train on which seventy-five unarmed Yankee soldiers were going home on leave—and killed every one of them; and the affair of Jesse James and the brothel.

James, as a young man, was extremely good-looking, and it required no great feat of make-up to disguise him as a woman. Thus apparelled, he applied for employment at an establishment in the state of Kansas. When he reported for duty, he was accompanied by a detail of Quantrill's men. As the brothel was much used by Federal troops, there was no shortage of victims. When the killing stopped, a dozen of them lay dead.

Colonel John S. Mosby was of quite a different calibre. He was a member of the Confederate cavalry who, as existing photographs of him show, wore the uniform with pride. In 1863, he recruited a force of irregulars which he named 'the Partisan Rangers'. However, as the next chapter will show, Colonel Mosby's operations were sometimes bizarre.

4 The Snatch

According to a contemporary newspaper reporter, the most compelling elements in the face of John Singleton Mosby were his eyes. They might, the writer suggested, 'have induced the opinion that there was something in the man, if it only had an opportunity to come out'. He was, in many ways, a disturbing companion. For much of the time, his mouth wore a sardonic smile—as if he were enjoying some private joke that he was not ready to share. Mosby's talent to astound first revealed itself when he was studying law at the University of Virginia. A campus bully named George Turpin had, as Mosby recalled in later years, threatened to 'eat me up'. The two young men met outside one of the boarding houses. Turpin—armed with substantial brawn, but nothing else—advanced. Mosby stood his ground. For someone who was about to be severely beaten up, he seemed remarkably unconcerned.

The reason for his coolness became clear a second or so later. He suddenly pulled out a pistol and squeezed the trigger. Turpin collapsed. Although far from dead, it would be some time before he could menace anyone else. Shooting fellow undergraduates was not to be tolerated, even though the cause may have been a good one. The court in Charlottesville ordered Mosby to pay a fine of $1,000 and to serve six months in the local gaol. However, public opinion was on his side—and so, it transpired, was the appeal court judge. When his case was reviewed the sentence was quashed.

When the American Civil War broke out in 1861, Mosby was twenty-eight years old. For the last six of those years, he had been practising as an attorney in Bristol, Virginia. Now, he joined the Confederate cavalry as a trooper. He fought under General J. E. B. Stuart at the first Battle of Bull Run; on 17 February, 1862, somewhat to his surprise, he was promoted to lieutenant and appointed adjutant to his regiment.

He saw action at the approaches to Washington. For the following months, he carried out scouting duties for Stuart. In December, 1862, the two armies—Federal and Confederate—glared at each other from winter quarters on either side of the Rappahannock river. Mosby, as always, was impatient. Eventually he persuaded General Stuart that he might be able to serve the Confederate cause better if he carried out a series of raids on the Federal outposts. By the end of the year, with fifteen men under his command, he was on the far side of the river, commanding what he called 'the Partisan Rangers'. As he remembered, 'In general my purpose was to threaten and harass the enemy on the border, and in this way compel him to withdraw troops from his front to guard the line of the Potomac and Washington.'

Self-sufficiency was the keynote of the Partisan Rangers. Whatever they needed, they took—usually from the Yankees. Many of their recruits, indeed, came to them from the enemy lines, and Mosby showed little curiosity about their unexplained changes of loyalty. When, for example, a sergeant named Ames deserted the 5th New York Cavalry and offered his services one winter's day, Mosby never examined his motives. As was the custom, Ames had to prove himself by taking part in two or three small operations. Once he had completed his probationary period and convinced Mosby of his integrity, he was accepted.

It was probably the arrival of this renegade sergeant that gave Mosby the idea for an operation that was either outrageously daring—or foolhardy almost to the point of insanity. The defence of Washington south of the River Potomac was in the hands of Brigadier General E. H. Stoughton, whose headquarters were in Fairfax Court House—a small town about fifteen miles west of the capital. Colonel Percy Wyndham—an English mercenary who had fought with Garibaldi in Italy—was in charge of Stoughton's cavalry.

Wyndham had referred to Mosby as a 'horse thief', and the Ranger resented it. Since his partisans had helped themselves to a good many Federal mounts, there was, perhaps, some justification in the charge. But their leader was sensitive about such matters. He was a member of the Confederate cavalry—a soldier doing no more than his duty. It offended his self-esteem to be dismissed as a common robber. Wyndham, he decided, should be kidnapped. And, while he was about it, Stoughton might as well come too.

Ames was of great help in planning the affair. He had been stationed in Fairfax; knew the positions of all the pickets guarding the small town, the lay-out of its streets, and the buildings where Wyndham and Stoughton had their quarters. It should not, Mosby told himself, be too difficult.

It was now early March; a time of melting snows and fine drizzle, a season of mists and chill, when men preferred to remain indoors at night, and the vigilance of sentries was not very sharp. There would be no moon on the night of Tuesday the 8th. It would suit Mosby's purpose very well.

The strength of the partisans was that they needed no formal discipline. After each operation, the unit broke up, each man finding his own accommodation and amusing himself in his own way. They could never be run to earth—*en masse*, at any rate—for they had no camp. Nevertheless, when word went round that their services were needed, they mustered with an alacrity that would have done credit to more regular troops.

For the operation against Fairfax, they assembled at a point twenty-five miles from the town. Mosby had dined that evening with a retired colonel named Colville. The meal had been good, which was just as well. Many hours were to pass before he had another. Now, in the faint light of a lantern, he inspected his warriors. He was wearing his habitual, rather shabby, grey uniform and his wide-brimmed, brown felt hat. The others wore an assortment of civilian and military garb— even, in Ames's case, a pair of Federal breeches. Each was armed with a couple of revolvers. Mosby himself had a dislike of sabres, which may seem strange in a cavalry man, and he discouraged his men from using them.

As a body of soldiers, their appearance was not very impressive. Nor was their strength. There were only seventeen of them. Fairfax itself was garrisoned by at least one hundred troops, and there were several thousands in the vicinity. But, to quote one of Mosby's favourite axioms, 'the enemy can't count in the dark'. Small though the company was, it might be mistaken for a unit in a much larger formation.

He had already taken Ames into his confidence. Now it was time to brief the others. In Fairfax, each man had a particular job to do, and for a while the company would be split up into even smaller units. In a low voice, and speaking with a precision that had characterised his pleas as a student to the Charlottes-ville court, he told them about the geography of the town; the points where danger might be expected, and the locations of the various objectives. There was no room for any error. An error by one man might land them all in prison—and, quite possibly (for their status as soldiers was not too clear) on the scaffold.

Ames contributed a few points from his knowledge of Fairfax, and the men asked questions. When the conference was done, Mosby stood for a minute or two, peering into the blackness that hid the road leading to Chantilly, and seven miles beyond it, Fairfax. Then he climbed on to his horse. Turning to the company, he murmured a phrase he had borrowed from Disraeli—'adventures are to the adventurous'. He had used it on other occasions; the men seemed to like it. It was, perhaps, a suitable motto for the Partisan Rangers. With a wave of his hand, he gave the order to march.

The night was just as he had hoped it would be: moonless and the stars obscured by an overcast of cloud. The melting snow on the ground was made even more slushy by the fall of light rain. It was cold and uncomfortable, ideal for such a mission as this.

For a good many miles, they kept to the road. As they approached Chantilly, however, they had to contend with a line of Federal cavalry pickets. There would certainly be a post on the highway, and Ames had warned him of others in the vicinity. The sergeant was now acting as guide to the unit—leading it over the thin snow that carpeted the floor of a wood, and then on a snakelike course between the trunks of innumer-able pine trees. Mercifully, the landscape appeared to be unpopulated. Mosby smiled to himself; the others rode obedi-ently behind him—apparently unaware that they were now behind the enemy lines.

He had, he had worked out, to be at the courthouse by midnight. If he were any later, he might fail in his intention to be back on the far side of the Federal lines—and, indeed, a good few miles removed from them—by daybreak. But now the timetable seemed to be threatened. In the darkness of the wood, the small formation became split into two, and neither half knew where the other was. For a full hour, the bisected Partisan Rangers rode round in circles, blundering between the trees, each unit desperately searching for the other. The matter was resolved when, by a fortunate accident, the two sections collided with each other. But now, the Rangers were behind schedule—they would have to hurry. A few minutes later, they arrived at the edge of the wood. Beyond it was a field, and then the lights of Fairfax station, which had closed down for the night. The town was a mile or two farther on.

For the headquarters of a general, the base from which much of Washington's defence was conducted, Fairfax Court House seemed remarkably quiet. There were sentries on duty outside some of the buildings, but they must have mistaken the Rangers for one of their own cavalry troops. At all events, they did nothing to impede their progress. Even when a challenge was made and ignored, nothing was done about it. As Mosby had foreseen, these men were probably cursing the chill of the night, and wishing themselves indoors before blazing fires.

The company now split up into its various sub-units, which set off down the dark streets on their errands. Ames had been given command of a squad assigned to capture Colonel Wyndham. The irony of it appealed to him. Before he deserted, Wyndham had been the commanding officer of the sergeant's regiment.

A trooper named Joe Nelson had been detailed to locate the tent in which the telegraph operator and his assistant worked, and to cut the wires. Others had to find the officers' quarters and round up the horses. Mosby himself, accompanied by six men, proposed to take Brigadier General Stoughton into captivity.

Sergeant Ames and his section met with only moderate success. Wyndham, as it happened, had been summoned to Washington, and had caught the evening train to the capital. However, they helped themselves to the cavalry commander's belongings, and collected several horses. For good measure, they also captured a couple of staff officers. One of them, a Captain Barker, had been Ames's troop commander.

Nelson made short work of the telegraph wires and took the operator and his helper prisoner. The men assigned to the officers' lines were no less successful. Indeed, if Mosby's account of events was not supported by other evidence—including a report by the Provost-Marshal of Fairfax (a Lieutenant Connor who, like Wyndham, had been out of town that night)—it might be tempting to dismiss it as fiction. But Mosby did not exaggerate. Convinced that these intruders must be Federal troops, the garrison of Fairfax Court house had submitted itself without protest—to what? An enemy raid, or a series of crimes? It was hard to tell.

Mosby did not waste time looking for Stoughton's lodgings; he simply stopped a passing soldier and asked the way. He was informed that the general had moved into the rectory—a few yards down the road. At the front door, he and his escort dismounted. When he knocked, an upstairs window opened and somebody asked who was there. Mosby snapped back, 'Fifth New York Cavalry with a dispatch for General Stoughton.'

About one minute later, the front door was opened. One of Stoughton's aides, Lieutenant Prentiss, stood on the threshold in his nightshirt. Mosby grabbed the unhappy man's garment, whispered his name, and told him to lead the way to the general's bedroom. Each of the other partisans had now drawn his revolver, but Prentiss, who had been fast asleep a few moments ago, was not in the mood for heroics. Shrugging his shoulders, he meekly led the party upstairs.

Mosby was in a mood to be playful—and, perhaps, for self-publicity. In Stoughton's room, somebody lit a candle. The general was enjoying a good night's repose. It must have given him an unpleasant shock when Mosby dragged off the bedclothes, pulled up his nightshirt, and gave him a hard slap on his bare back.

Seeing Prentiss standing by the bed, Stoughton assumed that this was some prank—an officer, perhaps, who was drunk and was now taking a liberty he'd long regret. He was about to employ a rich vocabulary of reprimand, when the quiet voice of his captor asked whether he had ever heard of a Confederate named Mosby. The General said that he had. It was now time to bluff. 'I am Mosby,' his unwelcome visitor said. 'General Stuart's cavalry has occupied the Court House. Be quick and get dressed.' In fact, Stuart and his division were miles away on the far side of Virginia. But Stoughton seemed to believe him. If Fairfax had fallen, it might not be long before the Confederates were in Washington. It was an alarming thought. If he had been more alert, he might have wondered why one of his staff officers had not woken him up; or, indeed, how it had been possible to sleep through what must have been a hard fought battle. But neither idea seems to have occurred to him.

He blinked at Mosby, heaved himself half out of bed, and asked, 'Is Fitz Lee there?' He was referring to Colonel Fitzhugh Lee, who acted as Stuart's deputy. The general had been a contemporary of his at West Point. Mosby said that he was; that Stoughton might see him as soon as he was dressed. Again he told him to hurry.

Two men had remained outside to guard the horses. A trooper named Frank Williams had accompanied Mosby into the house. The others were busy emptying the stables. The street remained as quiet as ever.

General Stoughton had the reputation for being a brave man in action. He was also something of a fop. Even in these desperate circumstances, he was determined to look his best. He dressed slowly in front of a mirror, taking great pains with every detail. Mosby was now impatient. He seldom became excited—never let slip a suggestion that his veneer of self-confidence might contain any cracks. But now he walked quickly up and down the room, glancing constantly towards the window. It could surely not be long before a Federal officer realised what had happened. Perhaps playing for time, the general attired himself as if he were about to attend a ceremonial parade.

At last he was ready. Treating him politely, Mosby led him downstairs into the lobby. But then the general complained that he had forgotten his watch. Might he go back for it? Mosby sent Frank Williams to get it. Then he hurried his captive down the street leading to the Court House.

By this time, his other sections were assembled there. The
scene was unbelievable. Without firing a shot, or being fired
upon, they had collected heaven knows how many horses. It
was impossible to count them in the dark—nor to make an
accurate estimate of the number of prisoners. But Mosby
reckoned that they must have outnumbered his own men by
about three to one. Was it really possible that he might get
away with it? The fact that the telegraph wires had been cut
made sure that no messages could be sent to units outside
Fairfax. Nevertheless, this strange procession had yet to make
its way back through the Federal lines.

In an attempt to mislead the opposition, Mosby had decided
to leave Fairfax as though he were travelling east. Once clear
of the town, he would swing round and follow the Centreville
road. It would take longer, but it was sensible. When the
balloon went up—as go up it must eventually—the pursuing
forces would almost certainly travel in the wrong direction.

On the way out of town, the raiders were identified at last—
though, in all honesty, it was their own fault. If it had been
left to Mosby, with his quick wits and persuasive tongue, the
occasion might have enabled them to dissemble still more.

They were trotting along one of the streets, when somebody
opened a bedroom window, and asked what they were doing.
One of the men, intoxicated by so much easy success, burst out
laughing. Others joined in, and the laughter quickly became
jeers. It did not require a particularly well informed ear to
deduce that whoever had inquired about their business must
be an officer of some seniority. Since squads of enlisted men are
not in the habit of mocking their superiors, this man must now
have gathered that there were strangers in town. As Mosby
saw the situation, there was only one course open. The man
upstairs would have to join the general in captivity. It would
further disrupt his carefully thought out schedule, but there
seemed to be no alternative.

He ordered three of his men to dismount and batter down
the front door.

As they rushed inside, they were met by a formidable middle-
aged lady, who seemed determined to block their way; to hold
her ground, if need be, to the death. She was also a very angry
lady, who told them that her husband was a Colonel Johnstone.

They had, she assumed, heard of him? He was in charge of the cavalry brigade during Wyndham's absence.

It made sense. The colonel had obviously been woken up by the clatter of their horses. Once aroused, he might well have wondered what was happening; especially since there were no patrols due to go out—no earthly reason why horse soldiers should be taking to the road at dead of night.

Mrs. Johnstone's determination paid off. While she was promising Mosby's troopers damnation at the hands of her husband—or, possibly, from an even higher source—the colonel was running down a staircase at the back of the building, and taking cover behind a clump of bushes in the large garden. It cannot have been a comfortable experience, for he was naked. But it was perhaps better than being taken prisoner.

There was too little time left. To search the garden for the missing colonel might take ages. Mosby told his men to remount and move off. Mrs. Johnstone would tell her husband which way they were going. Even if he managed to assemble a cavalry unit within the next few minutes (and assuming he could find sufficient horses), he would be looking in the wrong direction. Mosby congratulated himself on the wisdom of planting false clues.

Once clear of Fairfax, they swung round and headed into the woods. They planned to join the Centreville road two miles on the other side of Fairfax.

The column was now spread out over some distance, and it was impossible to control it effectively in the dark. Not long after they had entered the wood, Lieutenant Prentiss, who had admitted Mosby to the general's house, suddenly made a bolt for it and escaped. Several other prisoners went with him, and they managed to take away a number of horses. General Stoughton, on the other hand, showed no such inclination. There was really no incentive. The fact that a small force of Confederate raiders had been able to penetrate his picket line, and go unhindered about their business in Fairfax, meant that his military reputation was ruined. Henceforth, he would have to count himself fortunate if he was given any posting at all— let alone be entrusted with an important command.

As they approached the highway, Mosby ordered the column to close up. Then he halted it. Leaving Sergeant Hunter in

command, he rode forward to reconnoitre. Everything was
quiet. He now deployed the small formation with parties on
the flanks—a scouting group out front, and a rearguard behind.
Hunter was holding on to the bridle reins of Stoughton's horse.
He was not to release them under any circumstances.

'With Joe Nelson', Mosby recalled afterwards, 'I remained
some distance behind. We stopped frequently to listen for the
hoofbeats of cavalry in pursuit, but no sounds could be heard
save the hooting of owls. My heart beat higher with hope every
minute; it was the crisis of my fortunes.'

The sky was slowly brightening; the hills on either side of
the road coming into focus. The scouting party suddenly
stopped, and one of its men came trotting back down the road.
They had, he told Mosby, spotted a fire burning some yards
ahead. It surely belonged to one of the pickets, but there had
been no challenge—no shots. Mosby halted the formation and
rode up to investigate. The fire was there, and there were signs
that there had been soldiers and horses as well. But it was now
deserted. It was understandable. As Ames had told him, the
Federal cavalry mounted an outlying picket on the road every
evening at sunset, and withdrew it at daybreak. The officer in
charge must have decided that, as nothing seemed to be
happening and the early morning sky was now flushed with
light, it was safe to go back to camp.

Mosby now remained at the front of the column. He could
see other fires burning in the camps on the hills around
Centreville; he could even make out the shapes of cannon in
the redoubts. But nobody seemed to be showing any interest in
him and his men. The look-outs must have mistaken them for
a troop of their own cavalry going out on patrol. The Federal
uniforms worn by the captives may have helped to create this
impression—though heaven knows what they made of the garb
worn by the Partisan Rangers.

He was considering the matter, when he heard a shot to his
rear. A Ranger of Hungarian extraction named Jake was firing
at Captain Barker, who had suddenly dug in his spurs and was
trying to make his escape towards one of the redoubts. Jake
was levelling his rifle to take a second shot when Barker's horse
blundered into a ditch, fell over and tumbled on top of him.
The man and the animal were put back on their feet; the

journey continued. Even this episode failed to awaken any interest from the sentries on the hills.

They skirted the Federal positions at Centreville with brazen effrontery, by-passed the town and rode on in a westerly direction. They were now clear of the Federal lines; but surely, by this time, Colonel Johnstone had emerged from his hiding place in the garden, put on some clothes, and done something about the matter. In fact, Johnstone had acted very promptly, but Mosby's ploy of leaving Fairfax by a road heading east had been successful. Far from following the Rangers, Johnstone's horsemen were riding away from them.

With the houses of Centreville now some way behind them, the Rangers and their captives were now approaching Bull Run, where a bloody battle had been fought in the previous year, and where another would take place in the coming August (both of them victories for the Confederates). About half-way between Centreville and the battlefield, there is a stream named Cub Run. It is a tributary of Bull Run and normally of no importance. On this occasion, however, it had become swollen by the melting snow. Far from ambling peaceably, it was surging along with unexpected violence, and the water level was far higher than usual. Mosby paused before it. Would the horses be able to swim across? The alternative was to turn back and try another route, but this would bring them back into full view of the Federal soldiery. This time, somebody was bound to be inquisitive.

Shouting to the general to ride beside him, he and his horse plunged into the swirling waters. By the time they reached the far bank, they were wet and extremely cold. Stoughton, who had said little so far, now raised his voice in gentle reproof. 'Captain', he said to Mosby, 'this is the first rough treatment I have to complain of.'

The sun was now well up, and it promised to be a glorious day. There were still no signs of any pursuit, and Mosby was feeling elated. When, twenty miles farther on, they entered the small town of Warrenton, his spirits became even higher, for the entire population turned out to give him and his men a hero's welcome. It was all most gratifying. As it happened, one of Warrenton's leading citizens was a gentleman named Beckham. In this strangely small world, Mr. Beckham's son was another of General Stoughton's West Point class mates. He was, admittedly, now serving as an officer in the Confederate artillery, but Mosby considered this sufficient reason to call at the house and ask for breakfast. They were, as he saw matters, now safe.

General Stoughton met his old friend Fitz Lee thirty-six hours after the operation had begun—at the latter's headquarters in the town of Culpepper. Lee appeared delighted to see him, though his attitude to Mosby was somewhat less than cordial. 'He treated me with indifference,' Mosby complained. 'He did not ask me to take a seat by the fire, nor seem impressed by what I had done.' It was all rather disappointing, and suggested to Mosby that a Ranger officer was not a welcome figure at headquarters establishments.

In fact, General Stuart was very much more appreciative. When he heard about the kidnapping operation, he formally commissioned Mosby as a captain in the Confederate forces. In December, 1864, when there were eight of these companies operating in the field, the Ranger leader was promoted to colonel, and given overall command of them.

Back in Fairfax, the provost-marshal, Lieutenant Connor, was now sitting in his office, looking glumly at a sheet of notepaper. He had to write a report on the affair, but how could he explain the removal of twenty-five Federal soldiers (among them a major, a captain and two lieutenants), twenty-six horses and a good deal of equipment? In the end, he decided to pass the blame on to Colonel Johnstone—pointing out that the colonel had at first mistaken them for a returning Federal patrol.

Neither Stoughton (who was exchanged some while later) nor Johnstone ever recovered from the shame of the matter; both vanished from the army records with little trace. Abraham Lincoln, when he heard about it, remarked, 'I don't mind the loss of a general, for I can make another in five minutes. But I hate to lose the horses.'

What *were* these men: regular soldiers operating in small units, or (as Colonel Wyndham had suggested) characters who were little better than horse thieves? Doubtless recalling the depredations of Quantrill's men in Kansas, the Federal government decided to brand them as outlaws. In Quantrill's case, this was largely true, for many of the men employed by him were precisely that. In Mosby's case, however, the ruling was a harsh one—made even worse when some of his troopers were captured and hanged without so much as a trial. It was not until he had retaliated by hanging some of Colonel Custer's men who had been taken prisoner, that the executions ceased. Thereafter, the Partisan Rangers enjoyed the same rights as other prisoners of war.

The word 'commando' was adopted by the British Army in June 1940, when Winston Churchill was considering a series of sea-borne attacks on the German-held coastline of Europe. What were these raiding parties to be called? 'Storm troops', 'striking companies' and (more imaginative, perhaps) 'Leopards' were toyed with and cast aside. Eventually, Churchill's mind went back to the Boer War, which he had covered as a correspondent for *The Morning Post*. The Boer troops had been self-sufficient, mobile, crack shots, experts in the use of ground and cover—indeed, they had nearly all the military virtues that would be needed in these amphibious operations. So *Commando* was settled upon—the word had the right sort of ring to it, and a sound ancestry.

In its South African War context, 'Commando' applied to pretty well any formation—no matter whether it was made up of ten men or 10,000. Like the early United States Rangers, its members might be described as amateurs. Indeed, the very word 'soldier' was anathema to them. They preferred to be called 'burghers' or, even, 'farmers', and this was not inappropriate. Most of them lived off the land: they had not learned their craft on some barrack square, but on hunting trips.

Unlike most other armies, the rank and file elected their own officers—and, by the same token, could dismiss them. *All* important decisions were made by councils of war—*krijgs-raads*—where the majority opinion prevailed. On several occasions, generals were outvoted by, and had to yield to the views of, men who, in the British army, would have been mere subalterns.

Such democratic procedure may suggest a laxity of discipline. In fact, it worked very well, for the men often had to use their initiative without running to some senior officer for guidance.

As far as weapons were concerned, they were better equipped than the British forces, for they had the new Mauser rifles and the latest field guns from the Krupp factory in Germany. But, even more important, they did not depend on cumbersome supply lines. A Boer Commando, whatever its size, travelled light.

When a British army moved into battle, its general had to pay as much attention to his waggon train as he did to the fighting soldiers. If the former was destroyed, or if it did not arrive punctually at the right place, the consequences might be disastrous. But the Commandos had no such problems. Each man travelled on a small horse, equipped with a rifle and bandolier, a blanket, a sack of mealies and biltong (strips of sun-dried lean meat) and a bag of spare cartridges. If members of a unit ran out of food, they slaughtered sheep—or else bought eggs from the black Africans.

The saddled-up weight of a burgher and his load seldom exceeded 250 pounds, whilst that of a British cavalryman and his accoutrements was probably about 400 pounds. The result was that the Boer horses became less easily tired and could travel longer distances. Several instances were recorded of small commando units covering sixty—sometimes seventy—miles in one day.

In battle, the Boer attitude differed in several respects to that of the British. Heroic refusals to retreat (such as the conduct of British gunners at Colenso) were a luxury that only armies with large resources of manpower could afford. It might furnish the stuff of legends; but, to the Boer Commandos, it did not make sense. They would hold a position for as long as it seemed prudent to do so, and not one minute more. On several occasions, so skilled was their fieldcraft, they managed to extract themselves from such situations without the enemy being aware of it.

Unlike their namesakes in World War II, the Boer Commandos did not take part in any amphibious operations. Nor did their example, which might have been noted with a good deal more than interest, have any effect on the British attitude to warfare. Throughout World War I, the general opinion was that big battalions could, on the whole, be overcome only by bigger battalions; that might could be vanquished only by something mightier.

Nevertheless, the conflict between 1914 and 1918 produced two ideas that were to recur between 1939 and 1945. The first—which was another of Winston Churchill's inspirations—was never put into practice. It did, however, find a most useful application during the Normandy invasion of 1944.

It was conceived by Churchill shortly before he joined the Cabinet as Minister of Munitions in 1917. To intensify the blockade of Germany, and to prevent U-boats leaving for forays in the Atlantic, a naval base was needed on the enemy's doorstep. The German-owned Frisian Islands of Borkum and Sylt were selected as ideal sites. They might either be captured by landing troops in specially built bullet-proof lighters—covered by naval guns firing a mixture of gas and high explosive shells—or they could be by-passed, and a rather more ingenious expedient used.

Rather than put troops at risk in an invasion, Churchill decided, it should be possible to create artificial islands. On the banks of the Wash, the Humber, the Medway and the Thames, barges could be built from concrete. They could be towed across the North Sea and sunk in shallow water. When it was possible, suction dredgers would pump them full of sand and gravel. They would provide pens for destroyers and submarines; a landing strip for aircraft. Having conceived this idea, Churchill's imagination took matters a stage further. The principle could be applied to the construction of platforms for heavy guns; for oil tanks, store-rooms and even living quarters.

Inevitably, the German intelligence network would learn about the manufacturing of these strange concrete barges; but, he decided, their purpose would probably be misconstrued. They could be mistaken for devices intended 'for an attempt to block up the river mouths'—which, when he came to think of it, was another good idea.

Nothing ever came of the plan, but World War I had produced one excellent example of a large scale commando raid—carried out entirely by personnel of the Royal Navy and Royal Marines. It was the attempt to block up the Belgian port of Zeebrugge and prevent U-boats from using it.

5 The Stopper

The German mine-laying submarine *UC44* was not, by any standards, an important vessel. It had been built at the Vulkan works in Hamburg during 1916. On a gusty October night in the following year, while going about its business in the Irish Sea off Waterford it collided with one of its own mines and blew up. That might very well have been the end of the matter. The Royal Navy, however, was not prepared to let the wreck lie undisturbed on the ocean bed. The *UC44* was brought to the surface and carefully examined. Among the contents of the badly damaged hull was a set of papers that caused great consternation at the Admiralty. Indirectly, the papers were responsible for the raid on St George's Day (23 April) 1918, when part of the Belgian port of Zeebrugge was transformed into a very passable imitation of hell.

Encouraged by Vice-Admiral Sir Reginald Bacon, commander of the Dover Patrol, the Admiralty had been under the impression that the Strait of Dover was virtually closed to enemy submarine traffic. Guarded by an assortment of warships ranging from a monitor to armed drifters, protected by nets and mines, this narrow link between the North Sea and the English Channel appeared to be impassable. The U-boats, which were taking such a severe toll of Allied shipping in the Atlantic, *had* to be making their way to the hunting grounds via the north of Scotland.

One of the documents on board *UC44* completely demolished any such ideas. Headed 'Instructions to U-boat Commanders', it stressed that the quickest and safest route to the Atlantic was by way of the Channel. The passage was to be made on the surface at night. If a boat was compelled to dive, it should submerge to a depth of forty metres, and remain there until it seemed safe to come up again.

Admiral Bacon's measures were based on his assumption that the boats would be travelling submerged, and the mines were sited at what he judged to be a suitable depth. As this document made clear, the submarines were relying entirely on darkness for cover—using their diesel engines to make the best possible speed, and passing over the tops of the hazards. Far from being an impenetrable barrier, Bacon's defences were scarcely an obstacle at all. About thirty submarines a month were taking this route. During the past two years, only two of them had been destroyed.

Bacon received a copy of the captured instructions, but appears not to have acted on the information. It was no doubt foolish. Inevitably, the UC44's documents were examined at the Admiralty and eventually, Bacon's conduct of the war in the Strait of Dover was questioned.

Indeed, the mood in Whitehall was one of reconsideration. Sir Eric Geddes had recently taken over as First Lord of the Admiralty; Admiral Sir Rosslyn Wemyss had replaced a very weary John Jellicoe as First Sea Lord. But, even more significant, was the 45-year old officer who, on 28 September, 1917, had been appointed Director of Plans. His name was Roger Keyes.

At the outbreak of war, Keyes was employed as commodore of submarines. During the 1915–16 Dardanelles campaign, he had served with some distinction as chief-of-staff to the naval commander-in-chief, Admiral de Robeck. Now he was sitting restlessly behind a desk, wishing himself in action.

Keyes was short, slender and, socially, inclined to be shy. But he was also a man of immense energy—impatient, apt to fly into sudden rages that evaporated equally quickly and fiercely jealous of the Royal Navy's reputation. He also happened to be a personal friend of Admiral Wemyss.

Once this stormy and relatively young rear admiral had studied the German admiralty's advice to submariners, events moved quickly. Before his departure from office, Jellicoe had predicted that, unless something very drastic were done, the Allied war effort would perish for want of shipping. It was a view that had to be taken seriously, for the U-boats were exacting a fearful toll. But now, with this information in the navy's possession, it should be possible to hinder their progress towards the Atlantic.

Bacon was eased out of his position as commander of the Dover Patrol; Keyes, promoted to vice-admiral, was appointed in his place. He immediately introduced a system of flares and searchlights by which the Dover Strait was illuminated at night. He directed the mines to be laid closer to the surface, and increased the vigilance of the warships. During the first month of his residence at Dover, five boats were destroyed. One was sunk by depth charges; the remaining four were caught in the glare of the illuminations—compelled to dive for cover and were demolished by mines.

This, however, was not the end of the matter. Keyes was determined to strike at the very source of these forays; to prevent the submarine marauders from proceeding to sea at all. The key to such a plan seemed to be the Belgian port of Zeebrugge—and, perhaps, to a lesser extent, Ostend.

When the Germans overran most of Belgium in 1914, their purpose had been to take an easy way into France. But, when the war turned out to be longer and bloodier than they had expected, a bonus soon became apparent. Belgium could provide ports at the threshold of the Channel. It provided an excellent point of departure for U-boats.

The submarines themselves were berthed in the inland port of Bruges—the apex of a triangle with the North Sea as its base. One arm was a canal eight miles long, running in a straight line to Zeebrugge; the other, eleven miles long, connected Bruges to Ostend. In fact, the latter was too small to be navigable by these vessels, but the British Admiralty was unaware of this.

Ever since its occupation by German forces, Zeebrugge had been regarded as a flaw in the grand design for an Allied victory. From time to time, plans had been conceived to regain the port—or, at least, to neutralise its role as an exit for U-boats. Two such plans had been devised by Bacon who was seldom at a loss for an original idea. The admiral, not unreasonably, decided that the key to the problem lay in the lock gates through which the canal debouched into Zeebrugge

harbour. If these could be destroyed, the inland waterway
would be put out of action. For his first essay in destruction,
he designed a monitor armed with an 18-inch gun. The idea
was that it should approach the Belgian coast under cover of a
smoke screen, and pound the gates to pieces at the somewhat
improbable range of 24,000 yards. If this failed, coastal motor
boats would enter the harbour, and complete the work of
demolition with their torpedos. Since Zeebrugge was known to
be heavily defended, the likelihood of these boats returning
from the mission had to be reckoned small.

Later the ingenious Admiral Bacon produced a variation on
the plan. It was that the 18-inch gun would be landed
somewhere along the coast, transported into Zeebrugge and set
up in the Palace Hotel, where it would open fire from a
somewhat closer range. But this, too, had its snags. The shores
of Belgium were guarded by batteries of 12-inch guns; the
weight of Bacon's gun was all of 150 tons; and a very large
number of troops would be needed for a venture that, even
then, had to be accounted a gamble.

But the inventive Admiral Bacon was not yet done. Having
consigned these ideas to the wastepaper basket, he re-designed
a monitor named HMS *Sir John Moore*—equipping it with false
bows capable of withstanding a 1,000-ton shock, and fitting the
forecastle with a ramp along which (in theory, at any rate)
troops could disembark marching eight abreast. This, in some
respects, was nearer the mark—though, like so many of the
admiral's ideas, it never developed beyond the drawing board.

In 1916, Admiral Bayly produced a scheme for an elaborate
combined operation involving landings on the German Frisian
Island of Borkum—as well as at Zeebrugge and Ostend; and,
in the same year, Commodore Tyrwhitt put up a suggestion
for inserting a blockship into the canal mouth under a barrage
of poison gas. This, obviously, put those taking part at the
mercy of the wind (a sudden shift would be disastrous), and
had to be rejected.

The army, too, demonstrated its awareness of the Zeebrugge
problem—though to very little avail. The object of the third
Battle of Ypres—better known as Passchendaele—in July, 1917,
was to turn the German flank and drive a way to Zeebrugge
and Ostend. But everything became bogged down in a sea of

mud. The troops advanced for no more than half a mile—the purpose became forgotten, and the affair degenerated into the usual Western Front contest of seeing which side could slaughter the bigger number of opponents.

Soon after he moved into Dover, Roger Keyes took up the question of Zeebrugge yet again. Tyrwhitt's idea of blocking up the entrance to the canal seemed to be a good one; Bacon's notion of converting a warship into a large assault craft also had something to commend it. Each in its way provided a starting point. The question was: how could they be made to work?

Zeebrugge nestles in the shelter of its mole—which was at the time the longest in the world. One and a half miles long, it takes the form of an arc curving round towards the north-east, and guarding the canal's approaches. The entrance itself is about 500 yards long—a reasonably wide waterway that ends suddenly at the lock gates.

Reconnaissance flights by the 61st Wing of the RAF had shown that the mole and the adjacent shore were extremely heavily defended. Assuming that the correct solution to the problem was to stop up the seaward end of the waterway from Bruges, these obstacles would have to be overcome. If they were not, the blockships would never reach their destinations in one piece.

Batteries of big guns were clustered on the neighbouring shore; but Keyes had little doubt that these could be subdued by a heavy barrage from the equally substantial weapons of monitors. The monitors could also bombard the area inland and hinder the arrival of reinforcements to the 1,000-strong garrison of Zeebrugge. But this was the simple part of the undertaking. Such action, though vital, would not enable him to pierce the port's immediate defences.

Again and again, Keyes turned his attention to the mole—studying charts and aerial photographs, reading and re-reading the pilots' reports. This, he felt certain, was the key to whatever operation he might design. If only this huge breakwater could be occupied and its defences smashed, everything else would be possible.

The mole was divided into four parts. Its progress from the shore began with a 300-yard long causeway carrying a footpath, a road and a railway line. This was followed by a steel viaduct, also 300 yards long, that enabled the surge of the North Sea to sweep through and scour out the intruding sand from the harbour. After that, the business of the mole began in earnest; it widened considerably to accommodate the peacetime paraphernalia—such as sheds and cranes and wharves—required by cross-Channel traffic. This section was more than 1,600 yards long. Finally, there was a 360-yard breakwater reaching its conclusion in a lighthouse.

But this complexity of civil engineering did more than shelter the approaches to Zeebrugge; it also protected its various installations against the ravages of sea and storm. This was accomplished by a wall, sixteen feet high, with a road running along the top. Since it served as a highway, it, too, required shelter—which was provided by a second wall nine feet high. The extension leading to the lighthouse was more moderate in its needs: in this case, the parapet was only four feet high.

At high water, the distance between sea level and the top of the nine-foot wall was twenty-nine feet.

Doubtless, when working on his plan, Admiral Keyes often had occasion to curse the Belgian architects and their elaborate ideas. The German occupying power had, of course, made full use of their defensive possibilities. As the aerial photographs made fairly clear, there were two 3.5-inch guns and four 4.1-inch guns on the extension leading to the lighthouse; and a couple of batteries (probably of 5.9-inch guns) at the point where the causeway joined the shore. In the area of the railway station on the main section of the mole, four large hangars had been built to serve as a seaplane base—and a vast concrete structure provided living quarters for the garrison. In addition to all this, there were machine-gun posts, anti-aircraft guns, cannon specially made for firing star shells, barbed wire entanglements and breastworks for the protection of riflemen.

The Germans, rightly deducing that eventually Zeebrugge would come under attack, had transformed this once peaceable arc of concrete into an elongated fortress of most ferocious capability. Nevertheless, if blockships were to reach the canal entrance, it had to be overcome. The preliminary of this show of naval power, Keyes decided, would be the barrage of the monitors, which would pound the German gun emplacements

on the coast, and create havoc inland. Then, the agile motor
launches and coastal motor boats of the fleet would lay a
curtain of smoke to conceal the approaching armada. Having
done so, they would serve any purpose within their compe-
tence—from firing torpedoes at German naval craft, to picking
up survivors from the blockships and any other vessels that
might be sunk.

To root out the gunners on the mole and to smash their
emplacements was a soldier's job. Indeed, at first there was talk
of the army contributing men for this purpose. But then the
admiral had second thoughts. This was to be a naval occasion;
the action of a select band of warriors who would be asked to
perform deeds transcending even the normal standards of
heroism. Membership of this special assignment should be
confined to his own service. Only blue jackets and Royal
Marines should be allowed to participate.

But these men had to be conveyed to their destination. To
perform the task, he selected an aged cruiser that was deemed
to be expendable, and a couple of ferry boats that normally
went unmolested across the River Mersey—carrying passengers
between Liverpool and the Cheshire bank. The cruiser was a
veteran warship named HMS *Vindictive*, which had been built
at Chatham Dockyard in 1899. Displacing 5,750 tons, and
armed with ten 6-inch guns, nine 12-pounders and three 18-
inch torpedo tubes, it was powered by a triple-expansion engine
that, with coal-fired boilers at full pressure, gave the ship a top
speed of 19 knots. With its three lanky funnels and a far from
athletic hull, it looked like a vessel more suited to coastal
defence chores than to the present perilous assignment.

Vindictive, it seemed certain, would die. But at least its death
would be an occasion of fire and glory—and not the ignominy
of some breaker's yard. For the ferry boat role, the steamers
Iris and *Daffodil* were chosen on account of their manoeuvra-
bility and shallow draught. They, too, seemed hardly likely to
return to their more humdrum role on the Mersey.

Keyes now found himself heavily involved in the market for
unwanted warships. For the part of blockships, he engaged a
trio of cruisers each of which was even more elderly than
Vindictive—*Thetis*, *Intrepid* and *Iphigenia*, the youngest of which
was *Intrepid* (a not very sprightly twenty-four year old). But,

since the object was to sink them at the canal mouth, their
infirmities were no handicap.

In addition to all this, there were destroyers—and two very
old submarines. Keyes had thought of every possibility. He had
to accept that, once his intention became clear to the Germans,
more troops would be rushed to reinforce those on the mole.
But here the elaborate system of construction could be turned
to his advantage. The most vulnerable feature was the 300-
yard viaduct. If it were demolished, any such action would be
impossible. For this purpose, he picked a couple of obsolete
submarines, *C1* and *C3*. Each was to be filled with explosives
and steered to its final resting place amid the viaduct's piers.
Fuses would be ignited; the crews would depart in haste
(hopefully to be picked up by a motor launch) and, with a bit
of luck, this section of the mole would be blown to smithereens.

But there was more to it than composing a list of vessels.
The stars, so to speak, of the production had to receive special
treatment. The ferry boats, for example, needed armour to
protect them against the shot and shell that would be directed
against them. *Vindictive* itself was not yet adequate for its new
responsibilities; not least, because the topmost deck fell many
feet short of the mole's parapet—even at high tide.

The responsibility for adapting the cruiser to its new purpose
fell largely to the *Vindictive*'s executive officer, Lieutenant
Commander Rosoman. By building a false upper deck along
the entire length of her port side, he raised it sufficiently to
meet the occasion—though there was still the problem of
getting the Marines and sailors ashore. No doubt Rosoman
and his colleague, Engineer Lieutenant Commander W. S.
Bury, carefully studied Bacon's idea of a single eight-foot wide
ramp. The admiral was thinking along the right lines; but,
when it came to the hurried disembarkation of three companies
of Royal Marines and at least 200 sailors, it was not adequate.
Instead, they devised a system of eighteen gangways, each
twenty-seven inches wide, that would be lowered from the top
of the false deck.

In an attempt to increase the armament, an 11-inch howitzer
was mounted on the quarter-deck, and 7.5-inch guns were
installed on the false deck and on the forecastle. A flame-

thrower was incorporated on the port side—just forward of the bridge.

For the raid to stand any chance of success, it would have to take place during darkness, at high tide, and with the wind blowing from off the sea to nudge the smoke screen in towards the enemy. It would also have to be carried out quickly. As *Vindictive*'s commanding officer, Commander Alfred Carpenter, said afterwards, 'If it were carried out in the latter part of the night—that is to say, by the morning twilight when our ships could be seen from the shore, there was practically no chance of any ship getting away.' But, even if everything went according to plan, the likelihood of many returning alive had to be reckoned as small.

With such uncomfortable odds against survival, Keyes decided that volunteers only should take part—and that these must be unmarried men. Depots of the Royal Marines, the Grand Fleet, and commands such as Dover were asked to lend personnel for the occasion, and each applicant was carefully screened. The men (to quote Commander Carpenter) 'were given to understand that they were going on a hazardous enterprise', but, at this point, they were not told precisely what it involved. Indeed, when a near-replica of the mole was constructed on a hillside near Dover, the story was circulated that it represented a strong point behind the German lines on the Western Front. Nobody seems to have doubted it.

Eventually, three companies of Royal Marines were assembled at Deal. The force, which was known as the 4th Battalion Royal Marines, amounted to 740 officers and men. It was commanded by Lieutenant Colonel B. N. Elliot. Also destined for duty on the mole were 200 sailors (fifty of them volunteers from the Grand Fleet) led by Captain H. C. Halahan, RN. The Grand Fleet contingent was to be used mostly for demolition work.

By the time these volunteers—and there was certainly no lack of them—had completed their special training, 'we all (to quote one of the Royal Marines) knew the mole as though we had lived there'. What was more, each had a very thorough understanding of the overall picture. The possibility that all the officers might be wiped out could not be discounted. Under such circumstances, the men would have to manage on their own.

Originally, it had been intended to go forward with the raid on the night of 11–12 April. On the first of the month, aircraft from the 61st Wing carried out a final reconnaissance; on the 9th, bombers from the 65th Wing made a low-level attack on Zeebrugge. On the evening of the 11th, Roger Keyes's fleet put to sea from the Thames estuary on the 72-mile journey. The weather was poor at the outset; when they were a few miles from the Belgian coast, it became even worse. To attempt to land men under such circumstances would have been impossible. Keyes, in his flagship—the destroyer HMS *Warwick*—decided to turn back. The operation would have to wait until conditions improved.

For the next ten days, the weather continued bad, and the landing party was confined on board an ancient battleship of pre-Dreadnought vintage named HMS *Hindustan*. These men had become tuned to a certain pitch by 11 April; eager to do and, if necessary, to die. Now, faced with an anti-climax, their morale might have declined. A state of mind in which a man may eagerly face the prospect of death can quickly become replaced by resignation—and that, in its turn, by reluctance.

These sailors and Marines, however, even though they had been given time to think about it, never questioned the wisdom of their decisions to volunteer—nor the nature of the adventure which, if conditions improved sufficiently, might actually take place. Indeed, there was an uncommon eagerness to take part. The crews of the blockships were to be reduced to the minimum—for the very sensible reason that, when the time came to leave them, there would be fewer men for the motor launches to rescue. Nevertheless, the surplus ratings came close to mutiny, when they sent a deputation to their commanding officer. Why, they wished to know, should they be excluded from this chance to earn themselves some glory?

Other vessels found out in mid-passage that they actually had stowaways on board. When the time came to go ashore on the mole, the intruders picked up rifles and belts of ammunition, and took their chances with the others.

At last, in the late afternoon of the 22nd, the going appeared good enough. From HMS *Warwick*, from which Keyes's flag flew like a huge white sheet at the foremast, came the signal,

'Saint George for England'—a doubtless appropriate thought on the eve of Saint George's Day. Carpenter in *Vindictive*, an officer with a nice sense of humour who was seldom stuck for the apt phrase, replied: 'May we give the dragon's tail a damned good twist.' The game was afoot; the fleet of seventy-seven vessels ranging from the latest destroyers to the inoffensive ferry boats, from the fast-moving CMBs (coastal motor boat) to the lumbering *Vindictive*, set its bows towards the darkness of the North Sea. The future was anyone's guess, and nobody cared to consider it too minutely.

Owing to the bad weather, the aircraft of the 65th Wing had been unable to repeat their raid of the 9th; whatever was done to soften up the defences would have to be accomplished by the 15-inch guns of the monitors *Erebus* and *Terror*. But there were other hazards against which no precautions could be taken. This part of the Belgian coast was beset by shifting sandbanks upon which the larger vessels might become firmly lodged. And had the Germans put down a minefield at the approaches to Zeebrugge? There had been no reports to this effect, but it would have been a sensible expedient. Indeed, it would surely be surprising if a raid such as this, which had been so elaborately prepared over a period of two months, and then postponed should catch the enemy unawares. There must surely be German spies in the neighbourhood of Dover. If they were only moderately competent, they would have dispatched enough information to enable an astute commander to piece together a picture of Admiral Keyes's intentions.

Every man had a specific job to do. The task of Wing Commander F. A. Brock, was, perhaps, the least clearly defined. Brock was a remarkable man, who created some sort of record by holding the ranks of lieutenant commander in the navy, lieutenant colonel in the army, and wing commander in the RAF. The heir to a firm of firework manufacturers, he was a man of many inventions. His skill at pyrotechnics had devised the flares that had assisted Keyes in his attempt to illuminate the Dover Strait. He had produced a smoke float that emitted no flames—and consequently did not betray its source—and he had been responsible for considerable advances in the technology of such things as Very lights and signalling devices. Indeed, it was his smoke floats that, if all went all, would screen the approaching ships from the German look-outs. His main purpose in accompanying the raid was to study their performance in action—though he was also hoping to investigate some new German range-finding equipment that was said to be installed in a battery on the mole's extension.

The two submarines, now charged with explosives to demolish the viaduct, were towed towards their destination; *C1* by the destroyer HMS *Trident*, *C3* by HMS *Mansfield*. Somewhere in the middle of the North Sea, *C1*'s hawser parted, and she had to be taken back to Dover. *C3*, commanded by Lieutenant Richard Sandford, would have to do the job for both.

It was now nearly 11.30 pm. Twenty-three motor launches were out in front, ready to drop the smoke floats upon which so much depended. Everything seemed to be going in the expedition's favour. The wind was blowing from the north-east—from which direction it would drive the fumes in blinding clouds towards Zeebrugge's defenders. The sky was overcast, blotting out the pattern of stars and the waning moon. Although a swell was running, the sea was calm enough to make the landing possible.

Aboard HMS *Warwick*, Keyes was cautiously optimistic. In *Vindictive* and the two ferry boats, the Royal Marines had been issued with a ration of rum. Lieutenant Colonel Elliot was chatting to his men. They seemed in good heart—impatient to get on with their work. As for Commander Carpenter at his post in the cruiser's wheelhouse, he was listening contentedly to the distant thunder of the monitors' guns as they pounded the Belgian coast. 'It was', he afterwards remarked, 'one of the most heartening things I can remember.'

Punctually at 11.30, the first of the motor launches released its smoke floats. There was a scattering of fire from the shore; but, as the black fog rolled forward, it became erratic. Then it stopped. A light mist was turning into rain.

The wind is an unfaithful ally; capricious—even mean. At 11.56, it suddenly veered round to the south. This was the worst possible stroke of misfortune. The smoke, upon which the raiders depended for surprise, was now wafted uselessly out to sea. But it was too late to call the operation off. Vice-Admiral Keyes and the thousand or so men under his command were committed.

It was as if the wind's change of direction had acted as a signal. One moment, everything was dark; the ships no more than faint black blobs on the gently heaving sea. Now, suddenly, there was light. Star shells created artificial suns; searchlights groped at first, seeking their targets—and then steadied as they picked out one or another of the ships.

One motor-launch skipper professed to be grateful for it. 'We were', he said, 'really glad of the light, for we were not sure where we were. A searchlight was turned on me, but this was not at all powerful and caused no trouble.'

But he was in the minority. Once the German gunners were able to make out targets, their reaction was understandably savage. As one seaman put it, 'We steamed through the smoke screen, and then we caught hell. There is no other word for it.' And, from *Vindictive*'s CO: 'One had an extraordinary naked feeling when one saw how exposed we were—even though it was the middle of the night.'

The first shots had been fired by five or six guns on the mole at a range of about 300 yards. Every gun on the *Vindictive* replied, as the old cruiser slowly turned to go alongside. Commander Carpenter ordered extra speed to bring her round more quickly. She was now rolling heavily in the swell that surged against the great concrete structure. The task of landing the shore party was not going to be easy.

It seemed like hell itself; the sky aflame with bursting star shells—the mounting din as more and more guns joined in the chorus of destruction; and the figures of men, running this way and that, some pausing in a moment of final agony and falling down. But, within this context of violence, there was a strange orderliness. The ferry boat *Daffodil* took up station as if long used to such tasks, and pushed *Vindictive* sideways towards its berth on the seaward side of the mole. Then its landing party, and that of *Iris*, swarmed on to the cruiser's deck, waiting to disembark.

But the cruiser was now rolling heavily. Commander Carpenter noticed that, at one moment, the gangways were eight or ten feet above the wall; the next they were crashing down upon it. 'The way the men got over those brows', he said, 'was almost superhuman.' And there were now only four of them in any condition to be used. Enemy gunfire had accounted for several; others were smashed to pieces by the motion of the ship. Nevertheless, amid the racket of battle, somebody could be heard yelling, 'Over you go, Royals!' It was probably Captain A. R. Chater of the 4th Battalion, for it was he who led one of the first two parties ashore. The other, under Lieutenant Commander Bryan Adams, was made up of seamen. Both had to make their ways along the 30-foot ramps that were now tilted at an angle of 45 degrees. As soon as they stepped ashore, they were met by intense machine-gun fire.

As one of the Marines afterwards recalled, 'There was a perfect din from our bombarding fleet, the German guns replying, bombs, machine guns and the terrific explosions caused by our destruction parties. There seemed to be flames everywhere.'

During World War II, Commandos were lightly equipped. But these men, as they struggled up the ramps and on to the mole, were laden with Lewis guns, hand grenades and drums of ammunition. Even when they reached the ends of these perilous ramps, they might be confronted by a drop of eight feet. Nor were the men detailed to carry out demolitions on the German installations any more fortunate. The only available explosive was gun cotton—each slab about the size of a brick. To carry them to the targets, large baskets normally used to deliver parcels had been commandeered from the General Post Office.

Nothing was easy; everything was accomplished under extreme peril. Even the task of securing *Vindictive* to the mole exacted a price in lives. Colonel Elliot of the Royal Marines and Captain Halahan of the navy's storming party were both killed before the cruiser was alongside. Wing Commander Brock was last glimpsed hurrying towards the lighthouse on the extension. What happened to him afterwards can only be speculation—though a seaman said he had seen him charging a gun position. If this was indeed Brock, he died in the attempt.

It was not enough to come ashore; the German guns had to be put out of action before the blockships entered harbour. Everybody had to be on the move. When one man dropped, another had to take his place; if one section was wiped out, another had to assume its duties.

Lieutenant Commander A. L. Harrison was wounded while still on board *Vindictive*. His jaw was fractured and he was left behind—apparently unconscious. But now he, too, appeared on the mole, where he took command of a party of sailors. The objective was one of the 4.1-inch guns, but the way was temporarily barred by an enemy machine-gun post. The 4.1 was not demolished. Nevertheless, it presently ceased firing. Presumably, its crew had all been killed or wounded. By this time, Harrison, too, was dead.

The wall of the mole sheltered *Vindictive*'s hull from enemy fire, but her funnels and upperworks were receiving tremendous punishment. The howitzer was put out of action early on, and so was one of the 7.5-inch guns. The other was manned throughout the action, single-handed at times, by a company sergeant major from the Royal Marines.

C3 was fitted with automatic controls, which would enable it to home on the viaduct after its crew had made their getaway. But *C3*'s captain, Lieutenant R. D. Sandford preferred to leave nothing to chance. He personally took over the wheel and remained there until the small vessel was securely wedged in place amid the piles. Then, allowing his men time to make their escape in a tiny motor boat, he lit the fuses. Once this was accomplished, he joined them—only to find that the boat's propeller had fallen off, and they would have to row. German soldiers on the road above lost no time in opening fire with rifles and machine-guns as the sailors toiled at the oars.

The old submarine exploded with (as one man put it) 'a terrific uproar'. The timing, as it turned out, was perfect. A platoon of German infantry was hurrying towards the mole on bicycles. Suddenly the way ahead vanished; and, one by one, they free-wheeled into eternity. Shortly afterwards, the gallant submariners were picked up by one of the motor launches.

At twenty minutes past midnight, the three blockships rounded the end of the mole, and steamed cautiously towards their final resting places. Each came under fire, but the German gunners had much to think about, and they were being constantly harried by the Royal Marines and seamen on the mole. Consequently, it was by no means as heavy as it might have been. *Thetis* fouled an anti-submarine net near the harbour entrance. By now her engines had been shot out of action, and she was beginning to sink. Her crew abandoned ship; specially prepared charges blew out her bottom, and she settled across one of the dredged channels. It had not gone entirely according to plan; but, in this position, the ancient cruiser could be accounting a serious enough obstacle to enemy shipping.

Intrepid and *Iphigenia* both reached the entrance to the canal in spite of heavy fire. Then they, too, were sunk and their crews rescued by MLs, which were scurrying from point to point like sheepdogs as each gathered up its quota of stranded mariners.

Doubtless it seemed like an eternity, but the action at Zeebrugge that April night lasted for little more than one hour. Presently, the whistles on the ships were sounding the recall. But such things take time. For one thing, there was so much noise from the guns, that the signal had to be repeated several times before anyone heard it. And then there was the task of bringing the dead and wounded on board. All told, twenty minutes elapsed between Keyes deciding that his work was done, and the ships moving away towards the open sea.

Vindictive and the two Mersey ferries were badly damaged, but all three were still seaworthy. As they headed back into the North Sea, the enemy guns pursued them. Said Commander Carpenter, 'The shells seemed to fall all round the ships without actually hitting them. The German gunners had judged the speed correctly, but not the range. Regularly, salvoes plopped into the sea behind us.' At one stage in the action, *Vindictive*'s commanding officer had doubted 'whether there was anybody on board who really thought we should get back'. Now, as they headed back to Dover at full speed, and the action passed into the hands of the ships' surgeons who were busy trying to repair the wounded, everything seemed strangely quiet. Carpenter's last thought about the battle was; 'Really, now it is all over, it all seems like a dream.'

One of the men awaiting their return was a reporter from *The Times*. 'They keep returning here in driblets', he wrote, 'some hobbling and limping as best they can, and others able to march to the depot. They appear so exhausted by their hard fighting, that it is impossible to get a coherent and connected story of the enterprise.' However, one Royal Marine was able to say, 'All that I can tell you is that we landed, and that for more than an hour we were subjected to heavy fire, which we returned with compound interest.'

The Germans, predictably, asserted that the raid had been a failure. They announced that their naval losses had been 'of the lightest' and that 'no more than forty men succeeded in reaching Zeebrugge, and, dead or alive, they fell into our hands'. However, the Kaiser himself judged the operation to be of sufficient importance to pay a hurried visit to the port and inspect the damage. More to the point, was the observation of Captain Ion Hamilton, a motor-launch flotilla commander who, some months later, visited Zeebrugge. He noted that, 'The two blockships that got into the canal on 23 April completely blocked it.'

Afterwards came the rewards. Such was the heroism of that angry night, that the recommendations for the Victoria Cross surpassed all bounds. Among those who received it were Alfred Carpenter (now promoted to captain), Lieutenant Richard Sandford of the *C3*, and Lieutenant Commander Harrison (who received it posthumously). Admiral Keyes was awarded a knighthood; the names of the two Mersey ferries were prefixed by the word 'Royal'. For the *Vindictive*, however, the safe return to England was no more than a reprieve.

That same night, there had been an attempt to block Ostend harbour. It had been a failure. On the night of 9–10 May, a second was made—this time with the old cruiser in the role of blockship. For most of its life, its career had been unspectacular, but it experienced glory at Zeebrugge—and died serving a useful purpose. It was more than most ships of that generation could expect.

Among the designations tentatively applied to the early Commandos were the letters SS, standing for 'special service'. However, the Germans, too, used them as an abbreviation—in this case, for *Schutzstaffel*. Since these men were the assault troops of Hitler's body-guard (an élite of heroism or villainy according to your side), the coincidence was not a very happy one, and the letters were not widely used.

Indeed, to liken a Commando raid to an operation by the SS (Nazi version) may incur the wrath of the former's veterans. Nevertheless, the concern of this book is with actions rather than ethics, and it might be argued (at least one writer has done so) that World War II was actually started by SS raiders.

Some excuse, no matter how improbable, had to be found for Germany's invasion of Poland. There had been a number of shooting incidents along the German-Polish frontier, but they amounted to very little. They were certainly not sufficiently dramatic to lend any weight to an argument that German communities in these places were being oppressed. Reinhard Heydrich, head of the SD (*Sicherheitdienst*—the SS security service) and Gestapo chief Heinrich Müller considered the problem, and presently produced an idea. The proposed scene of operations was the small German frontier town of Gleiwitz. It was a place of little importance, except that, on the edge of it, there was a local radio station. This was the key to their plan.

A small party of SS men was to be dressed in Polish army uniforms. The raiders were to force their way into the station; overcome the staff, and broadcast a statement denouncing Hitler and Germany as warmongers. Since the range of Gleiwitz's transmitter was only a few miles, the speech was to be sent over a landline to Breslau—where it would be re-transmitted to the whole *Reich*. German public opinion would be inflamed; to the rest of the world, it might seem as if the 'Polish' action were provocation enough.

Alfred Naujocks, a young SD officer with few scruples, was chosen to lead the raid. Admiral Canaris, head of the military intelligence service, agreed to provide Polish uniforms, and by 5 August 1939, the preparations were almost complete. At the last moment, however, somebody suggested that it would be a poor reflection on German security forces if the raiders escaped without casualties. How much more convincing it would be if one of them were killed.

Müller agreed that the suggestion was a good one. A Jew with a sufficiently Aryan likeness should be selected from the inmates of a concentration camp, and shot. His corpse would be dressed in one of the Polish uniforms—the pockets filled with a packet of Polish cigarettes, Polish matches, and even letters and bills written in Polish. After the raid, it would be dumped at the radio station's entrance.

One afternoon in late August, seven men wearing civilian clothes and describing themselves as 'mining engineers', arrived in a couple of black Ford V8s at the Oberschlesescher Hof, Gleiwitz's leading hotel. They spent two days making their final arrangements. At dusk on 31 August, Operation 'Canned Goods' (as it was called) was put into effect. Still wearing civilian clothes and carrying suitcases, the men piled into a large black Opel and drove to the radio station—about two miles out of town.

Müller had personally selected a victim and supervised the execution. The corpse, now attired as a Polish officer, lay in the Opel's boot.

Within sight of the radio station, the men changed into their Polish uniforms. They stormed the premises, beat up the staff, and took over the transmitter. At the last moment, however, a snag occurred. Nobody could discover how to switch on the landline to Breslau. The speech, made by one of them, was transmitted—though it seemed unlikely that anybody beyond Gleiwitz had heard it.

Leaving the dead 'Polish officer' on the building's steps, they withdrew. The mission had, they ruefully decided, been a failure. However, news of the raid had been leaked to the Nazi party's newspaper *Volkisher Beobachter*, which published the text in full and made indignant editorial comment. Next day, on 1 September, German forces crossed the frontier into Poland. World War II had begun.

Alfred Naujocks distinguished himself again in November of that year, when he led a raid on the Dutch frontier town of Venlo. The object in this case was to kidnap two British secret service officers, Major S. Payne Best and Captain R. Henry Stevens. The operation had originally begun by SD security service chief Walter Schellenberg making trips into Holland with the object of penetrating the British intelligence network.

Pretending to represent a German general with strong anti-Nazi views, he had succeeded in making the acquaintance of Payne Best and Stevens. After several meetings, he put forward an entirely bogus peace plan that included the guarantee of withdrawing German troops from Czechoslovakia and Poland,

the holding of plebiscites in Austria, the Sudetenland and
Danzig, equal status for Jews in Germany, the arrest of Hitler
and the disbanding of the Nazi party.

Major Payne Best had been sufficiently impressed to provide
Schellenberg with a radio set for further communications, and
an invitation to London to discuss matters in greater details.
Schellenberg was congratulating himself on the prospect of
becoming a master spy when, on the night of 7 November, he
received an unexpected phone call from Himmler. The idea
would have to be abandoned; Schellenberg must cease his
attempts to deceive—instead, he must bring his contacts to
Berlin for questioning.

The reason for the change of plan was an event which had
occurred that evening in Munich. Hitler, as was his wont on 7
November, had been addressing Nazi party veterans in one of
the city's beer cellars. The object was to celebrate the anniversary of the 1923 *putsch*. Shortly after he had left the premises, a
bomb exploded. This, Himmler was convinced, was the work
of the British secret service. It was essential to find out more,
and it could best be achieved by the persuasive methods of the
Gestapo.

Next afternoon, Schellenberg had an appointment to meet
Payne Best and Stevens in a café at Venlo. At 3.20, an hour
late for the meeting, the two British officers arrived accompanied by a Dutch intelligence officer named Klop.

Schellenberg made a pretence of getting down to business,
when a grey Mercedes with Naujocks and his gang on board
hurtled towards the frontier from Germany, smashed through
the barriers, scattered the Dutch guards, and stopped with a
scream of tyres in the café's car park. Captain Klop was killed
in a shoot-out when his army revolver proved to be no match
for the Germans' pistols; the two Englishmen were frog-marched
across the few yards that led to enemy territory. Schellenberg
never made the trip to London; instead, Payne Best and Stevens
were taken to Berlin. They spent the rest of the war in
concentration camps.

On 4 June, 1940—eighteen days before France signed an
armistice agreement with Germany—two men in London
independently came to very similar conclusions. That after-

noon, Winston Churchill wrote a memorandum to his chief of defence staff, General Ismay. In it, he referred to 'The completely defensive state of mind which has ruined the French'. Such an attitude should not be allowed to occur in Britain. Raids must be carried out on enemy-occupied coasts wherever the population might be considered friendly. They should be the work of forces 'composed of self-contained, thoroughly equipped, units of say, 1,000 up to not more than 10,000 when combined. Surprise would be achieved by the fact that the destination would be concealed until the last moment.'

Two days later, the Prime Minister returned to the subject. This time, he referred to 'specially trained troops of the hunter class, who can develop a reign of terror down the coast, first of all on the "butcher and bolt" policy'. As he developed the idea, his imagination led him into more ambitious areas. It might even be possible to 'surprise Calais or Boulogne, kill and capture the Hun garrison, and hold the place until all the preparations to reduce it by siege or heavy storm have been made, and then away'.

June 4 had been a depressing day at the War Office. After a *blitzkrieg* lasting forty-nine days, the German army had overrun the Low Countries and France. The latter's military fortunes were in ruins, and it could be only a matter of days before the French government sued for an armistice. Britain would then have to face the full fury of the German war machine on her own.

As he walked home from Whitehall to his apartment in Mayfair's Stratton Street, Lieutenant Colonel Dudley Clarke RA, Military Secretary to the Chief of the Imperial General Staff—General Sir John Dill—considered the situation. He reflected on the successes of guerilla units in the Peninsular War, and on the manner in which Boer Commandos had harassed much larger British forces during the South African War. Surely, he reasoned, similar results might be achieved by raiding parties carrying out lightning assaults on the German-occupied coast of Europe—which now stretched from Narvik to the Pyrenees. That evening, he set his thoughts down on paper; next morning, he submitted them to General Dill. Dill like the idea and passed it on to Churchill. The Prime Minister agreed—providing that no unit was diverted from the defence of Britain. The British Commandos were born.

As it happened, a similar idea, operating under the name of 'Independent Companies', had been used in the ill-fated Norwegian campaign earlier that year. The venture had been conceived as early as 1 June, 1939, by a Major J. F. C. Holland, who was serving as head of the general staff's research department. Holland envisaged a guerilla outfit that would, in most cases, fight at point-blank range—either in the course of a raid or an ambush.

Holland had worked with T. E. Lawrence in Arabia during World War I, and the value of irregular warfare had remained in his mind ever since. He selected a contemporary of his, a gunner named Major Colin Gubbins (later Major General Sir Colin Gubbins), to work with him. Gubbins took the independent companies to Norway; and there is little doubt that, in their intended guerilla role, they would have brought havoc to the Germans' lines of communication. But then everything went wrong. Through force of circumstances, and certainly through no fault of Gubbins, they were compelled to function in much the manner of more orthodox troops. Little was proven by the experience—except, perhaps (and this became a feature of Commandos) that raiders could acquit themselves equally well in the role originally conceived for light infantry.

In all, ten Commandos—each commanded by a lieutenant colonel—were to be raised from volunteers serving in the army and in the Royal Marines. Candidates had to satisfy the following requirements:

(a) Youth and physical fitness.
(b) Intelligence, self-reliance and an independent frame of mind.
(c) An ability to swim.
(d) Immunity from seasickness.

Commanding officers could select their own men. According to a secret publication issued by the American War Department's Military Intelligence Service, the units were 'roving hit-and-run fighters'. 'Leadership rather than command', it informed its readers, 'holds these men together. Within the

Commando unit, leadership is absolute.' Discipline, certainly, was less formal than in more conventional outfits. There was, for example, no question of putting a defaulter on a charge, and no such punishments as confinement to barracks. Indeed, there was only one penalty: that of being returned to one's original unit (RTU-ed). A commanding officer could administer it without the need to give any explanation—and there was no appeal against it.

A Commando was composed of six troops (each commanded by a captain), divided into two sections (with a subaltern in charge of each), split into two sub-sections (commanded by sergeants). The men were not housed in camps or barracks, but had to find their own accommodation. For this, each received the sum of 6s. 8d. (33p) a day in addition to his wages; officers were entitled to double this amount. Apart from being used to pay for lodgings, the allowance was also intended to contribute to the cost of maintaining a civilian wardrobe.

The idea was that, before embarking on a raid, a unit should 'trickle' into the port of departure disguised as ordinary citizens. Any inquisitive eyes would be deceived—not only would the raiders' objective be a secret, but the very fact that they were there at all would be concealed.

In view of his success at Zeebrugge in 1918, Sir Roger Keyes was appointed to overall command of the Commandos and the naval units detailed to convey them to and from their assignments. Later, Captain Lord Louis Mountbatten (later Earl Mountbatten of Burma) replaced him as chief of combined operations. He was promoted to vice-admiral—and also given the ranks of lieutenant general in the army, and air marshal in the RAF. Like Keyes, he reported direct to the Minister of Defence (Winston Churchill, who combined the duties with those of Prime Minister)—thus being freed from the rigmarole of inter-service red tape.

The first raid was carried out on the night of 23–24 June, 1940, when Number 11 Commando made four landings along a twenty-mile stretch of coast in the neighbourhood of Boulogne. The operation was commanded by Lieutenant Colonel Ronnie Tod, though Dudley Clarke went along as an observer. Two German sentries were killed outside a large building occupied by the *Wehrmacht* at Le Touquet, and hand grenades were lobbed through the windows. At Boulogne, where a seaplane anchorage had been established, a troop stalked one of these machines with the wholly commendable intention of destroying it. Unfortunately, by one of those coincidences tat make mincemeat of good ideas, the pilot chose this very moment to take off into the sky. The men returned without achieving anything.

A third party landed on a stretch of deserted beach, explored the sand dunes in a vain search for enemy soldiers, and came away without finding any. In the fourth venture, Colonel Tod was nearly run over by a German patrol riding along the shore on bicycles. Tod attempted to ambush the intruders, but he lacked practice in the operation of his tommy gun, and the magazine fell off. The Germans opened fire; Clarke, who was nearby, was wounded in the ear; but by then, convinced perhaps that it had been a case of mistaken identity, the patrol went on its way.

The raiders re-embarked, and returned home across a calm sea; the clouds above slowly parted and the moon put in an appearance. Clarke was the only casualty, which may have suggested that the Germans were somewhat less than alert. The raid could not be accounted a huge success—still, it was a beginning.

Later in the year, a small raid was carried out on the German-held island of Guernsey. Due to problems of re-embarkation in a strong sea, three non-swimmers (they had, presumably, exaggerated their aquatic talents when they were selected) had to be left behind; one boat's skipper made a mistake in his navigation, and landed his men on Sark; and there was a good deal of anxiety when, moving away from the shore, the engine of another landing craft refused to start.

But the Commandos were now in business. In 1941, they carried out raids on Spitzbergen, parts of Norway, and at points in the Middle East and North Africa. When, on 4 March of that year, a sizeable force went ashore on the Lofoten Islands, the landing was unopposed. Indeed, the German population turned out to be no more than a few members of the Gestapo and one or two businessmen. But the raid was more than justified by the fact that a great deal of damage was done— including the destruction of large quantities of fish oil (used for manufacturing vitamin A and B capsules for the German army and as an ingredient in nitro-glycerine). For good measure, 315 of the islanders insisted on returning to Britain with the raiders—intent on joining the Norwegian forces in exile.

This operation can fairly be said to have had an economic target. The raid that took place at Bruneval on the French coast during the night of 27–28 February of the following year had a more singular purpose. Its object was to discover the secret of Germany's latest achievements in the technology of radar by actually bringing back the components to Britain. It may not have been a typical Commando exercise, but it had all the drama of a first-rate thriller.

6 The Secret

Among the mysteries of World War II to which there has never
been an answer is the authorship of a mysterious document
referred to as the 'Oslo Report'. One day in November, 1939,
when the first snows were falling on the Norwegian capital, the
British Embassy received an anonymous phone call—asking
whether some details of German technical developments would
be welcomed. Since British intelligence was woefully short of
such information, the answer was a cautious 'yes'. Shortly
afterwards, the promised manuscript arrived on the Naval
Attaché's desk.

The Oslo Report should have been an amazing windfall. It
contained facts about such devices as radio-controlled gliders
and torpedoes, remote-controlled shells for use against the
Maginot Line, an aircraft carrier that was under construction
at Kiel, and radar. In the latter category, there was data about
a 50cm installation that (to quote the report), 'sends out short
pulses which are narrowly directed by means of an electric
dish'. It was not only able to estimate the range of an aircraft
'very precisely'; it was also 'very resistant to interference'. The
name of this masterpiece, although it was not mentioned, was
the *Würzburg*.

When the Oslo Report reached London, its contents were
regarded with scepticism. What might have been a major
intelligence coup was largely wasted—mainly because it dealt
with so many topics of which there had been no previous
knowledge. Consequently, there was no means of evaluating it.
There was, too, the feeling that no single person could be so
well informed on such a diversity of subjects. In the light of

this, it was presumed to be a plant to mislead the Allies. In fact, it turned out to be the truth in almost every particular.

Throughout the war, only one member of the German military intelligence (*Abwehr*) collaborated directly with the Allies. This was an official named Paul Thummell (A-54), but he was mostly concerned with events in Eastern Europe, and he certainly could not have written the Oslo Report. The *Abwehr*'s second-in-command, General Oster, happened to be a member of the German resistance, but he confined himself to giving last-minute warnings of impending operations. He, too can be discounted.

No matter who composed the report, it had to be taken from Berlin to Oslo, and this suggested some degree of connivance— either by the Gestapo or, more likely, by Admiral Wilhelm Canaris, the head of *Abwehr*. This supposition, not unnaturally, seemed to reinforce the Whitehall view that the document was intended to mislead. In fact, had there been a better under- standing of Canaris' attitude, it might have been taken more seriously. His feelings for Hitler and the Nazi hierarchy fell a long way short of enthusiastic. Nor did he regard his country's plunge into World War II with favour. On the day German troops marched into Poland, he observed, 'This means the end of Germany.' Later when he was sent to Madrid with the idea of persuading Franco to join forces with the Axis, he went against his instructions. The Spanish dictator, he privately urged, should remain neutral. Franco accepted his advice.

Had Canaris survived the war, the mystery of the Oslo Report's author would no doubt have been cleared up. Unfor- tunately, he did not. He was hanged at Flossenburg concentration camp on 9 April 1945, for his alleged part in a plot against Hitler's life.

Among those who studied the report was Dr R. V. Jones, Student in Astronomy at Balliol College, Oxford. Dr Jones had worked in the Clarendon Laboratory of Frederick Lindemann (later Lord Cherwell). In 1940, Lindemann was to replace Sir Henry Tizard as the chief of air staff's leading adviser on scientific matters. Since Dr Jones had impressed his superior, it followed that he, too, would become involved. Indeed, he had been attached to the Air Ministry's staff while he was still at Oxford. His particular interest lay in the application of infrared as a means of detecting aircraft. Inevitably, he became concerned with radar and, no less predictably, he sometimes had to deal with intelligence matters.

In the early days of the war, Britain was more concerned with her own development of radar than with any enemy achievements in this field. The reason was simple: radar was regarded as an instrument of defence. Since Germany was on the offensive, it seemed unlikely that the matter need be of any particular concern to her. Nevertheless, in 1933, a state-funded company named GEMA had been set up in Germany to investigate its possibilities. GEMA had produced an 80cm system known as Seetakt, which was fitted to warships and which, when properly tuned, provided a considerable improvement on optical range-finders (especially at night or in poor visibility).

As later became clear, the state company had also produced radar for anti-aircraft purposes. In this case, it was rather more fancifully dubbed *Freya*. As students of Scandinavian mythology may recall, she was the god Odin's wife—who deserted her husband for the trappings of finery, and who became goddess of love and also (though there seems little logic to the twin responsibilities) of the dead.

In its original form, *Freya* had a range of thirty miles. Later, this was increased to seventy-five miles and the *Luftwaffe* used it as a tolerably efficient early warning system. It did not, however, present the RAF with any insuperable difficulties. As time went by, the scientists—and Dr Jones in particular— came to terms with *Freya*. They discovered how to jam it and, even, how to mislead it. There seemed little reason to suspect that it might unduly inhibit bombing operations.

During the early winter of 1941, however, the performances of German flak gunners and, especially, of night-fighter pilots, achieved a marked improvement. Of every 100 bombers that flew over occupied territory, at least four were shot down—and two-thirds of the casualty list was accounted for by enemy aircraft. Had *Freya* undergone some sort of transformation, or did the RAF now have to deal with some other system?

Reports filed by the French underground movement, supplemented by listening devices and aerial photographs, suggested that there was a newcomer to the German radar scene. If the

pundits in Whitehall had paid more attention to the Oslo
Report, they might have found this less surprising. *Freya* was
no longer working on its own. The *Würzburg* unit had arrived.

Unlike *Freya*, *Würzburg* was a product of private enterprise.
It was manufactured by a division of the Telefunken conglom-
erate on the edge of Berlin. The range of the set was a good
deal less than that of the older systems—only twenty miles—
and its beam was narrower. But it was amazingly accurate;
and, unlike its companion, it could reveal the altitude of an
aircraft as well as its direction. The only flaw occurred when a
plane was flying below 6,000 feet. In these instances, there was
rather a lot of ground interference. Nevertheless, it was responsible for an unacceptable toll of RAF bombers. Since it was
easy and not very expensive to make, there seemed to be no
reason why the whole of German-occupied Europe should not
soon be flanked by *Würzburgs*, each providing vital data for an
attendant night-fighter.

The intelligence reports suggested that it resembled a large
electric bowl fire, which was a reasonably good description. Its
aerial was in the form of a huge dish with a diameter of twenty
feet. The installation itself was reasonably small, and it was
mobile. When it was in use, the four wheels upon which it was
mounted were retracted.

Würzburg was the subject under discussion on 3 December,
1941, in the Intelligence Wing of the Photographic Reconnaissance Unit (or PRU) at Danesfield—a large country house
fifteen miles from RAF Benson in Oxfordshire. Among those
who looked in on the meeting was a squadron leader named
Tony Hill. He was one of the pilots at Benson who flew on
photographic missions for the PRU.

There had, it appeared, been reports of a *Würzburg* installation near the cliff top at Cap d'Antifer—between Le Havre
and Dieppe. Providing the weather was suitable, Hill volunteered to fly over it next day and to bring back whatever he
could in the way of pictures.

A remarkable man named Sidney Cotton had founded the
PRU in 1939. Much against the wishes of more orthodox
members of the RAF, who considered that every fighter was
needed for combat, he had been able to obtain a small number
of Spitfires. By removing their armament and modifying their

Rolls-Royce Merlin engines, Cotton was able to increase their
speed from 360mph to 400mph—to give each a range of 1,250
miles, and to raise their flight ceiling to 30,000 feet. They were
able to outfly anything that might be sent up to intercept them.
It was in one of these aircraft that Squadron Leader Hill flew
over Cap d'Antifer on 4 December. When he returned to
Benson, he was able to report that a radar set with an aerial
resembling a large electric bowl fire had, indeed, been installed
there. He proposed to go back next day to take pictures. The
venture was a complete success. When the film was developed,
it yielded more than sufficient evidence of the *Würzburg's*
presence, and gave a very good impression of its immediate
surroundings.

But, whilst this explained the heavy bomber losses, it did not
provide a solution to the problem. If the scientists were to
devise an antidote to *Würzburg*, they needed to know a great
deal more about it—much more than could be shown by aerial
photographs or deduced from the report of agents. It could
only be done if they discovered how the equipment worked—
and, ideally, if they could study certain components. The one
way in which this might be achieved was by a trip to France.

Lord Mountbatten had been on a special mission to the United
States in the early part of October, 1941. He was about to
accept an invitation from President Roosevelt to stay at the
White House, when a signal reached him from Churchill. The
text of it was: 'We want you home here at once for something
which you will find of the highest interest.' Thus he inherited
the Commandos from Sir Roger Keyes, who was now seventy
and, in the Prime Minister's opinion, ripe for replacement by
a younger man.

The first demonstration of Mountbatten's ability in his new
role took place on 27 December, 1941—when the Air Council
was still reflecting on the results of Squadron Leader Hill's
flights over Cap d'Antifer. Upon this day, Number 3
Commando, assisted by two troops loaned from Number 2, a
Royal Army Medical Corps detachment from Number 4, and
a party of sappers from Number 6, raided the Norwegian
Island of Vaagso. The object was to attack and destroy a
number of military targets in the town of South Vaagso. By ill

luck, the garrison had recently been reinforced by a detachment detailed to spend Christmas there. Consequently, there was fairly heavy fighting, and this marked the first occasion on which the raiders encountered any opposition when landing.

The operation against the *Würzburg* installation at Cap d'Antifer, code-named 'Biting', promised to be more complex. The set was located near the edge of a 400-foot high cliff, not far from the village of Bruneval. The best way of going about the business, Mountbatten decided, was to drop the raiding party by parachutes—and, when the men had completed their mission, to bring them home by sea. This involved the co-operation of all three services. When the matter was submitted to their respective chiefs-of-staff, the Air Force showed predictable enthusiasm for the project, the Admiralty was by no means keen, and the Army settled for some point between the two extremes. However, Winston Churchill approved of the idea and this was enough to ensure that it went forward.

The notion of landing a party of men who would help themselves to enemy equipment and then return to Britain more or less in one piece was outrageously daring. The marvel of Operation 'Biting' is not only that anyone had the courage to mount it, but also that it succeeded beyond its initiators' wildest dreams. A good while later, Mountbatten was to describe it as 'the most hundred per cent perfection of any raid I know'. But, before it could achieve this high degree of excellence, there were many things to be done.

Before the affair at Bruneval, there had been only one raid by British parachutists—when a small party was dropped in southern Italy and blew up a viaduct. Afterwards, they were all captured. For the present operations, a company from the 2nd Parachute Regiment, which was being formed at Hardwick Hall in Derbyshire, was selected. A troop from Number 12 Commando was detailed to cover the raiders' withdrawal from the beach; a detachment of Royal Engineers was required to assist with the more technical aspects of the assignment, and a radar technician from the RAF was essential.

In addition to all this, the French underground movement would have to co-operate. Beyond the evidence of the aerial photographs and some out-of-date maps, little was known about the surroundings of Bruneval and virtually nothing about

the state of the German defences. This gap in the planners'
knowledge had to be remedied as quickly as possible. Since the
operations would obviously have to take place at night, a full
moon was desirable. Likewise, for the evacuation, it was judged
imperative that the landing craft should be able to approach
the beach on a rising tide. If both considerations were to be
satisfied, a date during the last week of February, 1942, seemed
most appropriate—ideally, before the 27th.

Perhaps it is significant—a measure, possibly, of the youth-
fulness of the army's airborne enterprises at this time—that,
when 'C Company of the 2nd Parachute Regiment was detailed
for the mission, its company commander, Major John Frost,
had not yet completed his statutory three training drops. The
RAF's contribution in the person of Flight Sergeant Charles
Cox, who was currently performing the not very exacting duties
of a radar technician at Hartland Point, North Devon, had
never jumped by parachute at all. In peacetime, he had worked
as a cinema projectionist at Wisbech, Cambridgeshire—devoting
his leisure hours to ham radio. Falling out of an aeroplane,
supported in the sky by a mere blossom of silk, did not seem to
suggest a return ticket to Wisbech. Nevertheless, he had volunteered for the enterprise and, like Major Frost, he had to make
his way to the airfield at Ringway (on the edge of Manchester)
where a parachute training centre had been set up.

It took Frost, whose training had been interrupted by an
injured knee, a week to complete his course. Flight Sergeant
Cox qualified in twelve days—and found the experience rather
more pleasant than he had imagined. In the meanwhile, 'C'
company had moved from Hardwick to the more bleak
surroundings of Salisbury Plain. The location was Tilshead
Camp, which was then occupied by the 1st Battalion of the
Glider Pilot Regiment.

Almost immediately after 'C' Company's arrival (and Major
Frost's return to it), the unit was inspected by Major General
Frederick 'Boy' Browning, a former Guards officer and one-
time adjutant of Sandhurst, who was in command of all
airborne forces. General Browning was a stickler. At this stage
in their gallant career, the men of 'C' Company, skilled though
they may have been in the art of war, were not calculated to
bring a smile to the lips of a fastidious senior officer. Browning

regarded them as he might have looked at a tumbled-down
barn on his estate, and decided that they should be kitted out
with new uniforms.

Later in the day, his chief-of-staff, Peter Bromley-Martin,
put them, as the saying went, 'into the picture'. There had to
be some reason for 'C' Company's sudden departure from
Hardwick and the flurry of activity that had accompanied it.
Nevertheless, these men could not be kept in quarantine for
several weeks. There were, for example, bound to be outings
into Salisbury. As any other town frequented by soldiers in
wartime, its publicans were usually as well informed as the
War Office about any impending military operations their
habitués might be about to undertake. For this reason, Bromley-
Martin told a carefully prepared story.

It was, or so it seemed to be, in the nature of a public-
relations exercise. The Commandos had established themselves
by making several raids on enemy-held territory. The Parachute
Regiment, which might aspire to similar ventures, had carried
out one brief and not entirely successful foray (getting caught
did not add up to total success) in Italy. To improve its record
in this respect, it was necessary to convince Churchill and the
rest of the War Cabinet. Once they had become trained to the
necessary standard of efficiency, the men would perform a mock
assault on the Isle of Wight. Aircraft would take them there
and the Royal Navy would bring them home. It was, he
assured them, of the utmost importance to their future.

To Major Frost and, indeed, to most of the men in 'C'
Company, Bromley-Martin's discourse came as a severe
disappointment. Despite the fact that they were promised the
latest in weaponry for the exercise, it all seemed to be rather a
lot of fuss about very little. Next day, the chief-of-staff returned
to Tilshead camp. On this occasion, he spoke to Frost alone. It
had, he admitted, been a deception, but the fiction must be
maintained. The truth of the matter was... And he told Frost
about the intended operation at Bruneval.

'C' Company, now joined by Flight Sergeant Cox and a
section of airborne Royal Engineers commanded by Lieutenant
Dennis Vernon, trained hard. The majority of the paratroops,
like their leader, were Scotsmen. Frost himself had volunteered
for airborne duties while serving in the Cameronians; his

second-in-command, Captain John Ross, was from the Black
Watch—indeed, the only outsider among the officers was
Lieutenant John Timothy, who came from the Royal West
Kent Regiment. To enhance the Scottish atmosphere—and no
doubt to stir the fighting blood of the northern warriors—the
unit had its own piper.

Vernon and his sappers were Englishmen; but, after several
excursions on to Salisbury Plain, the unit became welded into
a whole. Originally, it had been intended that there should be
two representatives of the RAF to deal with the radar equipment, but the man who had been earmarked as Cox's colleague
fell ill. It was, the flight sergeant assured Frost, unnecessary to
look for a replacement. Lieutenant Vernon had shown such
aptitude for the work that he could provide all the assistance
that was needed. The Major agreed.

Number 51 Squadron, which was equipped with outmoded
Armstrong Whitworth Whitley bombers, had been selected as
the means of ferrying the unit to its target. Mechanics had cut
holes into the undersides of the aircrafts' fuselages, and then
covered them with trap doors. The method may have been
crude, but it supplied a satisfactory exit in aeroplanes that had
not been designed with any such role in mind. There were
certainly more comfortable ways of travelling—not least because
the Whitley was a notoriously chilly conveyance. But it would
have to serve—and the squadron's commanding officer, Wing
Commander Charles Pickard, was a man who inspired confidence.

He was a large man who smoked a pipe; a man in whom
experience and high spirits combined to create a certain
charisma. As a matter of fact. Wing Commander Pickard had
quite recently distinguished himself as a film star. To improve
morale and to show that Bomber Command was beginning to
take the offensive (even if in only a modest way) a film (*Target
for Tonight*) of a night's operations had been made. No professional actors were employed—in his role as captain of the
aircraft, Pickard had acquitted himself very well.

The squadron was stationed at Thruxton, not far from
Andover, and 'C' Company paid it a visit. The paratroops also
travelled north to Inveraray where, on the often difficult waters
of Loch Fyne, they did their best to master (not always very

successfully) the problems of embarking in landing craft. Nevertheless, this was a pleasant interlude. The parent ship was a vessel named *Prince Albert*, which had been completed in 1937 for the Belgian Government's passenger service between Dover and Ostend. Although she had been modified for her new task, and was now able to carry eight assault landing craft (LCAs), her accommodation was still a considerable improvement on that of Tilshead Camp—and so, too, were the meals served on board.

It was during the period when they were based on *Prince Albert* that Frost's mind was set at rest about a matter that had been troubling him. A member of the team who has not been mentioned so far was a private soldier named 'Newman', who wore the badge of the Pioneer Corps. The inverted commas are deliberate, for this was not his real name, and nobody discovered what it was. Private Newman, who was to serve as the Major's interpreter, was a German. His father, it seemed, had fled to England from the Nazis; he himself had led a cosmopolitan life in various European capitals. He spoke faultless English—and, it appeared, several other languages as well.

A great deal had been done to provide Newman with an entirely new life for the obvious reason that, should he be taken prisoner and his German origins revealed, he would certainly be shot. All this was understandable, but Frost was not entirely happy. Suppose, and the web of deception was complex enough, Newman was really a German agent—or suppose that, once he heard the chatter of his native tongue, he were to experience a change of heart. Might he not land them all inside a prison camp having accomplished nothing?

While they were training at Inveraray, Lord Mountbatten paid them a visit. He watched them trying to deal with the wilfulness of the LCAs on a difficult shore. Afterwards, on board *Prince Albert*, he asked Frost whether he had any misgivings. The Major mentioned their experiences with the landing craft. Then he brought up the question of Newman. Was he really to be relied upon?

The Chief of Combined Operations sent for the man. During the conversation that followed, Mountbatten surprised Frost by speaking fluent German. When it was over, he expressed himself entirely satisfied with the interpreter's credentials. 'Take him

along,' he told Major. 'You won't regret it, for he's bound to
be useful. I judge him to be brave and intelligent. After all, he
risks far more than you do; and, of course, he would never
have been attached to you if he hadn't passed Security on
every count.'

Ultimately, the man who would be able to put the results of
Operation 'Biting' to good use was Dr R. V. Jones at the Air
Ministry. It was, after all, he who was best qualified to make
whatever deductions were possible from the stolen components
and from any pictures they might be able to take of the
Würzburg. It was obviously necessary that he should give Cox
a briefing and it was equally desirable that Vernon should be
there too. The story of the mock attack on the Isle of Wight
was still being maintained—and, so far as anyone could tell,
being believed. Cox and Vernon, however, had been taken into
Frost's confidence, and so had Newman.

There could not, then, be any question of the two men being
sent openly on a visit to the Air Ministry. A cover story was
necessary—though it does not seem to have been very
convincing. By a curious quirk of fate, or so it was said, both
needed compassionate leave—and both required it at the same
time. They were fortunate for, as well as the trip to London,
each managed to spend a couple of nights at home.

At the briefing session, Dr Jones was accompanied by a radar
specialist from the experimental establishment at Swanage—a
man whose knowledge of the subject was enormous and who,
for the moment, might be known as D. H. Priest. However, for
the purposes of the operation, he should be referred to by his
personal code name 'Noah'.

The risk of such a well-informed scientist falling into the
hands of the enemy was obviously considerable. Indeed, it has
been suggested that, if he were about to be taken prisoner, one
man (unnamed) had orders to shoot him. He would not be
travelling with the parachutists, but in one of the landing craft.
The idea was that, if everything went off smoothly, and if the
opposition was almost unbelievingly small, he might be able to
walk up to the cliff top and supervise the stripping of the
Würzburg.

While the training for 'Biting' was being carried out in
Britain, members of the French resistance were making their

contribution to the forthcoming raid. The area in which
Bruneval was situated was the responsibility of a group known
as the *Confrérie Notre Dame* (CND for short), which was master-
minded by an almost legendary character known as 'Rémy'
(but actually named Gilbert Renault). Among his concerns at
this time was the surveillance of those twin giants of the German
Navy, *Scharnhorst* and *Gneisenau*, which were nearing the end of
their year-long sojourn at Brest. On 24 January, 1942, Rémy
was in Paris. As it happened, he was due to be picked up by a
Lysander from a field in Normandy for one of his rare trips to
London. On this day, however, the radio connection with
London brought him specific instructions. The signal contained
a request for, 'Firstly position and number machine guns
defending road at Theuville repeat Theuville on coast between
Cap d'Antifer and Jouin latter being seventeen kilometres north
Le Havre secondly what other defences thirdly number and
state preparedness defenders stop Are they on qui vive stop
Firstclass troops or old men stop Fourthly where are they
quartered fifthly existence and positions barbed wire'.

Rémy passed the assignment on to two of his agents, 'Pol'
(Roger Dumont) and 'Charlemagne' (Charles Chauveau) who,
on a cold day when there were thirty centimetres of snow on
the ground, booked themselves into an hotel at Le Havre. Next
morning, they drove to Bruneval, where they chatted with the
owner of the Hôtel Beauminet—an establishment on the small
road that wound through a gulley down to the beach. The
place, they soon discovered, was much used by German troops.

The proprietor informed them that there was a machine-gun
post at the Villa Stella Maris (farther down the road in the
direction of the beach), but he did not think that it was
manned all the time. Nevertheless, he explained, the garrison
of Bruneval, which was commanded by a sergeant, was quartered in his premises. The NCO seemed to be an efficient soldier,
and he suspected that his men could be brought into action at
very short notice. Yes—there were several German units in the
neighbourhood. Some of them were armoured.

'Pol' and 'Charlemagne' walked down towards the shore.
Presently, they came across a barbed-wire barrier placed across
the road. It was guarded by a private who seemed to be
reasonably friendly. They offered him a cigarette. Their cover

story was that 'Pol' was on a visit from Paris and that, before he returned home, he wished to catch a glimpse of the sea. Might they go down to the beach? Was it safe? The hotel keeper had suggested that it might be mined.

The sentry agreed that it was. Despite this, however, he escorted 'Pol' and 'Charlemagne' down to the edge of the sea and spent the next few minutes ambling about. As the two agents rightly deduced, it may have been the intention to plant mines there, but it did not seem to have been carried out.

They returned to their car. Later they took lunch at an inn some miles inland, where they copied out the names of German soldiers from the visitors' book. London, they knew, could identify their units from its records, and another part of the picture would fall into place.

With the information supplied by the industrious CND and more aerial photographs, the PRU at Danesfield was able to build up a fairly complete image of the land around the *Würzburg* installation and its defences. In a workshop situated in a cellar of the large house, craftsmen built a model—which was used for briefing Major Frost's men when, at last, the object of all their recent training was made clear to them.

It showed the *Würzburg* situated in a small pit, overlooked by a villa of elaborately Gothic design, which was referred to as 'Lone House'. About 400 yards to the north-east of this, there was a farm named Le Presbytère. German soldiers might be expected to be quartered here; and indeed, at 'Lone House'. To the north-west of the farm, on the edge of the cliff, there was another radar station—in this case, the installation was a *Freya* model.

The force, Major Frost explained, would be divided into three main groups, which would drop at five-minute intervals. The first, code-named 'Nelson', would have the responsibility for securing the line of withdrawal. In fact, it was composed of two sub-units. One, under Lieutenant E. C. B. 'Junior' Charteris and made up of three assault sections, was to storm the post at the Villa Stella Maris and any other opposition they might encounter. The other, led by Captain Ross, was to secure the beach and search it for mines—at the same time making arrangements to receive the landing craft.

Group Number Two was divided into three: 'Drake', 'Hardy' and 'Jellicoe'. 'Drake', under Lieutenant Peter Naumoff, was to stop the movement of enemy troops from Le Presbytère towards 'Lone House'. 'Hardy', of which Frost would take personal charge, was detailed to surround 'Lone House'—and 'Jellicoe' (A section under Lieutenant Peter Young) should protect the *Würzburg* (now code-named 'Henry') while Vernon and Cox went about their business. Finally, Group Three— 'Rodney'—was composed of thirty men commanded by Lieutenant John Timothy. Its task was to ward off any opposition that might arrive from La Poterie (a hamlet to the east of the target) and, when the mission was completed, to provide a rearguard.

Originally, Operation 'Biting' was scheduled to take place on Monday, 23 February. 'C' Company spent that morning packing their containers and checking over and cleaning their weapons. As Bromley-Martin had promised, they were, indeed, armed with the latest products of the armourers' skills. The officers were issued with Colt 45 automatics (priceless pistols in those days, though commonplace in the USA): the other ranks had rifles, Bren guns (the direct descendant of the more cumbersome World War I Lewis gun, and named after the Czech armaments factory at Brno, where it originated), and Sten guns (S and T were the initials of its inventors—the 'ens' was added to conform with Bren. This was a lightweight sub-machine gun; a utility version, so to speak, of the tommy gun. In its early days it was not very reliable).

Doubtless, those men who took their burdensome weaponry ashore at Zeebrugge would have envied the tools of a raider in 1942, who was able to travel without the encumbrance of heavy equipment. Nevertheless, there was one item missing from the list—and one for which, as things turned out, Major Frost would have been grateful: a 2-inch mortar.

At 2 pm, the containers were ready for dispatch to the airfield at Thruxton. At 5 pm, the men sat down to tea—and then the news arrived. The weather had turned bad, and any thought of the operation going forward was impossible. It was postponed for twenty-four hours. This was a fearful anti-climax, but there was nothing anyone could do about it.

The story of the next three days was similar, and then Friday
dawned. There was a sharp frost, but the sky was clear and a
bright sun beamed down on the camp. Dutifully, they once
again made the necessary preparations, though Frost was
doubtful whether they would serve any purpose. They were
now beyond the time limit set by the Admiralty, for the landing
craft would have to approach the beach on an ebbing tide.
Privately, he expected Operation 'Biting' to be put off for at
least a month. Instead of making a quick journey to France
and back, he imagined that his men might be sent on leave.

Had he known it, however, a signal had already been sent
by the Admiralty to Commander-in-Chief Portsmouth. Its text
read: 'Carry out Operation 'Biting' tonight 27 February'. HMS
Prince Albert, which was at anchor in Portsmouth harbour with
thirty-two men from Number 12 Commando abroad, was
already being prepared for sea. An escort of five motor gunboats
and two destroyers (HMS *Blencathra* and HMS *Fernie*) had been
brought to a state of readiness.

At 5 pm, just as the men were sitting down to another tea
at which the only cheerful person seemed to be Company
Sergeant Major Strachan, General Browning arrived unexpectedly at the camp. The business, he told Frost, had been set in
hand; they would fly to France that night. And he wished them
good luck. Wing Commander Pickard at Thruxton also wished
them good luck, though he seems to have been doubtful about
the whole enterprise. As he murmured to Private Newman
when the interpreter clambered abroad one of the Whitleys, 'I
feel like a bloody murderer.'

In huts around the perimeter of the airfield, 'C' Company
and its attachments had been fed with bully beef sandwiches
and treated to gallons of tea liberally laced with rum. It was
very nice at the time—though it was to make them aware of a
basic role concerning operations by parachute: do not, under
any circumstances, consume too much liquid beforehand.
Conditions aboard the Whitley bomber were austere. They
certainly did not include a toilet. There was, they had been
told, fairly thick snow in the dropping zone, and they could
expect to encounter flak. Both statements turned out to be true.
The snow was about one foot deep; and as they crossed the
French coast, the sky exploded. As they learned afterwards, the

Würzburg—'Henry'—had picked them up when they were about twenty miles from the coast, and had passed on the data to 88mm flak guns in the neighbourhood. Fortunately, however, there did not seem to be any night-fighters up.

On the flight from Thruxton, the men sat on the hard aluminium decks of the Whitleys, made the more uncomfortable by the ribs of the fuselages. Some of them sang; other played cards. A corporal named Stewart won a good deal of money; but, then, he usually did. If he was killed, he said, his victims could recover their cash from his body. Within an hour, they were over the target; dropping ten men to a stick, the racket of the Whitley's twin engines suddenly superseded by the deep silence of the night sky—punctuated now and again by a flak gun barking in the wake of the departing aircraft. The assembly area was in the cover of a line of trees about three-quarters of a mile from the target, and it was here that 'C' Company—or most of it—mustered. Unfortunately one group, the first to arrive, was missing. Somewhere in the dark landscape of north-western France, Lieutenant Junior Charteris and his three assault sections seemed to have gone astray.

The whole business of securing the line of retreat would have to be handled by Captain Ross. Since Ross's group was composed mainly of a few sappers—with responsibilities for mine-detecting on the beach, and laying anti-tank mines on the road up the gulley—the auspices for a successful withdrawal did not look good. Nor was the present situation to Ross's liking. For the better part of an hour, he and his men were pinned down by the machine-gun post in the garden of Stella Maris.

Quite obviously the landing of Frost and his men had caught the Germans completely by surprise. The Lone House, from which opposition had been expected, turned out to have only one man inside it. He was firing out of a window towards 'Henry', which was now a bedlam of exploding hand grenades and light machine-gun fire. What, precisely, he may have hoped to contribute to the *mêlée* is unknown. He was shot down before he had time to turn round and see the intruders.

'Henry' was manned by *Luftwaffe* personnel who, no doubt wisely, decided not to argue with the hell that Peter Young and his men were creating in their midst. Lit by the bright

moon, they hurriedly made their departure. One went the
wrong way; he fell off the cliff top, but was hauled back to
safety and captured. Vernon and Cox could now go about their
business with only small fears of being molested. They worked
quietly and with skill. The only snag came when Vernon began
to take photographs using a flash. The light attracted more
attention from the German troops (estimated at about 100) in
Le Presbytère and the fire from that direction intensified. Frost
ordered the sapper officer to put away his camera. Flight
Sergeant Cox would have to content himself with notes and
drawings.

Down in the gulley, Ross and his small force were engaged
in a heavy exchange of fire with the machine-gun post, and
now white flares were going up from the direction of the beach.
They suggested that the soldiers in Le Presbytère were moving
away from the cover of the farm buildings and that, before
very long, an attack might be expected from that direction.
There was still no news of Charteris and his missing sections—
but information of any kind was in short supply. The signallers
had been issued with No. 38 wireless sets for communications
within the company; with No. 18 sets for contacting the landing
craft and neither kind was reliable.

On the cliff top, the fire was increasing. Private McIntyre
was killed; Sergeant Major Strachan stopped three bullets in
his stomach but, by some miracle, survived. And Vernon and
Cox worked away. One vital piece of equipment, the pulse
unit, turned out to be impossible to remove by orthodox
engineering methods. The trouble was that the screwdriver
they had brought was too short. Eventually, they were able to
wrench it free with a crowbar.

Time was beginning to run out, and Frost urged them to
hurry. Had he known it, there was even less to spare than he
imagined. Units of Number 1 Company of the 685th German
Infantry Regiment had just returned to their billets in La
Poterie after an exercise. They were promptly put on the road
to Bruneval—where they had orders to occupy a hill to the
south-east of the village. The time was now 1.00 am.

Fortunately, the Germans imagined that, having wrought
their havoc with 'Henry', the paratroops might move up the
coast to tackle the *Freya* installation. It would obviously fall to

General Laurent Gouvion Saint Cyr, commander of the forces that besieged Fort Trinidad Admiral Lord Collingwood, commander-in-chief of the British Mediterranean fleet (*Jennifer Moore Personality Picture Library*)

An earlier action by Lord Thomas Cochrane off the Spanish coast in 1807. He commanded the sloop HMS *Speedy* in an engagement with the Spanish frigate *El Gamo* (*MARS, Lincs.*)

Admiral Sir George Cockburn,
architect of the plan to raid
Washington (*Jennifer Moore
Personality Picture Library*)

British troops under General Ross attack Washington
(*New York City Public Library*)

Midshipman Charles Lucas of HMS *Hecla* throwing overboard a live Russian shell during the bombardment of Bombarsund (*Jennifer Moore Personality Picture Library*)

French infantry building 'fascines' before the attack on the forts of Bombarsund (*Naval Historical Library, London*)

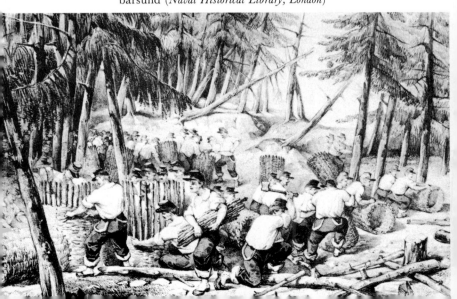

French Chasseurs charging Fort Tzee, Bombarsund
(*Naval Historical Library, London*)

The Russian governor of Bombarsund surrendering the island of Aland to the
British and French (*MARS, Lincs.*)

Colonel John S. Mosby, leader of the Fairfax raid (*Jennifer Moore Personality Picture Library*)

Mosby's Partisan Rangers during their earlier attack at Thompson's Corner, February 1863 (*MARS, Lincs.*)

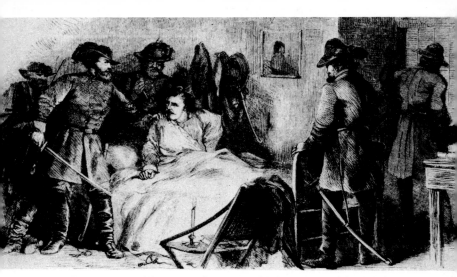

The capture of Brigadier General E. H. Stoughton at his lodgings
(*MARS, Lincs.*)

Typical Partisan Rangers at the time of the attack on Fairfax Court House
(*MARS, Lincs.*)

Vice-Admiral Roger Keyes, commander of the Dover Patrol, and the inspiration behind the Zeebrugge raid (*Radio Times Hulton Picture Library*)

German guns on the mole at Zeebrugge (*Imperial War Museum, London*)

The gap in the viaduct caused by the blowing up of the submarine C_3
(*Imperial War Museum, London*)

Major John Frost (*centre*) 2nd Parachute Regiment, who led the raid on Bruneval, with an officer of an airborne division (*Imperial War Museum, London*)

The *Würzburg* installation at Bruneval (*Imperial War Museum, London*)

Commandos dashing up the beach at Dieppe under the cover of a smoke screen (*Imperial War Museum, London*)

The aftermath of the Dieppe raid—tanks and landing-craft burning on the beach (*Imperial War Museum, London*)

One of the Churchill tanks captured by the Germans at Dieppe
(*Imperial War Museum, London*)

The flotilla of fast patrol boats that brought back the survivors of the Dieppe
raid (*Imperial War Museum, London*)

Mussolini with Hitler before the Italian collapse (*Bundesarchiv*)

The Storch ready for take-off (*Bundesarchiv*)

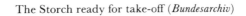

US infantry practise assault landings on a Devon beach in May, 1944
(*United States National Archives*)

Lt Colonel Rudder, CO 109th Infantry Regiment, leads his troops through
Colmar during the victory parade on 8 February, 1945 (*United States Army*)

US Marine artillery, part of the 1st Marine Division, in action with a 105mm howitzer on Guadalcanal, 12 September, 1942 (*United States Marine Corps*)

The wreck of a Japanese flying boat at Makin after the raid by the Marine Raiders (*United States Marine Corps*)

The table-top model of the Son Tay prison camp, used in the training for the raid (*MARS, Lincs.*)

Colonel Simons during a 'ticker-tape' welcome for returning POWs and Son Tay raiders in San Francisco, April 1973 (*United States Army*)

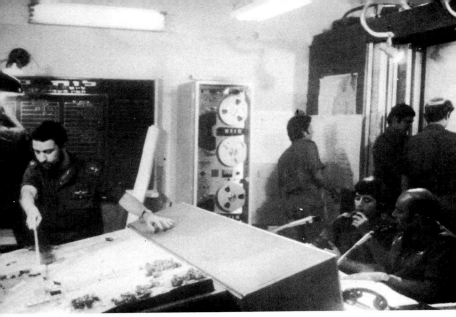

Operations room for the Israeli raid on Entebbe, from the film
Operation 'Thunderbolt' (*EMI Films*)

Israeli forces attacking the airport building at Entebbe, from the film
Operation 'Thunderbolt', (*EMI Films*)

the 100 or so men who were stationed in Le Presbytère to block
the route. For this reason, they may have held back when an
attack might very well have succeeded.

So far as Captain Ross was concerned, things were improving.
Charteris and his men had been offloaded from Pickard's
aircraft which flew at the head of the formation, and from the
Whitley immediately behind it. Consequently, they caught the
worst of the flak—with the result that, in the confusion, the
three sections were unleashed at a point 2 1/2 miles from the
dropping zone. But now, after running for most of the way,
they came up a road from the south-east and joined in the
action. The machine-gun position in the villa's grounds had
been sited in the expectation that any attack would come from
the direction of the shore. It was badly placed so far as the
present engagement was concerned. The arrival of Charteris
and his assault troops put an end to the opposition. In the
general exit, the telephonist, who had been at his post inside
the villa, timed his departure late. He was captured.

The force was now converging on the beach. The components of 'Henry' were taken down the road on a two-wheeler
trolley that had been specially built to carry them. At about
this time, Corporal Stewart was hit in the head. He was about
to hand over his gains from the card game, when a medical
orderly assured him that he would survive. He withdrew the
offer.

Some while previously, the eight LCAs had departed from
Prince Albert, which was now on course back to Portsmouth.
They should be somewhere not far off the coast, and Frost was
ready to summon them to the beach. The No. 18 sets, however,
remained stubbornly dumb and, used as a last-but-one resort,
the No. 38 sets did no better. Two green Very lights were shot
into the sky in the hope that they might be identified as British.
At the same time, the sappers played their final card. It took
the form of a small portable radio beacon named 'Rebecca'. It
was so secret that, like the fearless Mr Priest, it had a built-in
demolition device to prevent its falling into enemy hands.
Nobody had any great faith in Rebecca's ability to work, but
it was worth a try.

Somehow, the navy received part of the message, though a
little conversation over the radio sets might have helped. As

the leading landing craft approached the water's edge, the Bren gunners on board mistook 'C' Company for Germans and opened fire. But, now the No. 38 set suddenly mended its ways and it became possible to speak. The raiders hurriedly embarked in a manner that turned out to be a good deal more adroit than the training attempts on the shores of Loch Fyne. At 3.00 am, the LCAs were taken in tow by the MGBs; and, escorted by the two destroyers, several vessels in the Free French Navy, and by an air cover of Spitfires, the procession made its way to Portsmouth.

The British losses had been two men killed, two wounded (though CSM Strachan was the only one to be seriously injured) and six who were eventually taken prisoner. The German casualties added up to five dead, two wounded, and five missing (two of these were taken prisoner by the British).

In technical terms, the aftermath of Operation 'Biting' was impressive. It enabled Dr Jones and his radar experts to discover the weaknesses as well as the strength of the *Würzburg*, with the result that 'window' was created. Taking the form of strips of tin foil that were dropped by the bombers, it served to confuse the operators—producing an effect somewhat like that of a snow storm. In Germany, the raid marked the beginning of Admiral Canaris's fall from Hitler's favour until, on Himmler's insistence, the *Abwehr* was taken over in 1944 by the SD (*Sicherheitdienst*—the security service of the *Reich*). Why, Hitler wanted to know, had he not managed to lay his hands on any British radar sets? An *élite* unit known as 'the Brandenburg Division' had been formed for just such an operation. Why wasn't it used?

At the same time, the Führer turned his attention seriously to the state of Germany's defences on the coastlines of occupied countries—with the result that the Atlantic Wall was built. But this was too late to save 'Henry' from the depredations of these brave men who, indirectly, were responsible for saving the lives of many airmen.

'C' Company of the 2nd Battalion, Parachute Regiment, which distinguished itself at Bruneval, was made up mostly of

Scotsmen. Similarly, many of the Commandos had regional characteristics reflecting the more orthodox units from which their men were recruited. For example, Number 2 was composed largely of East Anglians and Liverpudlians. Lord Lovat's Number 4 had, not surprisingly, a strong nucleus from its commanding officer's own regiment—the Lovat Scouts (raised by his father for service in the Boer War). Number 12 was formed in Northern Ireland; the majority of its men came from Northern Irish regiments or else from the Welsh Division, which was stationed in Ulster at the time. Eight Commando was formed by Robert Laycock of the Royal Horse Guards (he later succeeded Lord Louis Mountbatten as Chief of Combined Operations). Many of its founder-members were from the Household Cavalry or else from the Foot Guards. It was this preponderance of socially very acceptable officers that caused Evelyn Waugh (himself in a Royal Marine Commando) to describe it as 'boisterous, xenophobic, extravagant, imaginative, witty, with a proportion of noblemen which the Royal Navy found disconcerting'.

It would, indeed, be utterly wrong to think of Commandos as bands of brigands with greater skill in strong-armed methods than in more cerebral pursuits. Surprisingly, this type of warfare seems to have had a pronounced appeal to robust and daring intellectuals. A random survey of the officers who served in one or another such unit reveals a poet, two novelists, a curator from the Victoria and Albert Museum, several journalists, a stockbroker, an economist, two schoolmasters and a civil engineer.

But, no matter where they came from, and no matter what their occupations in civilian life, all commandos had to measure up to certain standards of toughness, courage and endurance. Discipline may have been less formal than in the regiments and corps from which they came; they may have been a more companionable relationship between officers and men, but the training was hard and some of the raids may have seemed virtually impossible.

The university of Commando warfare was at Achnacarry in Inverness-shire—north of Fort William near the point where Loch Arkaig meets Loch Lochy. The instruction was nothing if not realistic. Of the 25,000 men who passed through the

establishment, no fewer than forty lost their lives there. To
introduce newcomers to a world of education in which death
was the ultimate rebuke, a line of false gravestones flanked the
approaches to the camp. In *The Green Beret*, Hilary St George
Saunders recalls the misadventure of one of the first US Rangers
to visit the centre. Apparently he decided that it was unnecessary to sit in the bottom of a boat—as ordered. Instead, he
preferred to perch on the side. His punishment was immediate:
he received a bullet in one of his buttocks.

Robert Laycock (then a lieutenant colonel) began his
Commando career in the Mediterranean as head of 'Layforce'—
a unit composed of Numbers 7, 8 and 11 Commandos (later
joined by 50 and 52, which had been raised in Egypt). Three
ex-merchant ships, now proudly prefixed HMS—*Glengyle, Glenroy*
and *Glenearn*—were put at 'Layforce's disposal. Each was
modified to accommodate small landing craft: twenty-four
LCAs, suspended from davits—and three LCMs (capable of
transporting a tank apiece), which were lowered by derricks.
There was room for 1,000 soldiers on board each vessel; but
only 400 could be landed in one flight of landing craft.

'Layforce', which was in business for most of 1941, carried
out raids on Benghazi, Tobruk, Rhodes and many other places.
It also assisted with the rearguard action during the evacuation
of Crete. But Robert Laycock's most spectacular, if least
successful, venture took place in mid-November of that year.
The object was to get the 8th Army's 1941 offensive off to a
good start by kidnapping—or, if necessary, killing— the supreme
commander of the Afrika Korps, General Erwin Rommel.

By this time, 'Layforce' had been disbanded, and most of the
men had returned to their units. Laycock, with six officers and
fifty-three other ranks, had remained behind in the Middle
East as a raiding force. Unfortunately, the plan for what
became code-named Operation 'Copper Flipper' was based on
an entirely false premise. It assumed that the German general
was living in a house at Beda Littoria—about 125 miles inland
from the coast of Cyrenaica. In fact, Rommel was never there;
nor, in any case, would the operation have succeeded. When
the raiders were due either to abduct or assassinate him, he
happened to be in Rome.

In early November, Laycock and his fifty-nine companions set off from Alexandria in two submarines, HMS *Torbay* and *Talisman*. The ill luck that was to bedevil the operation began as the boats approached the beach. A British intelligence officer, disguised as an Arab, flashed a torch to indicate the landing place; but a high sea was running at the time. Four of the rubber boats that were to ferry the men ashore were capsized and their occupants drowned. Eventually, only half the force managed to reach land.

With this resources of manpower severely depleted, Laycock had to revise his plan. He decided that Lieutenant Colonel Geoffrey Keyes, formerly of the Royal Scots Greys and son of Sir Roger Keyes, should lead the assault on Rommel's presumed headquarters. Another officer, Lieutenant Roy Cook, was to be responsible for cutting the telephone and telegraph wires that connected Beda Littoria with the world beyond; and Laycock was to do his best to safeguard the line of withdrawal.

The weather turned wet; the Arab residents in the area were ambivalent in their sympathies—doubtless calculating whether support for the Allies or the Axis would pay them best; and the 125-mile march from the landing place was very hard going. In the assault on the house, Keyes was killed by a stray bullet (he was awarded a posthumous VC). There was no General Rommel in residence. The second-in-command, Captain Robin Campbell, was shot through the leg by one of his own men— who mistook him for a German. And the survivors, led by Sergeant Jack Terry, made their way back to the coast, having accomplished nothing.

But the ill-fortune persisted. The weather was too bad for HMS *Torbay* to embark the commandos. The submarine would, her commanding officer promised, return on the following night. But, by then, it was too late. After attacks by Arabs who had been coerced by the Italians, and then by a German force, the party had to break up into small groups and make its way overland in the general direction of Egypt.

Only one party—Laycock and Terry—succeeded. After a trudge of forty-one days, they met advanced units of the 8th Army. During the trek, they were helped by friendly Arabs— intellectual stimulus came from a copy of *The Wind in the Willows* that Laycock happened to have in his haversack. Each

night he read the classic aloud to Sergeant Terry—though
whether the NCO appreciated these recitals seems doubtful.
His first words on reaching safety are purported to have been,
'Thank God I shan't have to hear any more about that bloody
Mr Toad!'

They had been fortunate in their treatment by the local
inhabitants, however. Four to five other wanderers were
murdered by less hospitable Arabs. But the Germans and their
Arab accomplices need not take all the blame for the raid's
casualties. The sorry truth seems to be that the operation
should never have taken place. In an entry in his diary dated
26 May, 1942, Evelyn Waugh recorded the remarks of an
intelligence officer in charge of a training course. 'Then',
Waugh quotes him as saying, 'there was that raid when Roger
Keyes's son was killed. All very gallant and quite useless. *We*
knew perfectly well that Rommel was away in Rome, but did
anyone trouble to consult us? No. So young Keyes's life was
thrown away.'

The enemy, it appeared, was not the only villain.

In Western Europe, the raid on the Würzburg at Bruneval
was followed, on 27–28 March, by Operation 'Chariot'—one
of the most successful and courageous Commando operations
of all. The target was an immense dry dock at Saint Nazaire
that, in peacetime, accommodated such giant transatlantic
liners as the *Normandie*.

Scharnhorst and *Gneisenau* had departed from Brest and had
returned, damaged, to their homeland. The battleship *Bismarck*
was safely at rest at the bottom of the ocean. Of the giant
foursome that had been built to inflict such heavy losses on
Allied shipping, only *Tirpitz*, now at anchor in a Norwegian
fjord, could be considered dangerous. If she broke out into the
Atlantic, the effect upon the trade routes to America might be
disastrous. But, to carry out such an operation, the *Tirpitz*
would have to depend on Saint Nazaire's dry dock. Nowhere
else was there an installation large enough to accommodate her
for repairs.

In some respects, the raid on Saint Nazaire can be compared
to Sir Roger Keyes's excursion to Zeebrugge in 1918—though
the effect was more damaging to the German cause. The idea
was that a former US Navy destroyer—once USS *Buchanan* and

now, ceded to the Royal Navy under the Lease-Lend agreement, renamed HMS *Campbeltown*—would be loaded with high explosives. She would cross the Channel from Falmouth to the mouth of the river Loire, steam upstream to the port, and then ram the dock gates. Having accomplished this, the ship would be sunk; the fuses would be lit and, with a bit of luck, she would erupt with devastating effect.

Campbeltown, launched in 1919, was an old ship and looked it. Four slim smokestacks suggested an earlier age of men-of-war—an impression that was in keeping with her performance. At full power she could manage a speed of twenty-five knots. Her modern counterparts could better this by a good ten knots.

To mislead anyone who might take an unwholesome interest in the ship's progress towards Saint Nazaire, *Campbeltown*'s funnels were replaced by a pair of chubbier stacks, which gave her a quite passable resemblance to a German Möwe-class destroyer. To complete the illusion, all the ships that sailed to France that night flew German colours.

Number 2 Commando, commanded by Lieutenant Colonel Charles Newman, was responsible for the military action, though demolition parties from eight other units were attached to it. All told, 611 men were involved. Seventy-five of them made the journey to France in *Campbeltown*; the others travelled in motor launches and motor gunboats—with the Hunt-class destroyers *Atherstone* and *Tynedale* acting as escorts.

The action on shore was exceptionally fierce, and in the end 169 men were killed and 200 were taken prisoner. For her part, *Campbeltown* successfully rammed the caissons at the dock entrance, was sunk according to plan and, later than had been foreseen, blew up. The explosion took place at about 10.00 am on 28 March—when the survivors were on their way back to England, and the captive commandos were being paraded on a nearby quayside.

For the rest of the war, the dock remained out of action. *Tirpitz* languished in Norway, where she was eventually destroyed by the RAF. Despite the heavy losses in personnel, the raid justifies Hilary St George Saunders's description of it as 'as classic operation of war'. Afterwards, five Victoria Crosses were awarded. Among those whose received them were Commander R. E. D. Ryder, who was in overall command of the naval forces; Lieutenant Commander S. H. Beattie, commander of *Campbeltown*; and Colonel Newman, who was taken prisoner when the reembarkation went less well than planned.

On 11 December 1941, the United States declared war on Germany and Italy—four days after Japanese naval units had attacked the American base at Pearl Harbour. In March of the following year, Winston Churchill congratulated President Roosevelt on his decision to form 'Commando forces on a large scale on the Californian shore.' The object was to harry Japanese forces that were widely spread out on islands in the Pacific. In most of these operations, the work was carried out by members of Marine Raider Battalions. In Europe and North Africa, America's adventures in the world of Commandos were performed by units of the US Rangers. The first occasion on which Rangers and Commandos fought side-by-side was at Dieppe on 19 August 1942. The code-name was 'Jubilee'—though, in all honesty, there was not a great deal to celebrate.

7 The Rehearsal

Dieppe is a pleasant resort town on the coast of Normandy; it has a port where cross-Channel steamers dock. Until 19 August, 1942, it had few claims to distinction; but then, one morning, its name suddenly leapt into headlines in the world's press. The reason was Operation 'Jubilee', a raid of such magnitude and such carnage that nothing like it had been seen before.

Operation 'Jubilee' had, it appeared, a political motive: to appease the Russians. Hard-pressed by the German armies, Stalin had been urging Britain to open a so-called 'Second Front'. This could only be achieved by an invasion of the Continent—an enterprise which, for the time being, was impossible. But, Winston Churchill and his colleagues decided, a large-scale raid might suggest that the Western Allies were not entirely indifferent to the USSR's pleas.

At the time, the military powers had neither the experience nor the resources to mount such a huge undertaking as an invasion—although that was to be the ultimate objective. Operation 'Jubilee' might fulfil the first of these necessities. The tragedy was that the price for such education was so extortionate.

The raid on Dieppe was originally code-named 'Rutter', and was scheduled to take place on 7 July, 1942. Reducing the geography of Dieppe to simple components, the town is at the mouth of a valley formed by the River Arques flanked by tall cliffs. It was on this high ground that the German occupying forces had established batteries of 5.9-inch guns. Each had a traverse of 360 and a range of twelve miles. For a force of any size to be landed on the beach in front of the town, the gun emplacements had to be put out of action.

In the 'Rutter' plan the gun positions were to be dealt with by parachute troops. Dieppe itself was to be invaded by the 2nd Canadian division commanded by Major General John Hamilton ('Ham') Roberts. An airborne unit had already given a good account of itself in the Bruneval raid. As for the Canadians, they had been encamped in Sussex ever since their arrival in England. The war appeared to have by-passed them, and they were becoming a little impatient. When Canadian Prime Minister MacKenzie King visited Britain during the early autumn of 1941, he told Churchill, 'I don't know how long I can go on leading my country while our troops remain inactive'. A raid on Dieppe might give them a breath of French air and a heightened sense of purpose.

The units that were to take part in Operation 'Rutter' duly assembled on the Isle of Wight, remained there for a while, and then dispersed without straying beyond the shore. Although they had accomplished nothing, there was one factor throughout this period that must have taught the planners something; the weather. Throughout the raiding force's brief sojourn on the island, it had been vile. The seaborne troops might just have survived the journey to France; from the point of view of the parachutists, it was impossible.

Opinion was divided on whether the idea should be revived. General Montgomery, who was then in charge of South-Eastern Command, was against it. As he pointed out, several thousand men had been briefed for specific tasks. They were now dispersed, and the probability of a hint dropped here, an unguarded word uttered there, was too great to be discounted. The Germans must, surely, know about it.

Churchill, on the other hand, took a different view. 'I thought,' he wrote, 'that a large-scale operation should take place this summer, and military opinion seemed unanimous that until an operation on that scale was undertaken no responsible general would take the responsibility of planning for the main invasion.'

His chief of combined operations, Mountbatten, agreed with him. As July drew to a close, the 'Rutter' plan, on which work had begun immediately after the Saint Nazaire raid, was taken out of the file once more. The parachute elements were replaced by Numbers 3 and 4 Commandos (the sea being a more reliable ally than the air), but otherwise it was largely unchanged. A combination of full moon and high tide during the early morning was needed for its execution. The last suitable date in August was Thursday, the 19th.

Once again, the forces assembled—though not on the Isle of Wight. Some of the units embarked at Portsmouth, others at Southampton; some at Shoreham in Sussex, one of them at Newhaven. The land elements involved were put under the command of Major General Roberts; the naval units, under Captain J. Hughes-Hallett, RN—who was also part-author of the scheme.

The first essential was to knock out the German batteries on the heights to the east and west of the town. Number 3 Commando, under Lieutenant Colonel J. F. Durnford-Slater, was given the task of eliminating the eastern batteries. Leaving Newhaven in their landing craft, the men were to come ashore at the base of the cliffs beneath the village of Berneval—about four miles from Dieppe. Having reached the top, they were to assault the batteries, which were thought to comprise four guns and which, for reference purposes, had been code-named 'Goebbels'. A party of the 1st US Rangers under Captain Roy Murray was attached to Durnford-Slater's Commando—plus a section of French Marines from the 10th (Inter-Allied) Commando. The unit practised its deployment in the area of Seaford, Sussex.

On the western side of the town, the gun emplacements (estimated at six and code-named 'Hess') were the responsibility of 4 Commando under Lord Lovat, to which, also, a detail of Rangers was attached. The landing places in this instance were to be near the mouth of the River Saane, not far from the village of Quiberville and about six miles to the west of Dieppe.

Dieppe itself was to be assaulted by a Canadian force amounting to about 5,000 men supported by twenty-four tank-landing craft, each of which was loaded with three of the latest Churchill tanks. Number 40 (Royal Marine) Commando was to take part in this sector with two possible roles. Either it would thrust its way into Dieppe harbour and cut loose German landing craft that were known to be moored there—assisting, at the same time, the Canadian sappers in demolition work; or

it would be held back as a floating reserve. The outcome of
events was the only thing that could determine what the Royal
Marines would do.

For fear of alerting the enemy, there was to be no large-scale
preliminary bombardment from the air. But, throughout the
operation and during the time immediately preceding it, the
US Army Airforce and the RAF would provide cover by
attacking selected German positions.

The plan looked good, and its advocates were enthusiastic.
Unfortunately, although the numbers involved in the operation,
which was now known as 'Jubilee', were roughly the same as
in the original plan, the opposition ranged against them had
been greatly increased. In that first week of July, the enemy's
strength had been correctly assessed an 'one battalion of low
grade troops' and a few supporting units. Since then, the 110th
Division had arrived as a respite from service on the Russian
front, and was now quartered to the west of the town; the 181st
Division had moved in—and, in reserve, a Panzer division was
stationed a few miles inland.

Surprisingly enough, this was a coincidence. There is nothing
to suggest that there had been any leak in security, nor that
the Germans had been inspired by guesswork about an
impending raid. But this was not the only unfortunate accident
of fate. The area commander liked to exercise his soldiers once
a month by closing them up on their positions. For his next
practice stand-to, he had chosen 18–19 August.

On the night of the raid, the sea was calm—silver-plated by
the full moon that shone in an umblemished sky. One by one,
the ships and the landing craft slipped their moorings, and set
out across the seventy miles or so of sea to Dieppe. On this
phase of the operation, Number 3 Commando had by far the
worst deal. While the other units travelled in the relative
comfort of Landing Ships, Infantry (LSI), most of which were
peacetime cross-Channel steamers adapted to carry LCAs from
their davits (though *Glengyle*, which had served 'Layforce' in
the Mediterranean, was also present), these men made the
journey in so-called Eureka (or LCP) landing craft. There are
many ideas about why these boats were constructed in the first
instance—among them, the possibility that they were designed
for studying marine biology on the lakes and rivers of North

America. But one thing is certain: they were not conceived with a view to landing troops on an enemy-held shore to the accompaniment of heavy fire. They were unarmed; their hulls were built from wood; and their maximum speed was ten knots.

And so the unfortunate men of Number 3 were crammed into these frail conveyances, packed twenty to a boat, and each sitting with his chin touching his knees in a strange contortion intended to occupy less space. By contrast, in one of LSIs, an officer was able to enjoy a breakfast of bacon, eggs and kidneys—followed by hot-buttered toast and coffee. If some were more equal than others, the occupants of the Eurekas were travelling in a maritime version of shanty town. Nor was this the end of the matter. In an operation that was so full of unkind coincidences, these small vessels were the most in need of armour during the Channel-crossing.

To add to the irony, the bewilderingly bad luck of this small fleet, this particular tragedy could have been averted. The culprits were a destroyer captain and (another feature of 'Jubilee') appalling communications.

Led by Steam Gun Boat Number 5, with Durnford-Slater and Captain Roy Murray on her bridge, and escorted by ML 348 and a flak boat (for anti-aircraft purposes), the small procession travelled in four columns. In mid-passage, a channel had been swept through the German minefield. At some point on their journey, the outward-bound Eurekas became mixed up with the homeward-bound sweeper. The confusion took time to sort out; afterwards SGB Number 5 (top speed: 35 knots) increased her speed—unaware, apparently, that the less athletic landing craft were unable to keep up with her. Four of them had to limp back to England with engine troubles.

Earlier that morning—at 1.24 am and at 2.44 am—the radar stations at Beachy Head and Newhaven had picked up echoes which indicated that a convoy of enemy ships was proceeding down the Channel between Boulogne and Dieppe. In a reasonable world, the information would have been transmitted to the destroyer, HMS *Calpe*—which, with General Roberts and Captain Hughes-Hallett aboard, was acting as command ship to the expedition. But no such signal arrived. One or two other destroyers picked up the report on their radios; but, for want of any instructions, their captains did nothing about it.

The convoy carrying 3 Commando plodded on, unaware that it was converging on the Germany Ships. Two destroyers, the Polish *Slazak* and HMS *Brocklesby*, had been detailed to strengthen the Eurekas' escort; but, at 3.47 am on that fateful morning, when the landing craft were about eight miles from the French coast, they had wandered from their stations and were more than four miles away. It was disastrous; for, at 3.47 am, the German and the Commando formations more or less collided.

Details are vague about the German convoy, though there were definitely five armed trawlers (escorting a tanker) and, possibly, other naval units. Certainly its fire-power was more than enough to deal with SGB5, ML348 and the flak boat (which had, after all, not been built to provide defence against surface vessels).

For the next few minutes, it seemed as if the twenty-three Eurekas and the 460 men of 3 Commando—minus, of course, the four boatloads that had been compelled to turn back—were doomed. The trawlers' 20-mm machine-guns alone were sufficient to tear the vulnerable wooden hulls to shreds and, in many cases, this is what they did. The steam gunboat's bridge was soon a shambles—the agony of blood and shattered equipment illuminated by enemy star shells. *Slazak* and *Brocklesby*, surely, must come to their senses and intervene. But they remained away, intent on whatever futile mission had engrossed them. Afterwards, *Slazak*'s captain—who was in command of the two destroyers—admitted that he had heard firing. But, he said, he had assumed that it was taking place on shore.

Ten minutes after the action began, SGB5 received a hit in its boiler room. SGB5 was now helpless, and the *coup de grâce* might be expected at any second. It never came. Unaccountably, the firing suddenly stopped, and the German convoy proceeded on its way. But it had done damage enough. With the gunboat bereft of power, neither Durnford-Slater nor Murray would be able to go ashore.

Indeed, the current was already dragging the helpless vessel in the wrong direction. The operation—or such of it that was still possible—was now in the hands of the unit's second-in-command, Major Peter Young. But there were now only four landing-craft in any condition to carry on with the raid. The others had either been sunk—or else so badly damaged that they were trying to struggle home to England. In at least two cases, the navel crews had all been killed or wounded, and the craft were taken over by commandos.

Durnford-Slater's plan was for the Commando to land on two beaches (Yellow 1 and Yellow 2), converging on 'Goebbels' from two sides. But all that remained of one group was Peter Young and eighteen men squashed together in a landing-craft commanded by Lieutenant Commander Buckee RN. As this solitary survivor of the Yellow 1 force resumed its journey towards the French coast, Young looked at his naval colleague inquiringly. What, he wondered, do we do now? Buckee was in no dilemma. 'My orders', he said, 'are quite clear. They are to put you chaps ashore, even if I have to wreck my boat doing it. I intend putting you ashore. OK?' Young agreed. He recalled a paragraph in his orders that said, 'The battery guns should be engaged by fire at the earliest possible moment and continually harassed by snipers if insufficient commandos get ashore for the planned attack.'

Amazingly, the Eureka crunched on to the beach at 4.50 am—five minutes early. Young and his men hurried ashore. They clambered to the top of the cliff, using ingredients in the pattern of German barbed-wire defences to assist them up a near-vertical slope. It was, perhaps, surprising that the enemy had gone to the trouble of putting them there; the cliff itself was obstacle enough. At the top, they took cover in a small wood, where Young briskly disabused his men of any ideas about this being a lost cause. The operation, he said, would go forward as planned. They might not be able to assault the gun positions, but there was the instruction about snipers. They might be able to cause more confusion than, at this moment, seemed probable.

Young and his warriors moved off briskly along the road that led to Dieppe, making for the village of Berneval. Just after dawn, they met a boy on a bicycle, riding in the opposite direction. The lad wished them well, and told them all that he knew of the German defences, which was really very little. In Berneval, they met a man who was carrying his mother in a wheelbarrow. She had, he said, been injured by a bomb fragment during the RAF attack that preceded the landings.

But, no: he had nothing against the English—far from it. His sentiments seemed to be shared by other members of the village's population, who came out of their front doors to greet the raiders.

The church at Berneval had a tall tower, and the top of it, Young decided, would be an admirable place in which to site a Bren gun. Unfortunately, the lower ten feet of the steps that led up to it had been cut away. Nor was there any ladder to make good this shortcoming. Instead, he moved his troops into a nearby wheatfield, where the corn gave adequate cover and where, firing from their knees, the commandos could snipe at the gun positions. They remained there for one and a half hours—never actually seeing a German, but obviously causing trouble. After a while, one of the guns swung round through 180° with the obvious intent of bombarding them. But it could not depress its barrel sufficiently, and the shells exploded harmlessly in the hinterland of France.

ut this could not go on for ever. When there were indications that the enemy proposed to attack them from the flank, Young decided that the time had come to return to the beach. The faithful Buckee had come back with his Eureka, and the tiny force was embarked with only one casualty. On the way back, they had preferred to travel down a gulley—rather than attempt a descent via the cliff face. During the latter part of the journey, Lance-Corporal White trod on a land mine and injured his foot. Nevertheless he reached the beach, still carrying the barrel of a 3-inch mortar.

The other force, under Captain Richard Wills, and amounting to about fifty men, had been less successful. Despite the heroic action of Corporal 'Banger' Halls charging a machine-gun post single-handed (and taking it), they had not been able to fight their way through the encircling Germans. During the action, Lieutenant Edwin Loustalot of the US Rangers was killed. He became the first American to be killed in land fighting during World War II.

When, at last, Wills and his men got back to the beach, there were no landing-craft. However, they had distracted the attention of 350 of the infantry assigned to the battery's defence, and this may have been achievement enough. Unfortunately, unable to make a getaway, they were all taken prisoner. In reprisal for treatment which, the Germans alleged, was being accorded to their own men who had been captured, their guards put them into handcuffs. But, with an ingenuity that many a criminal would have envied they released themselves within twenty-four hours. After this, the Germans tried rope, but it was even easier to break free from that than the more rigid metal of the handcuffs.

Number 4 Commando under Lord Lovat made the crossing in HMS *Prince Albert*, a cross-Channel steamer that, in peacetime, served on the Ostend run. The voyage had passed without interruption; and, ten miles offshore, the unit was transferred to LCAs. It was now divided into two groups. Number one, under Major Derek Mills-Roberts, was to come ashore on a beach referred to as Orange 1. Its purpose was to cover the attack by Group Two (under Lovat) on the six German guns, code-named 'Hess'—each of which was mounted on a concrete platform. Major Mills-Roberts had eighty-eight men under his command—including 'C' Troop, a fighting patrol on loan from 'A' troop, a 3-inch mortar detachment, and a party of signallers.

Group Two, which was to land on Orange 2, at the mouth of the Saane about 1 3/4 miles from Orange 1 and on the far side of a headland, was composed of 'A' Troop (minus the fighting patrol), 'B' and 'F' Troops, and a detachment of US Rangers. In view of the speed with which the operation had to be conducted, Lovat had decided to use only half his Commando.

Of all the forces that were committed to action in the area of Dieppe that day, this alone was completely successful. No doubt Number 3 Commando, had it made a safe passage, would have done equally well—which was probably a lesson that the planners bore in mind afterwards. For a combined operation to succeed, the first essential is that the men involved shall actually reach their destinations.

As Major Mills-Roberts and his commandos approached Orange 1, they saw the lighthouse on the headland flashing its customary signal. Then, suddenly, the beam was extinguished and some star shells were shot into the sky from a nearby semaphore tower. Nevertheless, the men came ashore without any opposition—without, indeed, getting their feet wet. The

gulley that they had intended to use for their ascent to the cliff
top turned out to be blocked by a fall of chalk. To the right of
it, there was another, but this was barricaded by barbed wire.
On the major's instructions, a bangalore torpedo was brought
up. This, a relic of World War I, was a tube, about eight feet
long, filled with 10 pounds of high explosive. It was extremely
effective—though, not unnaturally, it made an unholy noise.
Once it had been detonated, any hope of surprise—if such
there still was—would be destroyed along with the wire entanglements.

In fact, there were plenty of other sounds to engage the
German ears. The noise of Number 3 Commando's affray to
the north-east was already disturbing the early morning quiet.
By a happy coincidence, fighters from Number 129 Squadron
of the RAF chose that moment to make a low-level attack with
their cannons on the gun positions. In the prevailing cacophony,
the din of the bangalore torpedo's explosion seems to have
passed unremarked.

The route to the cliff top was now clear. Once up, the
commandos were able to double through a wood towards the
German batteries. On the way, they passed a cottage, where
an elderly Frenchman was watching their progress—clad in a
nightshirt and (a wartime replacement for bedroom slippers,
we must assume) buttoned boots. After a brief scrutiny, he
hurried inside—returning a few moments later wearing a black
jacket and a pair of striped trousers. He shook Major Mills-
Roberts vigorously by the hand, and offered him a glass of
wine.

'C' troop took up its position in a huddle of buildings at the
edge of the wood, about 250 yards from the Germany positions.
The fighting patrol from 'A' Troop set off to cut the telephone
wires leading from the lighthouse, and returned to report that
they had been accounted for. Each man as now the richer by
one newly laid egg, which had been presented to him by an
old lady whose cottage they had passed. Three of 'C' Troop's
snipers, their hands and faces painted green to improve their
camouflage, crept forward to within 150 yards of the enemy,
and the gun battle began.

Each man knew what had to be done, and he did it very
well. Corporal Frank Koons of the US Rangers was aware of

having shot a German, though he may not have realised that he was the first American to kill an enemy on land in World War II. He was suitably rewarded afterwards with the Military Medal. Gunner McDonough developed something approaching an obsession with a flak tower, on which two anti-aircraft guns were mounted, in the middle of the enemy position. He discharged something like sixty rounds from his Boys Anti-tank rifle (a weapon not unlike an elephant gun, the main feature of which was that it was virtually useless against tanks) in its direction—causing the crew to be replaced three times.

By now the 3-inch mortar had been brought up to the edge of the wood. The first round fell short, but the second more than made amends. As if by magic, it homed faultlessly on the battery's magazine, blowing up a batch of cordite charges which, in its turn, set off a greater explosion. Some minutes before, the snipers and three Bren gunners who were now keeping them company, had knocked out a trio of machine-gun posts. Major Mills-Roberts and his men had done well. Lord Lovat and the assault force could arrive whenever they chose.

Lovat and the rest of Group 2 landed at 4.30 am to find the beach littered with rather more wire than they would have liked. It took four men to dispose of it, but they were soon pressing on. The leading section, under Lieutenant A. S. S. Veasey, made shortish work of scaling the cliffs—using tubular ladders that had been brought along for the purpose. At the top, Veasey and his men stormed a pair of concrete pillboxes. One turned out to be empty; the other was briskly brought to a similar condition by a few well-aimed grenades. Not far away, a pole was supporting telephone wires, and this had to be dealt with. By now, there was heavy small-arms fire coming from the Germany positions. Undaunted by it, Trooper W. Finney climbed up, cut the wires, and—despite the fact that bullets were actually smacking into the pole—climbed down again. When the rewards were made afterwards, he became Trooper Finney MM.

Down below, near the beach, the enemy had obligingly marked the position of a minefield with notices written in French and German. Skirting it, Lovat and the rest of his group doubled along the left bank of the Saane. The going was

not easy, for the grass was long and the ground was flooded by
the river, which had recently inundated its banks. It was now
daylight, The noise of Group One's firing drifted down into the
valley; overhead, three Boston light bombers of the USAAF
obligingly streaked by at low-level, distracting the enemy's
attention for a few moments.

Presently, they arrived at the edge of a wood. Still hurrying,
they went through it, and through an orchard on the far side.
'B' and 'F' Troops now formed up for the assault. A 3-inch
mortar was set up to provide cover with its smoke bombs.

It was a strange mixture of peace and war. A German cook,
wearing a white cap, could be seen stretching himself somewhere
within the German position—as if he had just got up and was
looking forward to a pleasant day. Nearer to hand, a squad of
thirty-five *Stosstruppe* (assault troops) seemed to be preparing
itself for an attack on Major Mills-Roberts' commandos. A
burst of tommy-gun fire from 'F' Troop caused the men to
change their minds—or, that is to say, those who still had any
minds to change.

'F' Troop was indeed busy. The Germans, despite the apparently relaxed attitude of their cook, had been stung into a
lethal wakefulness. The Troop Commander, Captain R. G.
Pettiward was shot down. The second-in-command, Lieutenant
J. A. Macdonald, was killed at the same time. A sergeant
briefly took charge; and then he, too, perished in the heavy
fire. Not far away, Company Sergeant Major W. R. Stockdale
was firing his rifle to good effect from a sitting position, but
there was little else the CSM could do. half of one of his feet
had been blown off by a grenade. 'F' Troop, it seemed, would
soon be without anyone able to lead it.

At this moment in the tide of its affairs, Major Pat Porteous
providentially arrived on the scene. Major Porteous had been
acting as liaison officer between the two groups. Such services
no longer seemed to be necessary; 'F' Troop, he judged, was a
greater priority. He was in the process of arranging matters to
better effect, when a Germany sprang at him and shot him
through the hand. The Major's reactions were nothing if not
sharp. The enemy infantryman had no opportunity to regret
his impulsive assault. Porteous brought his surviving hand into
action and killed him instantly.

One hundred minutes after the landing, Lovat was able to order the attack to begin by firing a cluster of white Very lights into the sky. Mills-Roberts put down a screen of smoke, and then stopped firing. 'B' and 'F' Troops took off in the direction of the gun positions, and the first to arrive was the gallant Porteous. By the time he got there, he had been wounded twice more. Nevertheless, he bayoneted to death one gun crew—using only one hand. The feat afterwards earned him the Victoria Cross.

The engagement was brief and extremely bloody. Some time very near the end, the German battery commander and another officer were seen running away, rather futilely firing their pistols. Both were shot down. When it was all over, only four Germans were alive. The toll might had been less, had not some of the enemy soldiers been seen to kick the faces of wounded commandos who were lying on the ground. Such conduct did not put the men of 4 Commando in any mood to be merciful.

Immediately after the fighting stopped, the guns and their emplacements were destroyed by demolition charges. On Lovat's instructions, the unit's dead were placed at the foot of a flag-staff, and a Union Jack was run up. Then, in perfect order, the force withdrew back to the beach. The white-capped cook was among the prisoners, and so was a man who had suffered from frost-bite on the Russian front. He had, he complained, been excused by the medical officer from marching. Lovat was less lenient. The soldier was told to forget about his health and to lend a hand with the wounded.

All told, Number 4 Commando suffered two officers and ten other ranks killed. Three officers and seventeen other ranks were wounded, and thirteen other ranks were wounded and missing. The price was small for such an achievement, and Lord Lovat was later made a member of the Distinguished Service Order. From the moment Groups One and Two had disembarked to the time they were successfully reclaimed from the shore by their landing-craft, the conduct of the operation had been faultless.

There were many lessons to be learned that day. One of them was that aerial photographs cannot always be trusted; another was that, no matter how tempting it may be to launch an invasion at a place where there is a ready-made harbour, that temptation should be sternly resisted.

When Operation 'Jubilee' was planned, they knew about the gun positions on the cliff tops flanking Dieppe. The pictures did not, however, reveal that there were many others closer to hand, hidden by the high ground. Since they were not assumed to exist, nothing had been done about them. When the main force of about 5,000 Canadians came ashore, they marched into the nearest reproduction of hell that man can devise. They sailed across the calm, early morning sea from Southampton— the Royal Hamilton Light Infantry in the LSI HMS *Glengyle*; the Essex Scottish in the former Ostend boats *Prince Charles* and *Prince Leopold*; the Black Watch of Canada in the *Duke of Wellington* (before the war, known as the *Duke of York*, employed on the Heysham-Belfast service); the South Saskatchewan Regiment in the *Princess Beatrix* and the *Invicta* (after hostilities to ply between England and France on the Golden Arrow service); and so on. Although these men had not yet experienced battle, they were considered to be crack Canadian troops. Nevertheless, from the moment they stepped ashore, they were doomed. Unhappily, throughout most of the action, General Roberts, in his command post aboard HMS *Calpe*, did not realise exactly how badly things were going.

Originally, it had been intended that the river gunboat, HMS *Locust*—a ship that drew only five feet of water—should lead a flotilla of French *chasseurs* (fast motor launches) into the harbour. Each would carry a detachment of men from 40 (RM) Commando under Lieutenant Colonel J. P. Phillips. The Marines were to cut adrift the enemy landing-craft, and assist with demolition work. The naval units in this instance, were commanded by Commander Robert Ryder, who had handled things so well at Saint Nazaire.

But *Locust* and her followers never reached the basin. The gunboat was assailed by a heavy barrage from guns on the eastern headland of the harbour and, before long, suffered a good deal of damage. Ryder was not a man to hang back unnecessarily, but he was sufficiently realistic to realise that nothing would survive a second attempt. He ordered the captains to head out to sea again; at 6.30 am, he went on board *Calpe* to report the situation. Captain Hughes-Hallett accepted his opinion. Turning to General Roberts, he offered the Marines' services as a reserve unit. Roberts accepted, but now dense smoke was making it very difficult to see what was actually happening ashore.

The armoured regiment, known as the Calgary Tanks, had been transported with its Churchills to Dieppe in twenty-four tank-landing-craft. The plan was for them to push through the town and, working with the Cameron Highlanders of Canada, attack the airfield about ten miles inland at St Aubin. They never got near their target. The disembarkation itself came under very heavy fire and the operation could not, by any standards, be accounted successful. The captain of the first LCT to arrive misjudged his distance from the shore, with the result that the Churchills drove off the ramp into several feet of water. The drivers of the second flight had not taken the precaution of warming up their engines in readiness—with the result that, one after another, they stalled on the point of departure. When the third LCT approached the beach, the German gunners were in full command of the situation. The landing-craft was set ablaze. The first Churchill off shared the fate of those in the first flight and 'drowned' in ten feet. The second and third managed to get ashore, but not before the latter had slid backwards and crushed two wounded men who were lying on the LCT's deck.

As if to add to this chapter of misfortunes, the tanks had arrived fifteen minutes late—which meant that the infantry and sappers already ashore had no covering fire during this period. Once on the beach, the Churchills depended on wooden ramps to negotiate the sea wall (nobody had thought that the engineers might have included it among their collection of demolition targets). Afterwards, the hulls of the Churchills were able to withstand anything the Germans chose to fire at them. Their tracks, alas, were less robust and their engines were unreliable. Eventually, the advance of the Calgary Tanks died from sheer lack of locomotion.

On board HMS *Calpe*, the mood of the high command was still cheerful. It was a state of mind that could only have come from considerable ignorance. By 7.00 am, the Royal Hamilton Light Infantry had taken the Casino—a large building that jutted out over the beach—and there were Canadian tanks nearby on the promenade. General Roberts now decided to use the 40 (RM) Commando to reinforce them. This, he believed, would enable the RHLI to turn its attention to the guns on the western headland, which were seriously hampering the main assault.

It was the type of decision that may work very well on a tactical exercise (preferably without troops), but which can easily be fatal in real life. With all the smoke and confusion, the general could not see what conditions were really like. When somebody mentioned that the shore seemed to be clear of enemy, he assumed it was safe to put 40 Commando ashore on White beach (as it was called). At Dieppe, at this moment, nothing was safe, and any assumption that was not based on up-to-the-minute facts was dangerous.

The *chasseurs* surged through the fog of the smoke barrier, and then emerged into the daylight. The scene before them was terrible. According to Lieutenant M. Buist, commander of the flotilla, 'I realized that this landing was to be a sea parallel to the Charge of the Light Brigade. There was a barrage coming from the East Cliff, another from the West Cliff, and a wall of machine-gun fire from houses along the promenade, which showed only too well that White beach was under very heavy attack indeed. Added to which there was a blazing LCT on the beach, another abandoned alongside it, and shells were bursting ahead of us... I shouted to Colonel Phillips to ask what he thought about going in; but I doubt if he heard me. Anyway he merely waved his arms and grinned to show that he meant to land at all costs.' As the official report put it, 'with a courage terrible to see, the Marines went in to land determined, if fortune so willed, to repeat at Dieppe what their fathers had accomplished at Zeebrugge'.

Few reached the shore alive. Lieutenant K. W. Smale managed it; he took cover with what was left of his platoon in the lee of an abandoned tank, and went on fighting until he and all his men were dead.

Colonel Phillips quickly realised that, unless the landing was stopped, his entire Commando would be wiped out. To make his signals clearer, he put on a pair of immaculate white gloves and climbed on the prow of his landing craft. He had just time to turn back the following boats before being shot through the head. Had he been vouchsafed a last thought, he might have reflected that he had just saved 200 men from totally useless slaughter.

There was great courage at Dieppe; a fearful tenacity and a dreadful killing. At last it dawned upon General Roberts and his naval companion that the time had come to call a halt to 'Jubilee'. At 10.30 am, the order to withdraw was given; but, here again, there was confusion. After he had uttered it, somebody reminded the general about the timing of the RAF fighter cover that was to support the evacuation. Accordingly, he changed the instruction to read '11.00 hrs'. Not all units received the correction—with the result that a number of vital posts were abandoned half an hour before schedule.

In fact, the fighters did not arrive until noon; but, before that, a formation of Bostons put down a dense smoke screen. This may not have been the happiest of ideas, for it warned the Germans that the boats were coming in towards the shore, and they aimed their guns accordingly.

Of the 5,000 Canadians who fought at Dieppe, 907 were either killed on the spot, or else died as prisoners of war; 2,462 were taken prisoner—many of them seriously injured. It was a steep price to pay for experience, but neither Churchill nor Mountbatten would admit that the raid had been a failure. The chief of combined operations said that it was 'one of the most vital operations of the Second World War. It gave the Allies the priceless secret of victory. . . If I had the same decision to make again, I would do as I did before.'

Churchill wrote that 'it was a costly but not unfruitful reconnaissance in force. Tactically it was a mine of experience. It shed revealing light on many shortcomings in our outlook.'

If Dieppe had never taken place, one can only speculate what might have been the cost of D-Day.

Despite the fact that there had been nine Allied war correspondents present at Dieppe, there were no accurate reports of the raid in the press. Prodded, no doubt, by censorship, the verdict echoed Mountbatten's opinion expressed on the following day. It had, he said, been 'very satisfactory'. In Germany, the

Deutsche Allegemeine Zeitung came closer to the truth, when it remarked that, 'as executed, the venture mocked all rules of military logic and strategy'. Praise could not be expected from the enemy; nevertheless, this severe critique was not altogether unreasonable.

Nor were the Allied newspapers fair in apportioning whatever credit there was to be had from the operation. The British press omitted any references to the Canadians, and described it as 'a Commando raid', which was a considerable under-statement. In the United States, most of the papers gave the impression that this was a triumph for 'Captain Roy Murray and his detachment from the 1st United States Ranger Battalion. The *New York Post* headlined its story WE LAND IN FRANCE, which was certainly true—though somewhat to overstate the case for Murray (who had not, in fact, landed at all) and his intrepid men. The *New York World Telegram* worked itself up into a state of greater enthusiasm by saying U.S. TROOPS SMASH THE FRENCH COAST—which, if he read it, must have brought a quiet smile to the face of the *Deutsche Allegemeine Zeitung*'s man.

The body of Lieutenant Colonel Geoffrey Keyes VC, who was killed in Cyrenaica during the abortive attempt to kidnap General Rommel, was taken to Potsdam, where it was buried with full military honours. The commandos who were captured at Saint Nazaire were treated with strict regard for the Geneva Convention and accorded the status of prisoners of war (though the French, who mistook the raid for liberation and joined in, were ruthlessly shot). The captives taken at Dieppe were also respected as POWs, despite their initial ill-treatment.

Nevertheless, in 1942, there were certain signs that raiders— whether they travelled to their targets by sea or by air, and despite the fact that they wore uniform—could no longer expect to survive if they were caught. On 19 September of that year, twelve men from Number 2 Commando were landed by a Free French submarine on the Norwegian coast. After a day's march under extremely difficult conditions, they reached the hydro-electric generating plant at Glomfjord. A demolition party of two men blew up vital pipelines and components; then, its work done, the force withdrew.

On the way back, the men encountered a German patrol. During the engagement that followed, the party's commanding officer, Captain Gordon Black, and his colleague, Captain Joe Houghton, were wounded. They, and six other raiders, were captured. But, for Black and Houghton, there was to be no sojourn in a prisoner-of-war camp. Both officers were shot by the Gestapo.

Less than a month later (on 3 October) a party from 12 Commando landed on the Channel Island of Sark. During a tour of the island, they snatched five Germans from their beds in an hotel, and made their way back towards the beach. On the way, the prisoners attempted to escape. Four of them were shot down; the fifth was taken to England. After the raid, Churchill announced that 'There comes from the sea a hand of steel that plucks the German sentries from their posts.'

In Germany, however, the raid brought Hitler's concern over Commando operations to a dark climax. On 18 October, he issued the infamous directive (known as the *Kommandobefehl*), in which he wrote:

For some time now our opponents have been using in the prosecution of the war, methods that do not conform to the international agreements of Geneva. Especially brutal and cunning is the behaviour of the so-called Commandos who themselves (as has been established) are partly recruited from among hardened criminals [sic] released in enemy countries.

These 'sabotage parties and their accomplices', the Führer ordered, 'will be ruthlessly exterminated in battle by German troops.' In a covering letter, which was not to be seen by anyone below the rank of divisional commander and which was to be destroyed, he said, 'Should it prove advisable to spare one or two men in the first instance for interrogation reasons, they are to be shot immediately after their interrogation.' Any officer who went against these instructions, and treated his captives with clemency, might be tried by court martial.

However, the rule did not apply to those who were 'taken prisoner in open battle, or who surrender in the course of normal battle operations'—which, presumably, would have included Dieppe.

In Norway, the commander-in-chief, General Von Falkenhorst, was even more explicit. 'Even should these individuals, on their being discovered, make as if to surrender, all quarter is to be denied them,' he instructed. On capture, the raiders were to be handed over immediately to the security forces (the SD). 'It is strictly forbidden', the general wrote, 'to hold them in military custody, e.g., in prisoner of war camps, etc.—even as a temporary measure.'

The executioners had received their orders and, in most cases, they carried them out with zeal. For instance, on 19 November, 1942, two Horsa gliders carrying thirty-two airborne troops set off to destroy the heavy-water plant (used for nuclear research) in the Telemark Mountains of Norway. The aircraft ran into bad weather; the pilots mistook their positions and crashed. Of the survivors, the injured were poisoned by the Gestapo in hospital; the others spent nearly a month under interrogation and were then shot.

On another occasion a force of Royal Marines under Major E. G. 'Blondie' Hasler was landed at the mouth of the Gironde by HM Submarine *Tuna*. After making its way up river to Bordeaux in canoes, it sank four merchant ships by means of limpet mines, and then withdrew. Of the two canoes that made the return trip, one—containing Major Hasler and Marine W. E. Sparks—made a successful getaway. The other, manned by Corporal Laver and Marine Mills, was captured. Both men were shot.

And there were many other such cases.

When Hitler composed his *Kommandobefehl*, he might have paused to consider his own country's exploits in this field— and, in particular, the ventures of the so-called Brandenburg Division. This unit, which never operated in more than company strength and frequently in small groups, was formed in October, 1939. Its inception, perhaps, gave formal status to troops who, for over a year, had already been functioning in the Brandenburger style. Wearing civilian clothes, they had been active in Czechoslovakia during the Sudetenland crisis of 1938—carrying out espionage, sabotage, and preparing possible landing strips for aircraft. Likewise, they had been busy during the Polish campaign, especially in securing a vital pass through which the southern prong of the invasion must pass. This was accomplished despite the fact that they arrived rather early at the target; for, at the last moment, Hitler postponed the offensive for six days.

The purpose of the Brandenburg Division was to operate in front of attacking forces—to the rear of those in retreat. Sabotage and the supply of information were its merchandise; on the rare occasions when it took part in amphibious operations, its task (as in operations against the Russians on the shores of the Black Sea and the Sea of Azov) was to prepare the beaches for the invading forces. Had Operation 'Sea Lion' (the German plan for the invasion of Britain) gone ahead, a company of Brandenburgers would have been parachuted into Dover to take the port; other units would have been landed ahead of the main force at points between Dover and Lyme Regis.

During the 1940 thrust by the Panzers through the Low Countries, it functioned to excellent affect—producing chaos as well as destruction. Unlike the commandos, who relied on darkness for concealment, its members camouflaged themselves by wearing the enemy's uniform. A legal expert expressed the opinion that this did not contravene the rules of warfare, so long as no weapons were fired while the men were so garbed. Consequently, the idea was to be partially disguised (such as by wearing the opposition's brand of steel helmet, of overalls, or whatever). On going into the attack, these trappings would be cast off—rather as a ship, flying enemy colours, unfurls her own ensign at the moment of joining combat. But it did not always work out like this. In North Africa, for instance, General Rommel refused to allow Brandenburgers to masquerade in British uniforms.

Some of the disguises were, it had be to admitted, very convincing—with a nice sense of detail. In Holland, a unit of Brandenburgers pretended to be captured members of the *Wehrmacht* guarded by completely phony Dutch soldiers. During operations in Latvia, a Brandenburger unit posed as Red Army troops—suitably bandaged to give the impression that they were wounded.

The Brandenburg Division was finally disbanded in 1944, when its men were re-mustered in a *Panzergrenadier* division—though the idea of dissembling survived, and Otto Skorzeny's Special Formation achieved some small success during the Ardennes offensive of December, 1944. Disguised as an American unit, and using American equipment, it cut telephone wires, blew up ammunition dumps, and misdirected convoys.

Whilst the Brandenburg Division came under the orders of *Abwehr* chief Admiral Canaris, Skorzeny's Special Force was ultimately responsible to Himmler's *Reich* Main Security Office. Otto Skorzeny himself was an Austrian who, at the outbreak of war, was running a building business. A large man, 6 foot 4 inches tall, he was rejected for service in the *Luftwaffe* on account of his age (thirty-one). Instead, he joined the Waffen SS (the combat force of the *Schutzstaffel* which, among other things, provided Hitler's bodyguard). His Special Force, comprised mostly of Waffen SS men, was formed in 1942 to engage in Commando-style operations. The most sensational of these ventures was the rescue of Mussolini from his captivity in an hotel situated amid the Abruzzi Mountains of Italy.

8 The Rescue

On 10 July, 1943, British and American forces under the command of Dwight D. Eisenhower invaded Sicily. On the 26th of that month, the Italian dictator, Benito Mussolini—or 'Il Duce'—was dismissed by the King of Italy, Victor Emmanuel. He was succeeded by General Pietro Badoglio. Mussolini was last seen in the royal palace. After that, he vanished. . .

Hauptsturmführer Otto Skorzeny of the Waffen SS was, if such a character is possible, a German version of the British hero of several hard-hitting adventure stories, Bulldog Drummond. He was large, daring, and could have been considered handsome. With a considerable gift for self-publicity, he was well able to portray himself in the Drummond role. Indeed, it cannot have been chance that he led what amounted to a private army of warriors—usually scripting his own operations, directing them, and playing the leading roles. He was, perhaps, one of the last great actor-soldiers.

As well as having an innate sense of drama, Skorzeny (who insisted that his name be pronounced 'Skor-tsay-ny') had a sensitive nose for politics. In the higher echelons of German power, Canaris' *Abwehr* and Himmler's Department of Security were fighting a small war within the greater universe of hostilities. Skorzeny, with his flair for backing winners, threw in his military lot with Himmler. He went so far as to assert that: 'Canaris betrayed his country's military secrets to Britain directly and wittingly from the beginning of his career to the end.' The statement does not appear to be entirely untrue, but Skorzeny was promoting Skorzeny when he made it. Accusing the *Abwehr* chief was merely a means to his favourite end.

On 26 July, 1943, this paragon of irregular warfare was in Berlin with the second-in-command of his Special Formation, Karl Radl. At about 3.00 that afternoon he received an unexpected telephone call. He was to go at once to the Tempelhof airfield, where a JU52 was standing by to fly him to Hitler's *Führerhauptquartier* (the *Wolfsschanze*— Wolf's Den') at Rastenberg in East Prussia. Although Skorzeny was never lacking in self-assurance, he was surprised—even, nervous— to be summoned to such an exalted place.

That evening, Skorzeny was greeted by the Führer himself, who began the conversation by asking him what he thought of the Italians. Skorzeny replied, 'I am an Austrian'—and thereby won immediate approval. As anyone with a smattering of history knew (and Hitler himself was an Austrian), it implied several less than complimentary things about the subject under discussion. With their reprehensible ability to lose on every front, Hitler had lost patience with the Italians.

Skorzeny, the Führer suggested, had heard that Mussolini had been taken into custody—nobody knew where. The former dictator, he said, had been betrayed by his king, and this unsatisfactory state of affairs could not be allowed to continue. 'To me', exclaimed Hitler, ascending into rhetoric, 'the Duce is the incarnation of the ancient grandeur of Rome'. His visitor agreed, which was just as well. He was, the Führer informed him, to get work at once: find out where Mussolini had been hidden, and rescue him. The mission was to receive top priority and top security. Not even von Kesselring, the C-in-C of German troops in Italy, nor the German Ambassador in Rome, were to be informed of the plot.

That night, Skorzeny worked late in a room that had been put at his disposal. For some of the time, he was with General Kurt Student, the founder and now head of the *Fallschirmjäger*, (the German airborne forces, with whom he was due to fly to Rome on the following morning. Briefly, Himmler looked in. This was Skorzeny's first meeting with the man who was so important to his career and it did not augur well for the future. The *Reichführer* SS chided him for smoking cigarettes, castigated him for taking notes when the assignment was so secret, and generally gave the impression that, on this occasion, Hitler had not picked the right man for the job. Nevertheless, he gave him one or two introductions in Rome that might come in useful.

For much of the time, Skorzeny communicated with Karl Radl—either by phone or by teleprinter. During the next nine hours, the unfortunate Radl had to assemble all the troops and equipment that might be necessary. He was to select fifty members of the Special Formation; if they spoke Italian, so much the better, but they must be the *best*. He was to procure two machine guns for every group of ten men, making a total of twenty; machine pistols, such as the Maschinen Pistole 38 (or *Schmeisser*), which was light (10.5 lbs) and could produce fire at the rate of 500 rounds a minute from its 32-round box magazine; grenades, the best were the egg type, which could be carried in the pocket; 30 kgs of plastic explosive—preferably from the British stock that had been left behind in Holland (it was better than the German product); tropical helmets; rations for six days and emergency rations for an extra three days; Very light pistols; and, perhaps, some civilian clothes for the officers.

Radl excelled himself. He completed his task well within the time scheduled and even threw in a couple of priests' outfits— assuming, presumably, that such a disguise would go down well in Italy.

Skorzeny hardly slept at all that night. The room was uncomfortably stuffy, and he had a great deal on his mind. At some point, he thought about his wife and young children, and realised that he had not made a will. He got up and rectified this oversight.

Next morning, he and Student took off for Rome in an He 111—a bomber that had failed to distinguish itself during the Battle of Britain and had since been relegated to such tasks as towing gliders and carrying personnel. Skorzeny was pretending to be one of the airborne general's aides, but he had overlooked the fact that he was still wearing his uniform of the Waffen SS. For an officer of this corps to be dancing attendance on the head of the *Fallschirmjäger* would obviously cause comment. Consequently he had to endure several hours of a particularly hot Italian summer, wearing his fur-lined flight jacket. Eventually, at Student's behest, somebody found him a Parachute Corps uniform from a batch that had been intended for North Africa.

That evening, they dined with von Kesselring at the German headquarters in Frascati, about thirty miles to the south-east of Rome. Also present at the dinner table were two men that Himmler had recommended—Kappler, the German police attaché in Rome, and Herr Dollmann, who had lived in Italy for a good many years and who was supposed to have good contacts.

Kesselring did his best to explain the situation. On 25 July, Mussolini—against the advice of his wife—had sought an interview with the king. The last time anyone had seen him, he had been talking to the monarch. Nothing had been heard of him since, and it had been assumed that he had been arrested.

Badoglio had promised that the switch of power would have no effect upon German-Italian relations, and that his government would continue to fight alongside Germany. Canaris apparently believed this to be true and Kesselring agreed with him. Hitler was more sceptical. He had already produced a plan to disarm the Italian army and to introduce more troops into Italy if Badoglio capitulated. As it happened, he was right: the new Italian prime minister had been discussing the possibility of an armistice with Eisenhower for some while. Canaris, as head of Intelligence, must have known about this; it seemed to be an example of the betrayal to which Skorzeny was to refer some while later.

For the moment, as Kesselring was bound to admit, the German troops had to be spread somewhat thinly on the ground. There was a division of paratroops defending Rome and, elsewhere, there were six more, though each was under strength. With the Allied foothold in Sicily now secure, it did not seem sufficient.

On the day after Skorzeny's arrival at Frascati, the 1st *Fallschirmjäger* Division flew in—followed, on the 29th by Radl and the fifty men chosen from the Special Force. The plan was that, once Il Duce had ben located, a detachment from the paratroops under a major named Mors would assist in the rescue operation. But, before this could happen, the ex-dictator had to be located. The task was not easy; having seen his men quartered in wooden huts on the edge of the airfield at Frascati, and having ordered that they should carry out training exercises during the mornings and evenings (the afternoons could be spent in swimming and sport), Skorzeny changed roles. For the next few weeks, the intrepid raider assumed the duties, or something very like them, of a private eye.

Although he was not yet privy to the rescue plot, Kesselring, too, was anxious to know where Il Duce was hidden. As general officer commanding German forces in Italy, he took the opportunity to pay a call on Crown Prince Umberto, and to ask him whether he knew of Mussolini's whereabouts. No, Umberto said, his father had not told him. Was he speaking the truth? It seemed unlikely, but what could Kesselring do?

Hitler decided that there *was* something else that he might do. July the 29th happened to be Mussolini's 60th birthday. What could be more natural than that the Führer should send his old friend a gift? He dug out a de luxe edition of the collected works of Nietzsche and dispatched them to Frascati. The commander-in-chief must present them in person. After all, such a mission could not be entrusted to an underling. Kesselring was not hopeful, but he dutifully asked Badoglio for permission to make the presentation. The new premier was polite. But, no—he was sorry: it was impossible. The books would be sent to the prisoner, who would no doubt enjoy reading them. There could not, however, be any question of Kesselring—or any other German, come to that—visiting the captive (whose whereabouts he felt unable to disclose).

The policeman-diplomat Kappler was more successful. At Skorzeny's request, he questioned a senior *Carabinieri* officer. This man informed him that, after the interview in the palace, Mussolini had been driven in an ambulance to a police barracks in Rome. But, again, the trail died out. He had, this man believed, been transferred somewhere else.

The next clue was discovered by chance in a Rome restaurant. The proprietor happened to mention that one of his customers employed a maid whose fiancé was serving as a soldier in the penal settlement at Ponza—an island about twenty-five miles offshore between Rome and Naples. In one of his letters, he had mentioned that 'a very high ranking prisoner' (unnamed) had arrived a few days previously. But, once more, Skorzeny's hopes of bringing the matter to a quick conclusion

were crushed. Il Duce, it appeared, was continually being
moved from one place to another. On 7 August, an Italian
naval officer happened to mention that the dictator's captivity
on Ponza had been brief. He had been taken by a cruiser to
Spezia a few days later. Was he still on board the warship?
The officer did not know—though he suspected that it was
unlikely.

Everybody, it seemed, was playing the game of hunt the
Duce. When the report concerning the warship reached the
FHQ at Rastenberg, Hitler, jumping to conclusions as those
who are far removed from scenes of events so often do, ordered
Skorzeny to raid the man-of-war. Quite apart from its diplomatic consequences (after all, Italy was still, nominally at any
rate, Germany's ally), the operation was too difficult to bear
thinking about. Fortunately, evidence was soon produced to
show that he had been removed to another place. A German
liaison officer attached to the commander-in-chief of the Italian
naval station on Sardinia reported that Mussolini had been put
ashore on the island, and was now living in a villa on the edge
of La Maddalina. It was worth investigating. Disguised as
naval ratings, Skorzeny and one of his officers, Lieutenant
Warger (who spoke fluent Italian), were taken to La Maddalina
in a German minesweeper. Warger was instructed to make
inquiries in the dockside area.

The enterprising lieutenant decided to base his research on
the Italian fondness for gambling. One afternoon, not long
after their arrival, he was discussing Mussolini with a talkative
greengrocer. Il duce, Warger informed his companion, was
dead. He had died a few weeks ago—hadn't the man heard?—
from cancer. The tradesman denied it. Warger wagered that
he was speaking the truth; the vegetable merchant accepted
the bet. It was, he suggested, a shame to rob his misguided
friend. Not only could he prove that Il Duce was alive, he
could actually reveal a glimpse of him.

On that sweltering August afternoon, the two men walked
to a villa just beyond the town limits. The place was heavily
guarded, but there, sitting on the terrace, was a figure who at
least bore a very passable resemblance to Mussolini. Now,
surely, he was convinced? Warger paid up and made haste to
Skorzeny to relay the glad tidings.

To remove their quarry from a fortified house no more than
a mile or so from an important naval station was not going to
be easy. Before he considered his plans, Skorzeny decided that
an aerial reconnaissance was essential. To mislead any prying
eyes on the ground, he decided to fly over Corsica as well. The
trip was not a success.

On 18 August, an He 111 was put at Skorzeny's disposal.
Not long after take-off, the bomber was intercepted by a couple
of Allied fighters. It was shot down; minutes later, Skorzeny
and the air crew were adrift in a rubber dinghy—trying to
attract the attention of an Italian anti-aircraft warship. As well
as the indignity of a failed mission, Skorzeny now had three
broken ribs. Nevertheless, he believed that Mussolini might still
be on the island and that a raid was possible. With his chest
uncomfortably wrapped in plaster, he set off to Rastenberg to
seek further instructions. Present at the meeting were Hitler,
von Ribbentrop (the foreign minister), Keitel, and Jodl (of the
Oberkommand Wehrmacht), Dönitz (who had taken over from
Raedar as head of the navy), and, of course, Kurt Student.
From somewhere or other, Canaris had picked up a rumour
that Mussolini, his itinerant captivity obviously not yet over,
was now under guard on a small island near Elba. But this was
dismissed. The question at issue was: could a raid on Sardinia
be successfully mounted?

From his researches on the island, Skorzeny was able to
suggest that there were about 150 armed *Carabinieri* deployed
around the villa. If they needed reinforcements, they could
expect help from a barracks not far away, where 200 naval
cadets were quartered. But, he insisted, before a rescue operation
could be carried out, another reconnaissance was essential. The
meeting agreed, though Hitler was obviously becoming
impatient. Despite reports from Canaris and Kesselring, he did
not believe that Badoglio could be accounted an ally for much
longer. He was, the Führer believed, about to sue for an
armistice; and, when this happened, one of the terms would
clearly be that Mussolini must be handed over to the Allies.
Skorzeny would do well to hurry.

Prudently, the Special Force leader decided that, on this
occasion, it might be safer to travel to the island on board an
E-boat from the port of Anzio. Again, he was wearing the

disguise of a rating, but he might have saved himself a lot of trouble. When he approached the villa, nobody took the slightest notice of him. A soldier was standing at the gates, enjoying the sunshine and seemingly not taking his duties very seriously. When Skorzeny approached him, he appeared glad of a chat. Yes, he agreed, Il Duce had resided at the villa for a short while; but, earlier that day, he had left. He had been removed, the soldier said, in a white aeroplane bearing Red Cross markings. He had no idea where he had gone.

Disappointed, Skorzeny returned to Frascati. The investigation seemed to be getting nowhere; unless his luck turned fairly quickly, he might be in trouble. Nor was there much for Student's comfort. If Badogolio threw in his hand—if, say, he decided to do a turn-around and join forces with the Allies— the one airborne division in the neighbourhood of Rome would be threatened by seven Italian divisions. On the evidence of their performances in Africa, these troops had not amounted to much. But—7:1! The odds could hardly be judged acceptable.

There were a great many rumours, but little hard evidence. Travelling one day with Student on a tour of inspection along the shore of Lake Bracciano, Skorzeny was informed that the mysterious white aircraft had been seen, flying above the Apennines. Since the range of mountains is 800 miles long, the report was of small value. In any case, there had been so many false trails that he had become dubious about such tittle-tattle.

Meanwhile Kappler had been beavering away. The policeman was fond of taking colour photographs, and he often used to make an early morning drive along the Appian Way in search of attractive scenes for his camera. As it happened, he also used these trips as cover for meetings with a highly placed contact within the Italian Ministry of Home Affairs. On one of these expeditions, he received the key that had eluded them all for so long. His friend passed him a signal that had just been received by the Ministry. It read 'Security measures around Gran Sasso completed'.

Gran Sasso is a mountain in the Abruzzi range—a peak that rises to a height of 9,560 feet on the edge of a plateau known as the Campo Imperatore. Normally the region had no importance other than as a tourist resort. There could be no possible reason for taking 'security measures' there unless they were for

the reception of a prisoner such as Mussolini. Suddenly the
report of the white aircraft over Lake Bracciano began to make
sense. Suppose that it had been a seaplane coming in to land
on the water? In which case, Il Duce's next journey might well
have been by car to the Abruzzi Mountains, and what more
inaccessible place of captivity could there be than in the shadow
of the Gran Sasso d'Italia? This, certainly, merited serious
scrutiny.

There was a hotel—called the Hotel Albergo-Rifugio—on
the Campo Imperatore, which had been built in 1938. Skorzeny
decided that this was most likely where Il Duce had been
interned. The difficulty was to obtain any reliable maps of the
neighbourhood. Since it had so recently been constructed, the
hotel was not marked on any of them. The only material they
could find was a brochure put out by a travel agency—and the
testimony of a German living in Italy, who had spent a winter
sports holiday at the hotel shortly after it had opened. This
gentleman explained that there was no means of reaching the
plateau by road; for the last stage of the trip you had to travel
by a funicular in which the cars, each carrying four people,
were suspended from wire ropes.

Skorzeny and Radl made their way to the airfield at Frascati.
They were directed to an He 111 that was fitted with a camera
which would, its air crew explained, take pictures automatically. To avert suspicion, it was decided that they should fly
over the target at a height of 15,000 feet. Skorzeny was still
wearing his lightweight Afrika Korps uniform and, at this
altitude, he found conditions rather chilly. The cold became
even worse when, thirty kilometres from the plateau, they
discovered that the automatic camera had developed a fault
and could not be used.

Fortunately, there was also a hand camera aboard the
aircraft, but it turned out to be impossible to take pictures
through the perspex windows. With commendable resourceful-
ness, Skorzeny managed to cut a hole large enough to
accommodate his head and shoulders through one of the panels.
He exposed sufficient film, and they flew on northwards. On
the return trip, the unfortunate Radl submitted himself to this
ordeal by cold and took more pictures.

To attack the hotel by land was obviously impossible. It might be done, Skorzeny estimated, if an entire division of mountain troops was put at the raiders' disposal, but this was out of the question. On the other hand, he had noticed a triangular meadow adjoining the premises. It seemed possible that gliders might be able to land there.

On the He 111's return to the airfield, it looked as if misfortune had dealt the project another blow. While they had been flying over the Abruzzi, Allied bombers had carried out a raid—destroying, among other things, the house in which Skorzeny and Radl were quartered and, more to the point, the photographic laboratory. A small dark room on the perimeter had survived, but it could not produce enlargements of sufficient size to serve a really useful purpose. As for gliders, the nearest squadron was stationed in the South of France. They were ordered to proceed to Frascati, but it was a long journey, and there was a danger that they might be intercepted by Allied fighters *en route*. Once again, the unseen hand of fate seemed to be conspiring against this act of liberation.

Hitler had been right when he suspected Badoglio's intentions. On 8 September, when British and American troops came ashore at Salerno in South Italy, the Italian prime minister capitulated. Not long afterwards, a broadcast from Eisenhower's headquarters announced that Mussolini had been brought to North Africa in an Italian cruiser and was now an Allied prisoner. Skorzeny did some quick arithmetic. The Italian fleet had indeed put to sea from Spezia with the object of surrendering itself to the Allies. But a simple calculation suggested that none of its units could have reached Algiers by the time of the transmission. The Americans, it seemed, were bluffing. However, all Italians must now be regarded as hostile, and this appeared to put the rescue operation at even greater risk. The commanding officer of Student's parachute forces went so far as to suggest that it might be impossible. He predicted that, if it went ahead, eighty per cent casualties might be expected.

It seemed unlikely that Hitler would be satisfied with any such excuse, and Skorzeny had no intention of abandoning the operation. Some days before the capitulation, he had met the *Fallschirmjäger* Division's medical officer, who, by a fortunate coincidence, was worried about the convalescent facilities for soldiers who had fallen ill with malaria. The Albergo-Rifugio, Skorzeny had suggested, might very well provide the answer to this problem. The medico agreed to explore its possibilities. When he returned a day or two later, he reported that he had not been allowed to visit the plateau. He had been turned away pretty sharply by guards at the foot of the funicular. He was, he confessed, surprised.

General Student and Skorzeny (assisted, we must assume, by Major Mors, whose part in the operation has probably received less attention than it deserves) drew up a plan. The idea was that paratroops commanded by Mors should be landed in the valley at the base of the plateau, and that they should seize the lower funicular station. The Special Force and some of the airborne troops would travel to the objective in a dozen gliders, each accommodating ten men. Zero hour was defined as 6.00 am on the morning of 12 September. At this time, it was estimated, the treacherous air currents, which might put the gliders at risk, would probably be at their weakest.

The trouble was that the gliders had still not arrived from the South of France and that, very shortly, Mussolini might expect to be removed into Allied custody. Indeed what might Il Duce's reaction be to the landing of German forces? Would he trust them? To make sure that he did, the services of a senior officer in the *Carabinieri*, a General Soleti, were enlisted. Still, apparently, viewing the Germans with friendship, he might provide the raiders with an adequate reference.

At last, after a flight that had been bedevilled by bad weather and the unwelcome attentions of Allied aeroplanes, the gliders arrived at 11.00 am on the 12th—nearly eight hours late. Zero hour had now been put back to 2.00 pm which, in terms of weather conditions, did not augur well for the enterprise. However, Skorzeny now had 108 men under his command, and he was determined to go on, whatever the perils. They were preparing to embark when somebody noticed that General Soleti was missing. Radl was sent off to Rome where, not without difficulty, he ran him to earth. The general, it seemed, was beginning to regret his commitment to what was obviously going to be a dangerous assignment.

The plan was that the gliders and the aircraft that towed them should travel in line astern. Ideally, groups 1 and 2 would land first and provide cover for the rest of the force. Skorzeny had elected to travel in number 3—which, assisted by the men in number 4, would force an entrance into the hotel. The remainder would deploy themselves in the light of any opposition they encountered. Whatever was done must be accomplished quickly; for, as Skorzeny had pointed out, Il Duce's guards might very well have been given orders to kill him rather than allow him to fall into what were now enemy (or almost enemy) hands. The password for the operation was 'Take it easy'—a phrase that Radl had often to utter to his tempestuous leader, as he fretted at the delays. Radl, in this partnership, was the calmer though less practical, member. He was, Skorzeny once remarked, 'a poet by temperament'. He must also have been extremely patient.

It was estimated that the flight to the Campo Imperatore would take about one hour. But, almost at the last moment, it seemed as if the operation might have to be postponed yet again: for, at 12.30 pm, the air-raid alarms sounded. The sound of bombs exploding could be heard from somewhere not far away, and the force was compelled to take cover. But the intruders left the airfield in peace and, half an hour later, they departed. Immediately, before there could be any more trouble, Skorzeny and his men climbed into the gliders, and the aerial armada took off. The cloud base was at 9,000 feet, which seemed ideal. Flying above it, the aircraft could approach the landing zone unseen.

But all was not entirely well. As Skorzeny soon discovered, groups 1 and 2 were not leading the formation; they had in fact never got off the ground. As he learned later, their towing aircraft had crashed into bomb craters. This seemed to be a severe setback, for the assault party could no longer count on any covering fire. Nor did the omens improve as the gliders slipped their lines and began their descent. Skorzeny found that he could not see properly out of the window and so he cut a hole in the canvas body of the glider. The view it revealed was not encouraging. The landing ground, he observed, 'was triangular all right, but so far from being flat, it was a steep, a very steep hillside! It could even have been a ski jump'.

What with a sharp wind blowing outside, and Skorzeny heaving his considerable weight about inside, it was, perhaps, a miracle that the pilot, Lieutenant von Berlepsch, managed to carry out his instructions to crash land as close as possible to the hotel. But he brought down the DFS230 sufficiently close to the target and more or less in one piece. The parachute brake was released and, not without a few ruptured components, the glider at last came to rest. They were within fifteen yards of the hotel and none of the guards, so far, had fired a shot.

There was no time to lose. The first door they came to admitted them to a small room in which an Italian soldier was seated at a wireless set. His chair was kicked away from beneath him; several blows from one of the machine pistols made sure that the equipment would never transmit nor receive again. Unfortunately, there was no exit to the rest of the hotel and they had to return to the terrace outside and make for the main entrance. There was a machine-gun post at either end, but neither seemed to be in any hurry to open fire. Skorzeny caught a glimpse of a face at one of the windows on the first floor. There was no mistaking the features; Il Duce was still in residence.

Everything happened very quickly, and still there was no firing. As they ran towards the entrance, a stream of *Carabinieri* began to emerge from it. It seems unlikely that they had much stomach for a fight, but there was no point in taking chances. One after the other, they were assaulted by machine pistols that were now being used as clubs.

Without, apparently, paying much attention to what was happening to the rest of his force, Skorzeny and his small party of picked men thrust through the hotel lobby and ran upstairs. Luckily, he was able to locate the room in which Mussolini had been briefly glimpsed. The ex-dictator and two Italian officers were standing in the centre of the room. Prodding them with his Schmeisser, Skorzeny ordered the officers to stand with their backs against the wall until they were removed to safe custody by an NCO named Untersturmführer Schwerd. The following dialogue then took place:

MUSSOLINI:

So everything's all right. I'm very grateful to you.

SKORZENY: Duce, the Führer has sent me. You are free.
MUSSOLINI: I knew my friend Adolf Hitler would not leave
             me in the lurch.

The Scarlet Pimpernel could hardly have done better.
Skorzeny had only seen the Duce once before, and then at a
distance. Nevertheless, he remarked that he had aged a lot,
and that he looked ill. He was wearing 'an ill-fitting and far
from smart suit', but he had no complaints to make about the
conduct of his guards. He had been treated more as a guest
than as a captive.

Now, there was the sound of firing in the distance, which
probably indicated that Radl and the other gliders had arrived,
and that the Italians were offering at least a token opposition.
It did not last for long. Within a minute or two, the commander
of the *Carabinieri* guard was brought in by two of Skorzeny's
men. He was protesting volubly, but Skorzeny cut him short.
Any attempt at further resistance was, he said, futile. He might
as well surrender at once. The officer pointed out that such
matters were not to be decided upon lightly. He needed to
think. Skorzeny promised him one minute: no more. Sure
enough, the colonel returned after the permitted sixty seconds,
this time carrying a glass of red wine. The game, he agreed,
was up: a white bedspread might be hung from the window for
want of any purpose-built flag of capitulation. The other ranks
would lay down their arms in the hotel dining room. As a
generous gesture, the officers were allowed to retain their
revolvers.

The whole business had taken twelve minutes.

Major Mors and his detachment had secured the funicular
railway. Of the other gliders, two had been compelled to
abandon the mission shortly after taking off, one had crashed
on to a rock face, the others had arrived safely. But the
immediate problem was how best to leave. The troops could
travel down the funicular and return to Frascati by road. Such
a method, which involved a journey of over 100 miles through
potentially hostile territory, did not seem suitable for Mussolini.
He must, Skorzeny decided, be flown to safety.

Two Fieseler Storchs, (the German equivalent of the
Lysander) had managed to come down on an airstrip down in
the valley. One of them had damaged a wheel in the process,

but the second, flown by Captain Gerlach, had taken off again and was now on the plateau.

Originally, there had been three possible plans for Mussolini's journey. 'A' was to use an airfield at the entrance to the valley, where three He 111s would be used; one to transport the illustrious passenger, the other two for escort purposes. But this depended on a radio link with Rome to call up the aircraft. Up here in the mountains, the wireless was unable to make contact, and the idea had to be abandoned. The second plan was to use the Storch that had remained down below, but the pilot reported that it was too badly damaged. All of which left Plan C and Captain Gerlach. Having landed on the plateau, it seemed probable that he would be able to take off from it. The added weight of Il Duce seemed to pose no particular problem, but matters became more complicated when Skorzeny decided that he must keep Mussolini company. With characteristic drama, he wrote in his memoirs, 'If there was a disaster, all that was left to me was a bullet from my own revolver'.

In vain, Captain Gerlach tried to point out that, by adding his not inconsiderable weight to the Storch's payload, he was more likely to cause a disaster than to avert one. Skorzeny was determined to go and, in this frame of mind, he would brook no opposition. He involved the names of Hitler, Himmler and various other members of the Nazi hierarchy, and in the end Gerlach capitulated. Mussolini, now wearing an overcoat and a dark brown hat, listened to the exchange with an unhappy expression on his face. As a pilot with 17,000 hours to his credit, he must have realised the dangers involved.

Acting somewhat on the principle used to launch an aircraft from a carrier, the raiders held the Storch back until Gerlach had gunned the engine up to its maximum rpm. Then they let go. It lurched forward, covered thirty yards without showing any signs of becoming airborne, plodded on until it crossed the 100-yard mark and eventually reached land's end. Far from climbing eagerly into the sky, it more or less flopped over the edge.

But the remarkable little aircraft in the hands of a master pilot recovered, grabbed at the thin air, and with great effort hoisted itself into the sky. About an hour later, it landed at Rome, where Mussolini was transferred into an He 111 en route for Vienna—and thence to the *Wolfsschanze* FHQ at Rastenberg, where Hitler was waiting to greet him.

Afterwards, Skorzeny, who took nearly all the credit for an operation that was largely conceived by Mors and Student, was rewarded with promotion and that much-coveted decoration, the *Ritterkreuz*. Mors received nothing, but he was just a simple soldier. He did not have Skorzeny's nose for politics, nor did he belong to the Waffen SS. If there were any awards to be handed out, the Führer would make sure that his own *élite* corps would always be the first to receive them.

Almost from the moment America entered the war Churchill had been urging President Roosevelt to form a unit along the lines of Commandos. The 1st United States Rangers, commanded by Lieutenant Colonel Bill Darby, was the point of origin from which all other such units developed. It was recruited from American troops stationed in Northern Ireland. Two thousand men volunteered for service in its ranks; 500 of them were selected. The chosen men duly underwent the somewhat severe initiation to Commando warfare at Achnacarry. At first, there had been an idea that they, too, should be called 'Commandos'. But General Eisenhower, not unreasonably, took the view that this was an essentially British concept, and that the UK raiders had earned themselves the exclusive use of the name. Recalling the exploits of Major Robert Rogers in the 18th century, he suggested that 'Rangers' might be more appropriate.

Since the Rangers had learned their art from the Commandos; and since, on at least one occasion, the latter wore Rangers' uniforms, it may have been difficult sometimes to tell which was which. But there was a difference. The Rangers were organised in battalions and usually went into action as such. They might, perhaps, be regarded as super-infantry. 'Butcher and bolt' raids on the French coast, the comings and goings of small parties during darkness—an act of sabotage here, the snatch of a prisoner there—were not for them. Essentially, they were shock troops. During a landing operation, for example, theirs was the responsibility for overcoming strong points—such as gun positions—and thereby making the beach-head safer for the main force. The ventures of Numbers 3 and 4 Commandos at Dieppe serve as a reasonably good example.

The first occasion on which the Rangers fought in strength was Operation 'Torch'—the landings of the Allied armies on the North African coast at Algiers and Oran and at Casablanca. Churchill had taken pains to assure Roosevelt that this was to be an essentially American operation. 'We British', he told the president, 'will come in only if and when you judge expedient. This is an American enterprise in which we are your helpmeets'.

In another letter, he wrote, 'We have plenty of troops highly trained for landing. If convenient, they can wear your uniform. They will be proud to do so'. The men of Number 6 Commando did, indeed, attire themselves as Rangers—though with the object of receiving a more sympathetic reception from the Vichy French. They certainly found the US-style steel helmet (being deeper in the crown) an invaluable tool for bailing when their landing-craft became filled with water, and they were glad to get their hands on the Garand automatic rifle (the invention of John C. Garand), which gave the US Army the distinction of being the only one to enter World War II with the automatic rifle as standard equipment for infantrymen.

The force that eventually went ashore in North Africa was a blend of American and British. At Casablanca, the invasion was, indeed, an all-American enterprise. At Oran, where Colonel Darby and his Rangers distinguished themselves, 18,000 Americans were landed, but their ships were escorted by the Royal Navy, and they were guided to the beach by canoes manned by members of the British Special Boat Section. And, at Algiers (where the Royal Navy again provided the escort), there were 9,000 British troops. Numbers 1 and 6 Commandos, which were involved, fought with, and as part of, Ranger battalions.

But, before the invasion took place, there was a nice—if somewhat fruitless—example of inter-Allied co-operation. America was not officially at war with Vichy (the puppet State that Hitler had created in France, which had its headquarters at Vichy and was not, on any account, to be confused with the Free French); consequently, it still had a diplomatic representative in Algiers. This man, Robert Murphy, pointed out that Major General C. E. Mast, who was in charge of troops in the

Algiers sector, seemed to be sympathetic to the Allies. If a meeting could take place between him and a senior American officer, the result might well be to the invaders' advantage.

Eisenhower chose his second-in-command, General Mark Clark, for the assignment. Clark was to be taken from Gibraltar to a point off the Algerian coast in the British submarine *Seraph*. He would then be secretly put ashore at dead of night by members of the Special Boat Section—who, later, would return him to the submarine. The meeting with Mast was to take place in a villa by the shore—sixty miles west of Algiers.

The affair could not be judged a complete success. *Seraph* arrived off the beach too late for Clark and his aides to be landed before daylight, and they had to remain on board, submerged, until darkness returned. At the discussions, Clark was a great deal less than frank with Mast—who, in any case, was not the overall commander of the sector. At some point, the Vichy police raided the villa, and the visitors had to hide in the building's empty wine cellar. And, on the return trip, Clark was nearly drowned when his canoe capsized.

On the day of the invasion, 8 November, 1942, some units fared better than others. Colonel Darby and his 1st Rangers took the batteries at Oran with only small casualties. At Algiers, Number 1 Commando, working with the American 168th US Infantry Regimental Combat Team, arrived two hours late at one of its beaches—to find that other events had almost caught up with it, and that there was not a great deal to be done. However, one of the Commando's troops secured the surrender of the airfield at Blida.

Number 6 Commando, which also went ashore with Rangers from the 168th RCT, fared less well. The unit had been taken to its destination near a fort to the west of the town in HMT *Awatea*—a converted merchant ship whose crew had received little training in the launching of landing-craft. Before sailing from Britain, they and the rest of the 3,000 passengers in the *Awatea* had been treated to a few not very well chosen remarks by Major-General Charles Ryder, the assault force's American Commander. 'Some of you', the General said, 'will not make the beaches, but you will be immortal'. It was a promise that, no doubt, they would have preferred to forego.

To add to the hazards, HMT *Awatea* was equipped with a new type of landing-craft that, since—like the Eurekas—it was made from wood, was not very reassuring. In the event, the merchant seamen muddled the launchings. Several of the craft came near to sinking (those American tin hats became very useful as extempore bailers), and the troops arrived several hours late for their appointment with immortality. Nor was the navigation of a very high standard. Major A.S. Ronald of Number 6 Commando and part of Number 9 Troop were mistakenly set ashore on the Ilot de la Marine, which was the most heavily fortified part of the harbour. Major Ronald and several of his men were killed; the rest were captured. However, those that did eventually end up in the right place were less unfortunate—though they cannot be credited with taking their objective. After enduring an attack by Albacores belonging to the Fleet Air Arm, the fort's garrison eventually succumbed to the threat of naval bombardment.

Dieppe should surely have taught the lesson that forays into the mouth of hell were not to be encouraged. Nevertheless, the 3rd Battalion of the US 135th Regiment was ferried into Algiers harbour by the destroyers HMS *Malcolm* and HMS *Broke*. The idea was that its men should land on the mole, occupy the batteries and prevent any attempts to scuttle the ships that were berthed in the port. The price of such folly was that the destroyers came under point-blank fire. *Malcolm* was very badly damaged; *Broke* was sunk while trying to disengage itself. Two hundred and fifty of the soldiers were taken prisoner.

In the months that followed, Rangers and Commandos fought much as ordinary infantry—though with the doubtful privilege of being accorded the really tough nuts to crack. Later, they assisted at the landings on Sicily, at Salerno in Southern Italy, and at Anzio. In all these places, they secured the beaches by assaulting the gun positions.

But, by 1944, the event for which Dieppe had been the merest rehearsal, the great climax of combined operations—the big feature for which everything else had been little more than a curtain-raiser, was in preparation. The Normandy invasion was being translated from a pious dream into a concrete plan. Among the many units that were to be involved in its cast of thousands were the 2nd and 5th US Ranger Battalions.

9 The Cliff

One of the more amusing avenues of historical speculation is to rearrange facts—to distort them a little, if need be—and to see whether they can produce some other conclusion. Consider for a moment or two the movements of a French resistance worker named Jean Marion on the morning of Monday, 5 June, 1944. Marion, who lived in the village of Grandchamp near the mouth of the River Vire in Normandy, had been aroused early that day. As sector chief of the local underground, an agent had called on him to report a newly arrived German flak battery at a site about one mile away. It seemed important to verify the information before passing it on to London. At the same time, he might carry out another task. Was it true, Allied intelligence wanted to know, that the Germans had installed long-range guns in positions near the Pointe du Hoc—a headland about two miles from his house?

Marion set off on his bicycle. Aided by a forged pass that identified him as a worker employed on the construction of the Atlantic Wall, he had no difficulty in making the trip. He discovered that five batteries of a motorised flak assault group— amounting to twenty-five heavy and light AA guns—had indeed moved into positions straddling the river mouth. The crews appeared to be working unusually hard at preparing them, which gave Marion pause for thought. Did this sense of urgency suggest that the Germans had received information about an Allied invasion—and that such an event might be imminent? The possibility of a leak in security worried him.

Having satisfied himself about the flak guns, he rode on up to the headland to inspect the other artillery locations. A quick

examination showed him that, whilst the concrete emplacements had been built, the weapons themselves were still some
way from their final positions. This intelligence, too, should be
sent to London. The problem was now one of communications.
The nearest radio transmitter was at Caen, about fifty miles
away. Marion was too busy to go there in person; any thought
of trying to use the telephone was out of the question. He
would have to enlist a chain of couriers who, with a bit of luck,
would get the message through. In any case, since the Pointe
du Hoc guns were still two miles from their destinations, this
particular item did not seem to be particularly urgent.

But Jean Marion was grievously wrong; it was, indeed,
urgent. At that moment he knew more about the situation on
the cliff top at Pointe du Hoc than General Eisenhower and
his entire intelligence staff. While he was making his brief
survey, three companies of the Number 2 Battalion of the US
Rangers were already embarked in ships riding at anchor in
Weymouth Bay. The men were biding their time before setting
off on a voyage to attack batteries that, in fact, were not there.
In quest of this non-objective, 135 men out of a complement of
225 Rangers were to die.

The question, hypothetical though it may be, is: what would
have happened if Marion had been able to transmit the news
earlier? Would the 135 lives have been saved? Would the
invasion plan have been modified to exclude Pointe du Hoc as
an objective? The taking of it was considered to be the most
hazardous of all the D-Day undertakings. To have written it
off might have been a relief.

Number 2 Battalion of the US Rangers had sailed from the
United States in the peacetime luxury liner *Queen Elizabeth*
during November of the previous year. For a while, the unit
had been quartered at Bude in Cornwall, and then on the Isle
of Wight. More recently, it had moved to Swanage in Dorset,
where the cliffs bore a passable resemblance to those on the
Normandy coast. At this point, Companies 'D', 'E' and 'F'
were detailed for what was referred to as 'advanced training'.
In other words, they toiled away for day after day, practising
the often dangerous business of ascent. They used ropes and
rope-ladders, and were taught the use of an ingenious device,
very high on the secret list, that shot lines and grapnels to the

cliff top by means of rockets.

By the time it was over, wrote the historian of Company 'E' in a monograph published at the end of the war, 'the men were tops in cliff-climbing, and bursting with confidence in their ability'.

At the end of May, the battalion travelled to a marshalling area near Dorchester. The duties were tolerably light, though calisthenics and rope-climbing exercises were carried out twice a day. The purpose, the Rangers were told, was to keep the palms of their hands suitably hard. On 1 June, they embarked in the former cross-Channel steamers (now converted into landing ships, infantry) *Amsterdam* and *Ben-my-Chree*.

For the next few days, the men read, played cards, argued about their chances of survival, wrote long letters home (one of them, a corporal, anticipated events. He addressed a note to a girl he knew in Paris, suggesting a date in early June), and marvelled at the assembly of shipping—all of it gathered to blast an entrance back into Europe.

The plans for the Dieppe raid were kept so secret that no words were committed to paper. Those for the invasion of Europe (Operation 'Overlord') were slightly less reticent—though a good deal of deception was carried out with the purpose of misleading Hitler. In an exercise code-named 'Quicksilver', General Patton—whose presence at any invasion was regarded as inevitable by the Germans—was posted to a largely fictitious command with its headquarters at Knutsford in Cheshire. Under another name, 'Fortitude', a good deal of hocus-pocus was staged to convince the enemy that the blow would come from across the Dover Strait.

But, despite all such precautions, and despite the huge force of men, ships and aircraft at his disposal, Eisenhower had sufficient anxieties. Among them were the weather—unusually bad for early June—and the lesson of the Dieppe raid. As the British Chief of the Imperial General Staff, Field Marshal Sir Alan F. Brooke (later Lord Alanbrooke), was to write, 'Several of the less rigid military planners had been profoundly shaken by the Dieppe casualties. . . and considered that it would not now be. . . possible to stage any large-scale cross-Channel operation before the summer of 1944.'

As events showed, they had been right. But was even this prognostication too optimistic? Eisenhower, certainly, believed that the experiences at Dieppe did not promise well for an easy success on the beaches of Normandy. Especially, he was concerned for the landings of the 1st United States Infantry Division on what was referred to as 'Omaha', and of the 4th United States Infantry Division on 'Utah'. Between the two stood Pointe du Hoc—an immense white cliff about 100 feet high. For want of any other information, it had to be assumed that both beaches were covered by batteries on the headland comprising half a dozen 155-mm guns of long range, capable of bringing devastating fire to bear on either.

It was the responsibility of Companies 'D', 'E' and 'F' from the 2nd Ranger Battalion under the command of Lieutenant Colonel James E. Rudder, to climb the cliff (estimated to be as high as a nine-storey building), and to put the guns out of action. Only the Germans and a handful of French underground workers knew that, in fact, the guns had not yet arrived.

But, as planned, the 2nd Ranger Battalion was not to be entirely on its own. Travelling in its wake were 500 men of the 5th Rangers. Once the 225 soldiers of the 2nd had taken the cliff top, the 5th, under Lieutenant Colonel Max Schneider, would land in support. H-Hour was 6.30 am. When Rudder's men reached the summit, the cue for the 5th's landing-craft to move inshore would be given by the firing of flares. If, by 7.00 am, no such signal had been seen, the 5th would assume failure and divert to 'Omaha', four miles away. Similarly, if any mishap occurred during the journey from the LCIs to the shore, the code-word 'Tilt' would be transmitted—again causing them to sheer off towards 'Omaha'. On landing, they would swing round in an arc and attack the guns from the rear.

At 4.00 am, when the two ships were ten miles off the Normandy coast, the loud-speakers crackled into life. 'Rangers', remote metallic voices commanded, 'man your craft'. Few of the men had slept; now, anxious, moving as if in a waking dream, they shuffled to their stations. The weather was better than it had been for the past few days; but, as the heaving of the *Amsterdam* and *Ben-my-Chree* suggested, the sea was by no means calm. To leave the comparative comfort and undoubted security of these vessels for the hazards of that unkind stretch of water, with heaven knew what perils at the journey's end, was the beginning of an ordeal that would become more terrible as the day wore on.

Still, they had been told that the landing-craft (LCAs manned by personnel from the Royal Navy) were unsinkable. As if to reassure them about their mission, the US battleship *Texas* was firing shell upon shell on the cliff top above the landing beach. Minutes later, as the small vessels struggled towards the shore, low-flying aircraft bombed the German positions. It was impressive. Nothing, it seemed, could survive this saturation by high explosives.

But by this time, some of the LCAs were in trouble. The men were crammed into them shoulder-to-shoulder; nervous, cold, uncomfortable, many of them were almost prostrate with seasickness. As the waves crashed inboard, the craft filled with water—and, once again, the American version of the tin hat showed its value as an extempore bailer.

The myth that landing-craft were unsinkable was soon destroyed. The first of the heavily laden supply boats foundered before it had covered one-third of the distance to the shore. Most of the crew were rescued by a motor launch that was serving as protector to this assembly of LCAs on the ink-black, turbulent sea. When, ten minutes later, another sank, there was only one survivor. In yet another, now almost water-logged, a sergeant was throwing stores overboard in an attempt to lighten the boat—rations, clothing packs, anything that could be shifted, was ruthlessly tossed into the ocean.

But worse was to come. In LCA860, the sea had been hurling itself on board at an alarming rate. The men had been bailing hard; but nothing, it seemed, could keep pace with the waves that were crashing over the landing ramp. Before very long a cry for assistance was heard over the radio. 'This is LCA860', its commander called. 'LCA860. We're sinking! We're sinking!' And then, with a final sigh of despair: 'My God, we're sunk!' Happily, most of the men were snatched from the sea by the industrious crew of the escorting ML.

There were nine landing-craft in the convoy, plus a couple of tank-landing craft laden with DUKWs (amphibious boats) carrying turntable ladders that had been loaned for the occasion by the London Fire Brigade. The fittings normally used to secure hoses had been adapted to accommodate light machine-guns. The idea was to employ them to give covering fire during the extremely hazardous attempt to scale the cliff face. A great deal would depend upon their safe arrival.

The sky above was alive with the racket of shells from *Texas*, streaking towards Pointe du Hoc with a sound like that of express trains rushing through a station—until they smashed to an explosive conclusion on or near the target. But now there was more trouble. The commander of the LCA with Colonel Rudder on board had mistaken his bearing. Instead of heading for the emaciated stretch of beach that was the objective, he was on course to another headland, Pointe de la Pércée, three miles to the west. Rudder eventually noticed the mistake, and briskly ordered a change of direction.

The error added forty minutes to the journey which, under these circumstances, was little short of disastrous. The gunners on board the USS *Texas*, keeping to their precise schedule, ended the bombardment at 6.30 am. The Germans—or those that had survived it—were given an unintentional respite. They had time to shake themselves from the stupor caused by incessant shell bursts and to resume their role as guardians of Pointe du Hoc.

When half an hour beyond H-Hour had passed without any flares illuminating the headland, Max Schneider in the convoy carrying the 5th Rangers had to assume that the landing had failed. He gave the code-word 'Tilt'; the LCAs swung away on a new course, heading for 'Omaha'. Whatever was now accomplished would have to be done by Rudder's three companies on their own.

For the final minutes of the voyage, the landing-craft had to travel within 100 yards of the shore. No doubt the shells from *Texas* had reduced the number of defenders, but there were still sufficient to bring heavy fire to bear on the LCAs. Two destroyers, USS *Satterlee* and HMS *Talybont*, closed in towards the headland and attempted to repair the situation. But their lesser armament was a poor substitute for the big guns of the battleship.

At last the grim journey was over; the 2nd Rangers, now diminished by forty officers and men, waded ashore. The beach, that small stage at the foot of the towering Pointe du Hoc, was so pitted by the explosions of shells, so hilly with piles of fallen cliff, that the DUKWs were unable to negotiate it. A gunner in the stern of one LCA was more successful, when he scattered some Germans on the summit. But there was now another enemy—the headland itself. Somehow, Rudder's Rangers had to climb it.

It was then discovered that the waters of the English Channel had come to the Germans' assistance. Four-foot waves crashing into the interiors of the landing-craft had drenched the climbing lines, which should have been fired by rocket to the cliff top. Heavy with water, few of them were able to soar into the sky, deposit their grapnels in the chalk above, and provide a reasonable, if not easy, way up.

At the same time, the Germans demonstrated yet again a truth of warfare that had been revealed in battle upon battle— ever since the beginning of World War I. No matter what the scale of the preliminary bombardment, there is no such thing as total saturation. At the end of it—shaken, perhaps, and their morale reduced—there will, nevertheless, be sufficient survivors to render the business of assault extremely hazardous.

The next half-hour or so marked the nadir of the 2nd Rangers' misfortunes. Nor was the situation improved when a shell from one of the destroyers removed another slice of cliff, which fell on Rudder and his staff, burying them briefly.

With a desperate courage, the men scrambled, clawed, cut steps with knives, dug their toes into laughable footholds, grasped at whatever could be held by hand—and, in several cases fell or slithered back to the beach below. One sergeant had to make three attempts before he reached the top. A GI, who had gained a point near the overhang at the summit, lost his grip. His fall could have only one conclusion.

Each landing-craft had carried 112 feet of light tubular ladder, pre-assembled in seven 16-foot lengths. These, and the few ropes that had reached their destinations, made it easier for some, but the German posts above were now doing all they could to hinder the ascent. They hurled down 'potato-masher' stick-grenades, splashed the cliff face with machine-gun fire, and even lowered 88-mm shells by means of wires—each carefully fused to explode where it would wreak most havoc. In several cases where a rope had been established, an enemy soldier found and cut it. In one instance, an enlisted man was nearly thrown from his ladder, when his Mae West accidentally inflated itself.

But, again and again, the Rangers attacked this seemingly impossible obstacle, and, in about thirty minutes, they conquered it. To speak of miracles would be unfair to the men in Companies 'D', 'E' and 'F'. In fact, it was a matter of sheer determination, a desperate bid to overcome the impossible. And now, despite a great many casualties, they achieved it. Round about 7.30 am, Colonel Rudder—now disinterred and established in a niche at the cliff edge—received what must surely have been one of the best pieces of news he had ever heard. With a small smile, his signals officer, Lieutenant James Eikner, handed him a radio message. It read: 'Praise the Lord.' It meant that the three companies were now established at the top.

But some had not made it. Down on the beach, the Rangers' medical officer was doing his best to repair the wounded and to provide some comfort for the dying. If, at this point, it had been possible to carry out a roll call, it would have revealed that only ninety of the original 225 men were in any condition to fight.

The plan had been for Company 'E' to be divided into four equal sections. One of them was to ascend the cliff to a point less than twenty-five yards from number 3 gun and its casement and to destroy both. The second was to push forward as fast as possible to the road running close to the cliff edge from Vierville-sur-mer to Grandchamp; to take up a position astride it and to prevent the arrival of enemy reinforcements. The third section was to demolish a concrete observation post that had been built to control the fire of the six guns; the fourth was to assist number three section and then to move on to the road and reinforce number two. Companies 'D' and 'F' were to concern themselves with the destruction of the remaining five guns.

One hundred feet, the height of a nine-storey building! The distance was so short and yet, measured in terms of that cliff-face, it had been prodigious. With his force now reduced by more than fifty per cent, Colonel Rudder's plan lay in shreds, and he would have to improvise. Nevertheless, he was still in business. Somehow, men had gained the top; they had recovered from the exhaustion of the climb, and they were now grouping together as a striking force. A section of Germans in a nearby pillbox had endured as much action as it could stand. Encouraged by the Rangers to step outside, the enemy soldiers meekly surrendered.

Looking around, it was hardly surprising. The flat, grass-mantled summit of Pointe du Hoc bore silent testimony to the gunfire of USS *Texas* and of the bombers that had assisted in the barrage. There was scarcely a foot of soil that had not been smashed into a crater. It looked like the surface of the moon, or the rough skin of some pock-marked giant. Not surprisingly, once the men had reached it, the initial resistance was small. The amazing thing was that, on the way up, the opposition had been so ferocious.

To those who had survived that ascent through hell, this should have been a triumph. But the victory, if such it was, concealed a flaw. It might be a while before the guns that promised to cause such havoc on the beaches of 'Omaha' and 'Utah' could be blown to fragments, for the supply of demolition materials had been buried by a cliff fall. But the batteries could at least be captured and insulated against any attempts to replace their crews. And so the Rangers hurried to their objectives and located them, only to discover what the sector leader of the local resistance, Jean Marion, had known for twenty-four hours: there were no guns there.

Some while later as, dodging from crater to crater, they fought their way through what remained of the opposition towards the Grandchamp road they uncovered part of the mystery. The camouflage was so perfect that a patrol composed partly of men from 'E' Company and partly of survivors from 'D' stumbled upon it almost by accident about one mile from the cliff edge. But there it was: five 155-mm guns and a substantial pile of ammunition. Although they had obviously never been fired, nobody could comprehend that these weapons had not been installed at the emplacements on Pointe du Hoc. The assumption was that, in the heat and fury of the bombardment, they had been withdrawn.

By the time the advanced units reached the road, the enemy, doubtless reinforced, had recovered from the initial shock and

was now vigorously contesting the 2nd Rangers' hold upon this
Normandy headland. By late afternoon, a force of Germans
had pushed through the gap that separated the outpost on the
highway from Rudder's command headquarters. With uncomfortably accurate fire from 88-mm guns, mortars and machine-
guns, it isolated the Rangers—to such effect that men who were
wounded, and more properly belonged to the security of a
medical post where their injuries could be tended by doctors,
were now fighting for what remained of their lives.

When the Rangers had scaled the cliff and arrived in this
strange and cratered world, there had been a blessed silence. It
was as if the war had suddenly stopped. But this had been no
more than an interlude. Now the battle was resumed in all its
fury, and Colonel Rudder's signal to the command of V Corps
was not encouraging. 'Located Pointe du Hoc. Mission accomplished. Need ammunition and reinforcements. Many casualties.'
It was brief almost to a fault for, with the opposition becoming
more confident, the patrols covering the road now seemed
dangerously likely to be cut off and surrounded. Nearer at
hand, a German outpost was still giving an uncomfortably
good account of itself. It maintained its fire until a fortunate
hit from a warship's gun removed it and the few square yards
of cliff upon which it was situated—sending the lot in a neat
package down to the beach below.

But naval guns could not achieve everything. A flak battery
had to be dealt with by the Rangers and the storming of it
caused more deaths. By the end of the day, there were only
seventy members of Companies 'D', 'E' and 'F' still able to
bear arms. Nevertheless, there was one item on the credit side.
At 11 pm, a patrol from 'E' Company managed to fight its
way to the command post; later, the whole force was re-
deployed around Rudder's headquarters.

Throughout the 7th, there were incessant counter-attacks.
Naval gunfire broke up some of them; others were dispersed by
accurate small-arms fire from the beleaguered Rangers. As 'E'
Company's historian wrote, 'Late in the day, strong patrols
were organised from members of all companies to aid in the
destruction of... an ammunition dump which the Jerries had
used as a source of supply and refuge.' What was more, the
observation post had been ripped into fragments of concrete by

demolition materials dug from their tomb on the beach.

Now the situation was calming down. When, that night, reconnaissance patrols were sent out to seek information about the enemy, they returned with little to report. Nor, once evening had set in, were there any more casualties.

Over to the left on 'Omaha', the 5th Rangers had landed with relatively few casualties. In company with the 116th Regimental Combat Team, they were now fighting their way towards Rudder's command post. Apart from desultory fire from a few snipers concealed in craters, the opposition had ceased at Pointe du Hoc. Indeed, at about the time the relief force arrived, three men from Company 'E', who had been missing presumed killed, walked into the headquarters. They had, they explained, been cut off. For the past thirty-six hours they had been lying in a ditch concealed by undergrowth to avoid detection.

The 2nd Rangers, or what remained of them, had done all that anyone could have expected of them. Death is an occupational hazard of soldiering; he who fears it should seek some other occupation, and he should certainly not volunteer for units such as the Rangers or the Commandos. But death should have a purpose. Unless it is the necessary price for some accomplishment, it is a wretched waste of life. In this instance, 135 men had been the forfeit demanded by a flaw in the pattern of intelligence. They had been cut down in an endeavour to rub out guns that were presumed to be there; but of which, obviously, there was no proof.

If only Jean Marion had made his bicycle ride a day earlier; if only there had been a radio transmitter nearer to hand than the one fifty miles away at Caen; if only.... It may be interesting to wonder about what might have happened, but no conjecturing can bring men back to life.

A map of the world would be required to chart the operations carried out by raiders in World War II, and the shores of each hemisphere would be littered with dots marking the scenes of particular actions. The names and compositions of the forces varied, but there can be little doubt that all owed their inceptions to the formation of the Commandos during the dark summer of 1940.

One feature common to nearly all of them was flexibility. A small unit could be detached for a swift hit-and-run raid; or the larger unit—Commando, Battalion (whatever its name)—could function as a whole in much the manner of ordinary infantry of the line. There are, indeed, times when one gropes for a definition. What was a raider? Do, for example, the six brigades of Chindits raised by Major General Orde Wingate qualify? For several months, they operated behind the Japanese lines in Burma. But their task was not, according to one of the Brigadiers, Mike Calvert, 'meant to be "guerilla warfare" '. The name of the game, in this instance, was 'long range penetration'.

Merrill's Marauders—more correctly known as the 5307th Composite Unit (Provisional)—recruited by Brigadier General Frank D. Merrill—had a similar purpose, but then they had been trained in India under Wingate's supervision. They conducted their operations in northern Burma, and earned themselves the citation of being '... the United States first ground combat force to meet the enemy on the continent of Asia'. The operation referred to was the taking of Myitkyina airfield (on the Irrawaddy about sixty miles from the frontier with China) on 17 May, 1944. But, significantly perhaps, when they were disbanded in August of that year, they were re-mustered as the 75th Infantry Regiment.

The Chindits and Merrill's Marauders worked inland. On the coasts of Burma, Malaya, Sumatra, wherever the Japanese were in occupation, the raiders were at work. Australia raised four independent companies that distinguished themselves on islands in South-East Asia and in the Pacific. They gave warning of the Japanese advances at the end of 1941 and at the beginning of 1942. The company designated '2/2' spent a prodigious eleven months on Timor, bringing chaos and insecurity to the Japanese occupation force; '2/5' Company spent thirteen months on the northern shores of eastern New Guinea to similarly good effect.

In 1942, the Japanese forces were occupying a line of islands in the Pacific that threatened to cut off the United States from any contact with Australia and New Zealand. Looked at this way, the blobs of land and their hostile incumbents were a menace. However, from another point of view, they were an opportunity. They provided excellent targets for raiders.

During the 1930s, the US Marine Corps had been experimenting with raider-type forces. By 1935, the first *Tentative Landing Manual* had been compiled; and the annual Fleet Landing Exercises (known as FLEXs) were including forays by raiding and patrolling parties that went ashore in rubber boats—either from fast transports or else from destroyers. In February 1941, a feature of FLEX-7 was the demonstration of 'Provisional Rubber Boat Companies' that had been formed from Companies 'A', 'E' and 'I' of the 7th Marines.

During the six months following the bombardment of Pearl Harbor on 7 December, 1941, the military fortunes of the United States took a turn for the worse. In such times the word 'Commando' was apt to crop up. Churchill certainly encouraged President Roosevelt to raise such forces—though the president needed little urging. Doubtless, the fact that his son, James Roosevelt, was serving as a captain in the US Marine Corps may have helped.

Indeed, one month after Pearl Harbor, James Roosevelt submitted a memorandum to the Commandant of the Marine Corps (Major General Thomas Holcomb), in which he outlined ideas for a unit 'for purposes similar to the British Commandos and the Chinese Guerrillas'. In the latter case, he noted how considerable had been their successes against extended Japanese lines of communication. 'It is submitted', he wrote, 'that the position of our forces in the Pacific would be greatly aided by similar action on Japanese positions in the Mandated Islands, and perhaps later the Philippines by units based to the South; even more devastating action frontly by landing on Japan proper. . . would certainly demoralize the enemy.'

Holcomb liked the idea—as it happened, he was already thinking along similar lines. The British Commandos might serve as an example, though he did not favour use of the name. 'Marine', he noted, was sufficient; it would 'indicate a man ready for duty at any time'. 'The injection of a special name, such as Commando, would be undesirable and superfluous.' Nevertheless:

The organisation, equipment, and training of infantry units of the Marine Divisions should, in practically all respects, be identical to that of 'Commandos'... in general, it may be stated that the training of all units in the two Marine Divisions prepares them to carry out either offensive operations on a large-scale, or small-scale amphibious raids of the type carried out by 'the Commandos'.

Holcomb's original idea was to adopt an army man, Colonel William J. Donovan, for command of a raider project and to give him the rank of Brigadier General. However, the Commanding General, Amphibious Force, Atlantic, and his colleague with responsibilities for the Pacific, both looked askance at the idea. It should not, they suggested, be necessary for the Marine Corps to look beyond its own ranks for a leader. Colonel Donovan was rejected. Some while later, he was appointed Chief of the Office of Strategic Services (OSS), which was the forerunner of the CIA.

Eventually, after a good deal of discussion, two Raider Battalions (first called 'Separate Battalions'), the 1st and the 2nd, were raised. Lieutenant-Colonel Meritt A. Edson was given command of the former; Lieutenant-Colonel Evans F. Carlson, of the latter. Edson had been a Marine pilot; he had captained the Marine Rifle and Pistol Team; and he had observed the Sino-Japanese war from points around Shanghai. Carlson had actually travelled with the Communist Chinese Eighth Route Army guerillas. His executive officer was James Roosevelt, now promoted to major. Edson's executive officer, Major Samuel B. Griffith, had been to Scotland to watch the Commandos in training.

The purposes of the newly formed battalions were threefold:

When amphibious landings were carried out by larger forces on beaches that were thought to be inaccessible, they were to act as a spearhead.

They were to conduct raiding expeditions in which those inseparable twins of the art, surprise and high speed, were required.

And they were to conduct guerilla operations for long periods behind the enemy lines.

In early September, 1942, the name Edson became immor-
talised in an action that might have been more properly fought
by an infantry battalion—though, to have achieved the same
results, the foot soldiers would have to have been of singularly
high calibre. On 7 August, the 1st Marine Division under
Major General Alexander Vandegrift had landed on Guadalcanal in the Solomon Islands and, with little opposition, taken
the airstrip named Henderson Field. The Japanese were
obviously not content to allow the situation to remain unchal-
lenged; by the end of the month, they had built up large
concentrations of troops to the east and west of the Marines'
perimeter. During the night of 30–31 August, 2,200 soldiers
belonging to Colonel Akinosuka Oka's 2nd Battalion of the
124th Infantry were put ashore by destroyers eight miles to the
west of the Marine lines; at the same time, a further 2,900
troops under Major General Kiyotake Kawaguchi were landed
on the eastern side. General Kawaguchi was in command of
the 35th Brigade, which was reinforced with artillery units,
engineers, and other, more specialised, units.

On 8 September, Edson's Raiders came ashore and captured
or destroyed all Kawaguchi's reserves of food, ammunition,
weapons and medicine. Nevertheless, there had to be a
reckoning. As Vandegrift realised, his opponent would have to
attack at once—before his supplies ran out; and, indeed, it was
not long before the barrage by aircraft and gunfire began.
Edson's men, with two under-strength parachute companies
attached, were directed to a grassy ridge, 1,000 yards long,
that reared up above the thick jungle of the island. The date
was now 12 September. They had enjoyed a three-day rest
since the raid on Kawaguchi's base. Despite this, many of them
were suffering from malaria, gastroenteritis and 'Jungle Rot'—
maladies that were uncomfortably common in this hot, wet,
and densely vegetated part of the world.

In wars that were less full of heroic encounters, the Battle of
Edson's Ridge would have become a classic—a 'thin red line'
in the annals of defensive operations. The stand of the British
squares against the French cavalry at Waterloo; the action
when the Gloucesters fought back to back in Egypt; the deeds
of the 1st Raiders on the ridge—these were in the tradition of

such things, the material from which legend is created.

The action began at 11.00 am on the morning of the 12th, when forty-two Japanese bombers attacked the Marines' positions. At 9.00 pm, a single enemy aircraft dropped a flare over Henderson Field, and four Nippon warships began a twenty-minute barrage. Half an hour later, the 35th Brigade went into the attack. Throughout that night and during the next twenty-four hours, the battle blazed. Platoons were cut off by the Japanese; companies were decimated. At 10.30 on the evening of the 13th, Kawaguchi's men put down a mortar barrage, and then stormed towards the top of the ridge yelling in English 'Gas attack! Gas attack!' Edson's men, or those who survived, were not impressed. Company 'A' fought its way back to where Company 'C' was grouped around the Colonel's command post on a knoll. Company 'B', now reduced to sixty men and with both its flanks exposed, was ordered to pull back and join them. It was estimated that Company 'B' and the parachutists had been under attack from two battalions.

At least a dozen more assaults were made by the Japanese that night. It was pitch dark with, now and then, a flare shot into the sky to illuminate the action in which men fought with guns, with knives, sometimes with stones and with their fists. The 11th Marine artillery, making its contribution to the holding of the ridge, despatched no fewer than 1,992 rounds—often at ranges of as little as 1,600 yards.

By daybreak the Japanese attack had spent itself. In the words of the 1st Marine Division's historian, 'The Battle of Edson's Ridge was the most critical and desperate battle of the entire Guadalcanal campaign.' After it, Kawaguchi's force was no longer to be reckoned with. Colonel Edson was awarded the Medal of Honour for his part in the action; Major Kenneth D. Bailey (killed later in the Guadalcanal campaign) received it posthumously for 'leading his troops in hand-to-hand combat for over ten hours on the ridge'. The Japanese suffered over 1,500 casualties; the 1st Raider Battalion's losses were thirty-nine dead and 103 wounded.

During a correspondence concerning the present book, an official of the United States Marine Raider Association pointed out to the author that 'Edson's Ridge was a *battle* and not a raid'. True. More appropriate in this context, perhaps, is an operation carried out by Carlson's 2nd Raider Battalion on 17–18 August, 1942. It may not have been of great military significance, but it was a beginning that taught much that was to be useful in subsequent ventures. It was also something that took a great hold upon public imagination. The scene was an unprepossessing girdle of coral named Makin Atoll.

10 The Surf

Makin Island is one among dozens of atolls that litter the Pacific. It lies at the tip of the Gilbert group; some 200 miles north of the equator and about 500 miles west of the international date line. It is shaped rather like an upside-down coat-hanger. On the northern side, its arms embrace a lagoon which is screened from the ocean by tiny islets of coral. On the southern shore, the Pacific rollers chase one another in a turmoil of surf.

In August, 1942, the only evidence of one-time European occupation were Government House and Government Wharf. A nearby warehouse displayed the name of its owner, On Chong. A 'native hospital' catered for the needs of the islanders; and there was a rather down-at-heel Japanese trading post and that is just about all. At its widest, the island is little more than 1,000 yards across; there was one road that travelled its length (less than eight miles), a village named Ukiangong where the local inhabitants lived, a mangrove swamp, and a great many palm trees.

At the beginning of August the management of this inconsequential arrangement of land was in the hands of a Japanese sergeant major named Kanemitsu who had about seventy men under his command. Ambitious though Kanemitsu may have been, he must have sometimes admitted to himself that his present responsibilities did not amount to very much. Indeed, had he been privy to the thoughts of US Marine Corps General Alexander Vandegrift, he might have been surprised. Major General Vandegrift, despite all his other pre-occupations, was thinking a good deal about Makin Atoll.

Vandegrift and 19,000 other Marines had landed at Guadalcanal in the Solomons on 7 August. Anything that might
distract the enemy from reinforcing its garrisons in this part of
the world was to be welcomed. If Makin Island were raided—
no elaborate operation but a quick in-and-out job lasting for
no more than a day—the Japanese high command might decide
that Sergeant Major Kanemitsu required reinforcements. It
might even come to the conclusion that Makin Atoll might be
a more important place than they had supposed. If this were
so, troops and supplies would be diverted towards it, and the
lot of Vandegrift and his Marine Division would be made more
satisfactory.

The Commander-in-Chief Pacific Fleet, Admiral Chester W.
Nimitz, agreed with this reasoning. The task, he decided, should
be entrusted to the 2nd Raider Battalion under Lieutenant
Colonel Evans F. Carlson. The raiders were currently at Pearl
Harbor. Makin Atoll was about 2,000 miles away to the south-
west, and there would certainly be a screen of Japanese warships
somewhere in between. For this reason, the voyage had best be
made in a couple of submarines.

Colonel Carlson's career had been unusual. Now aged forty-
six, he had enlisted in the US army at the age of sixteen. By
the end of 1917, he had become a captain in the field artillery.
He served briefly in Germany with the Army of Occupation,
and then returned to civilian life. He did not remain there for
long. In 1922, he joined the Marine Corps as a private soldier.
He was promoted to second-lieutenant in the following year,
and won the Navy Cross in 1930 when, as a first-lieutenant, he
led a dozen Marines against a force of 100 bandits in Nicaragua.

After three visits to China, he became so concerned about
the danger of Japanese aggression in the Far East that he once
again resigned his commission—preferring to adopt the role of
propagandist, with a civilian's freedom to write and lecture. In
1941, when the peril he had envisaged was becoming a reality,
he returned to the Marine Corps with the rank of major. He
assumed command of the 2nd Marine Raider Battalion during
the following year.

Each man has his own style of leadership; Carlson's was
personal and, sometimes, theatrical. He believed in taking his
troops into his confidence, in explaining carefully what was to

be done, and in embellishing his instructions with some nice touches of rhetoric. To assist him in this, he took a portable public-address system with him wherever he went.

For the Makin raid, he was accompanied by his executive officer, Major James Roosevelt, thirteen other officers and 208 other ranks—members, that is to say, of Companies 'A' and 'B', each minus one rifle section. They sailed from Pearl Harbor under cover of darkness in the US submarines *Argonaut* and *Nautilus*. Once they were out at sea, the two boats separated. If everything went according to plan, *Nautilus* would reach Makin Island first—and allow Carlson to spend a day making a reconnaissance at periscope depth before *Argonaut* joined her. The date of the raid was scheduled for 17–18 August.

The fears that they might be intercepted by Japanese naval units seemed to be groundless, and the voyage passed without incident. For most of the time, they were able to travel on the surface. Life on board the submarines was not comfortable; with so many men on board, conditions were very crowded. Since it took three hours to feed them all, it seemed that at almost any hour of day or night somebody was eating a meal.

The men from Companies 'A' and 'B' had been carefully chosen—as had all those in the 2nd Marine Raiders—and, despite the discomforts, their morale was high. From his days in China, Carlson remembered the war cry 'Gung Ho!' Now it was a kind of motto—a phrase that might be shouted in action to counter the Japanese '*Banzai*.' The Colonel also occasionally talked about *The Three Musketeers*. He approved of their declarations to be 'one for all and all for one'. This, he said, should be the attitude of his raiders.

Nautilus arrived off Makin Atoll without hindrance at 3.00 am on the morning of the 16th. *Argonaut* joined her some hours later. The island looked reasonably harmless, with no signs of Kanemitsu and his troops. Nevertheless, this was no cause for complacency. Intelligence reports had estimated the garrison's strength at 250—and had suggested (also wrongly) that a shore battery was installed to cover the entrance to the lagoon. There were known to be substantial reserves at Jaluit, 200 miles away in the Marshall group. If need be, they could be flown in at very short notice.

Throughout the 16th, Carlson and his companions studied
the island through *Nautilus*'s periscope. There was a scattering
of clouds in the sky; the sea, whilst not calm, appeared unlikely
to endanger the business of going ashore in rubber boats. After
all, the raiders had undergone so much training in their use
that they prided themselves on their expertise. It might, perhaps,
have been better if they had been less self-assured. In the
venture of Makin Island, the ocean—more than the Japanese—
was the raiders' enemy.

The submarines had taken up station 500 yards off the shore.
Nineteen rubber boats, each powered by an outboard engine,
were assigned to take the Marines to two beach-heads. Company
'A' under First-Lieutenant Merwyn C. Plumley was to hurry
across the strip of land that divided the island's seaward side
from the lagoon. Once there, it had to take control of Makin's
only highway and occupy Government House. There were
thought to be three radio stations from which appeals for
reinforcements could be transmitted to Jaluit—one at the
Japanese trading post, one at Government House, and one at
On Chong's wharf. These, obviously, must be destroyed as
quickly as possible.

Meanwhile, Company 'B' would be crossing the island to
wreak havoc in the eastern half of the village—eventually
linking up with 'A' on its right-hand flank. Communications
between the raiders and the submarines would be by radio and
Aldis signalling lamps. It was just as well that the Marines had
taken a signalling lamp with them, for none of the radio sets
could be made to work. And the outboard motors on the
rubber boats, though excellent in calm waters, tended to break
down on the wave-battered coral strand.

During the hour or so before first light on the 17th, the boats
were brought up on the submarines' decks and inflated. Now,
for the first time, it became obvious to Carlson that the landing
was not going to be as easy as it may have seemed. Had it not
been for the empty threat of a gun position at the entrance to
the lagoon, he might have done better to approach his targets
from the other direction.

First of all, there was the sheer noise of the great waves
smashing on to the distant reef. For one of the few times in his
life, the colonel was rendered inarticulate. It was not that he

had nothing to say—indeed, he had many orders to give. The trouble was that, with the prevailing din, nobody could hear him.

Once afloat, matters were no better. What with some engines stubbornly opposing attempts to start them, and the rubber craft being hurled about by the heavy swell, it was quite impossible to keep to the original plan. Company 'B's boats had become mixed up with those of Company 'A' and nobody knew which was which. To land in good order at two beach-heads would be impossible. Somehow, Carlson managed to convey instructions to most of them that they should follow him—and, with luck, all end up in the same place.

Fifteen of the nineteen boats made it. Three were wrenched off course and were eventually thrown on to land at a point about one mile to the north. Another, with First-Lieutenant Oscar Peatross and eleven men on board, was driven on to the beach 1 1/2 miles to the south of the appointed position. Within the small geography of Makin Island's defences, Peatross and his Marines were now behind the enemy lines.

By some miracle, the Japanese seemed to be unaware of what was happening not all that many yards from their positions, and they did nothing to hinder the Marines. Unfortunately, the shortcomings of their own sentries were made good a few minutes after the disembarkation, when one of the raiders discharged his rifle by accident. Sergeant Major Kanemitsu rose from his bed, and hurriedly alerted his men.

Although the two submarines had been allowed to travel in peace for more than 2,000 miles, their progress had not been entirely unremarked. A few days before the landing took place, Kanemitsu had been advised by his superiors that his lonely garrison on this island of no importance might be in for a spot of trouble. He was advised to make suitable arrangements.

His precautions were to prepare a number of machine-gun positions, and to exercise his snipers even more thoroughly in the art of climbing palm trees. These men, clearly, were selected for their agility as much as for their marksmanship. The large fronds at the top would, the sergeant major suspected, provide admirable concealment.

It was as if that accidental rifle shot had been a signal to begin the operation. Company 'A' set off quickly on its errand;

within fifteen minutes, it was able to report that its platoons had occupied Government House and likewise Government Wharf. Shortly afterwards, however, it encountered trouble on the highway.

The Japanese had reacted quickly. Travelling from their billets in trucks, on bicycles and on foot, they were now ready to oppose the raiders with four machine-guns, a flame thrower, two grenade launchers, and a number of lesser automatic weapons. The snipers were already in their positions atop the palm trees.

Over to the right, Company 'B' was moving forward; and, in the enemy's rear, Oscar Peatross and his men, left to their own devices, were filling in the time profitably. They blew up one of the radio stations, set fire to a supply dump, and created extempore ambushes to deal with runners linking one Japanese unit to another. Nevertheless, Kanemitsu had been able to transmit a radio message to Jaluit, and the reaction came quickly. At about mid-morning, just as Company 'B' was breaking through the Japanese line to link up with Company 'A', two ships steamed into the lagoon. One was a small inter-island transport of about 3,500 tons; the other, a 1,500-ton patrol vessel.

But, by this time, the two submarines had moved round from the seaward side and were able to open fire on the intruders with their 6-inch guns. All told, they fired twenty-three salvos. Both ships were sunk.

It was afterwards estimated that they had about sixty soldiers aboard. There were no survivors. The men were either picked off as they tried to swim towards the shore; or they were shot down as they scrambled on to the beach. So far, everything seemed to be going in favour of the raiders.

While the sergeant major and his small garrison did their best to pin down the invaders, the Japanese on Jaluit were obviously busily engaging themselves. The two ships must have been on passage to some other island; or else they were making a routine call at Makin—something that had been planned before Carlson and his raiders stepped ashore. If any further assistance were to be brought from the Marshall Islands, it would have to come by air.

The first evidence of this occurred shortly after the two vessels had been sunk. The time was getting on for noon, when two reconnaissance aircraft flew in from the north. For fifteen minutes, they circled the island; then, dropping a couple of bombs as a farewell gesture, they departed. Once their pilots had made their reports, it would surely not be long before a more substantial number appeared. It arrived at 12.55, when twelve aircraft—two float planes, four Zero fighters, and six reconnaissance-bombers—bombarded the Marines for the better part of an hour. At some point during this action, two large four-engined 'Mavis' flying boats of the Japanese Navy's Air Corps landed on the lagoon. In spite of all the other hell that was being let loose, the Marines were able to open fire on them with their .55 anti-tank rifles.

It was amazingly effective. One flying boat was set on fire as it floated on the water; the other was destroyed when it attempted to take off. Nearly all of the thirty-six soldiers they had brought to Makin had lost their weapons as they struggled in the lagoon. Now, as they tried to come ashore, they were mercilessly killed.

Around this time, another squadron of aircraft was approaching a point where Company 'A' was embattled with Japanese soldiers and suffering casualties from the snipers cunningly sited in the palm trees. There seemed to Carlson to be no reason why the enemy aircraft might not be put to some useful purpose. Leaving one platoon behind to safeguard his left flank, he quickly ordered the others to withdraw over a distance of about 200 yards. The ground here was more open; and, as he rightly anticipated, the snipers climbed down from their lofty positions to give chase. It was beautifully timed. As they left the cover of the trees, the aircraft swooped into the attack, blazing away with machine-guns and dropping bombs on their own men.

As the afternoon wore on, the opposition seemed to slacken off. In fact, Sergeant Major Kanemitsu was probably already dead by this time, and his surviving men had given up hope of receiving reinforcements. Most of them were no doubt wondering how best to escape from this hellish place—once such a peaceful retreat from the agony of war, and now made hideous by the arrival of the Marines.

But Carlson was unaware of all this. The opposition had made three counter-attacks that day. Although none of them had succeeded, he had to concede that they had been well executed. Moreover, as he saw the situation, the garrison would almost certainly be considerably strengthened during the night. He had received no news of Peatross and his men—now the lesser by three who had been killed—and he did not realise that any demolitions had been carried out. Nor had he taken any prisoners—who might have been useful for interrogation. It would soon be evening, and he needed to be back on board the submarines. He gave the order to pull back to the beach as the last of the light began to drain from the sky above Makin.

The sea had been his enemy on the way to the objective. Now, with the mission—or most of it—accomplished, it became even more hostile. Some boats were capsized in the surf. The outboard motors, drenched by waves, became even more recalcitrant. None of them would start. Fighting the breakers' attempts to hurl them back on to the beach, some Marines managed to paddle towards the submarines. Other boats, with wounded on board, never got far beyond the beach. As Carlson afterwards recalled his own experience:

We walked the boat out to deep water and commenced paddling. The motor refused to work. The first three or four rollers were easy to pass. Then came the struggle. Paddling rhythmically and forcefully for all we were worth, we would get over one roller, only to be hit and thrown back by the next before we could gain momentum. The boat filled to the gunwales. We bailed. We got out and swam while pulling the boat—to no avail. We jettisoned the motor.

For about three hours, there had been no signs of any enemy activity. At 9.00 pm, however, a sentry named 'Red' Hawkins was challenged by a Japanese patrol of eight men. He opened fire with his automatic rifle; they replied. With his first shots, he killed three of them. Seconds later, however, he was lying on the ground—seriously wounded in the chest. But he managed to keep on firing and, presently, the Japanese retreated in confusion.

'Our situation at this point was extremely grave,' Carlson recalled. 'Our initial retirement had been orderly, but the battle with the surf had disorganized and exhausted us and stripped us of our fighting power.' At midnight, he spoke to the men. Each could make his own decision. He could either have another try at getting back to the submarines; or, he could wait until next day, when Carlson intended to move to the northern end of the lagoon and attempt to reach *Nautilus* and *Argonaut* by using native outriggers.

All told, seven boats carrying about 100 men made the trip successfully. Among them was Oscar Peatross. In a radio interview some years later (he was then Major General Peatross), he said, 'One group that came back to our submarine, the *Nautilus*, said, "They're talking about surrender." They said that Carlson had told everybody that the able-bodied were left on their own to get off the island—because, they said, "Carlson says he's got forty or more wounded here and can't get them off." ' Carlson, it seems, reached his decision when 'Red' Hawkins came under fire. Peatross quoted his informants as saying, 'So Carlson thought, "This is the end. They're attacking in this area, and we can't get the wounded off." '

But there were no more attacks. Soon after dawn, four more boatloads of Marines managed to reach the submarines. Carlson, no doubt rightly, considered that he should remain behind with the wounded. He sent his executive officer, James Roosevelt, back to *Nautilus* to act as his deputy afloat.

At 7.40, there was a brief glimmer of hope when a boat, its engine still working, sheered off from one of the vessels with five volunteers aboard. One man swam ashore with a line and a message from the naval commander, a veteran submariner named Haines. The gist of it was that the boats would remain offshore until the evacuation had been completed. The idea of the line was to haul the surviving rubber dinghies through the turbulence. Unhappily, the attempt came to an abrupt end when a Japanese aircraft swooped down and shot the rubber boat to pieces. Nothing more was ever seen of its crew.

This was the first of several air raids that day. *Nautilus* and *Argonaut* were now in danger, and their captains decided they must submerge. With a brief flicker of the Aldis lamps, they informed Carlson that they would be back again at 7.30 pm, when darkness would frustrate any more air attacks.

By now the party that remained on the beach was in need
of food. Leading a small patrol, Carlson set off to search for
supplies—and also to find out what exactly the enemy was
doing. During the next hour or so, he discovered what he
estimated to be eighty-three Japanese dead (an exaggeration—
after the war it was discovered that forty-three had been killed,
three were declared missing, and twenty-seven survived). Near
Government House they came across two survivors, who were
shot. The rest, presumably, had fled to another island.

The Japanese Trading Post yielded cans of meat, fish and
biscuits; and, even more to the point, there was a small sloop
with an auxiliary motor anchored off its pier. When he returned
to the beach in the early afternoon, the Colonel decided to
move his men and the four surviving rubber boats to the shelter
of Government House. This, presumably, had been Kanemitsu's headquarters for, on closer inspection, they found several
charts and enemy documents that seemed to be worth taking
away.

When a lieutenant and two men volunteered to row out to
the sloop and explore its possibilities as a means of escape, they
were fired on by a Japanese Marine, who pointed his pistol
through one of the portholes. They replied by throwing in a
grenade. It demolished the enemy Marine; unfortunately, it
also wrecked the boat. They would have to revert to Carlson's
plan for the use of outriggers.

The day wore on. The aircraft now seemed to be devoting
their attention to Little Makin Island, a small strip of coral to
the north-east about three miles off-shore, and to the native
village at Ukiangong. Latish in the afternoon, another patrol
came across a store containing 1,000 barrels of aviation gasoline.
They set it ablaze with a charge of TNT. After sunset the fire
served as a useful beacon for the submarines.

So far, twenty-one raiders had lost their lives on Makin
Island. In return for a payment by Carlson, the islanders—
who were well disposed to the Marines—agreed to give them a
Christian burial. They also provided an outrigger to escort the
rubber boats to the submarines that had surfaced off Flink
Point, the western prong of the tiny mainland.

'All five boats [four rubber dinghies and an outrigger]were lashed abeam of each other', Carlson said. 'Two boats had motors although only one worked throughout. With what few souvenirs of the battle our limited space could accommodate, we set off across the lagoon at 20.30.

'The passage was distressingly slow, but there was no surf to intervene. Ashore, the only indication of life came from the billowing flames of the gasoline fire. Off Flink Point we flashed a signal and received an immediate response from one of the submarines. At 23.00 we arrived alongside'.

Minutes later, *Nautilus* and *Argonaut* set course for Hawaii. Everything seemed to have gone very well—and, with a pile of dead, a great deal of damage to buildings and stores, two aircraft and two ships to the raid's credit, it might be accounted a success.

There was, however, one flaw in this magnificent pattern. During the withdrawal to the submarines, nine raiders had somehow been left behind. To mislay one man might be considered a misfortune of war; nine, on the other hand, suggested carelessness. Surely, there should have been a roll call—a counting of heads to see who was there?

Against this, of course, it might be argued that there had been a great deal of confusion. It was hard to tell who had reached the submarines and who had not.

None of this, of course, was of any comfort to the men concerned. In fact, they had embarked in a rubber boat and, having lost their paddles, they had drifted helplessly downwind. When the Japanese returned to Makin Island next day, they were captured and taken to the Japanese base at Kwajalein in the Marshall group for interrogation. A few days later, on the orders of Vice-Admiral Koso Abe, they were ceremoniously beheaded and buried in a mass grave. The execution was witnessed by a Marshall Islander. After the war, Abe was tried and hanged for the atrocity. Captain Yoshio Obara, who had been ordered to carry it out, received a ten-year prison sentence. But he had protested to the Vice-Admiral against such inhuman conduct.

Whether the raid on Makin Island achieved its purpose may be doubtful. Did it really divert the Japanese from sending supplies and reinforcements to Guadalcanal? It seems unlikely.

But, as Merwyn Plumley (now Colonel Plumley), who had led Company 'A' reflected many years later, 'No matter what the attitude adopted towards Makin, there are several factors which cannot be denied. We were there! We were ready physically and emotionally! We were trained and when the job was to be done, *it was completed.*'

You can't be fairer than that.

One of the stranger examples of genealogy is that which makes it possible to trace the ancestry of a crack United States fighting establishment to an eccentric English civilian who died from an overdose of sleeping tablets in 1948. The name of the former is the Army Special Forces; of the latter, Geoffrey N. Pike.

Born in 1894, Mr Pike was a man of imagination whose ideas sometimes took him into the realms of science. Shabbily dressed (it was said that he wore spats to conceal the fact that he never washed his socks), bearded, and almost impossible to endure socially, he might have been dismissed as a failure. Nevertheless, there were a few who dared to suggest that he was a genius. It would have been hard to substantiate, though Geoffrey Pyke would no doubt have agreed with them. In 1916, this monstrously erratic personality had persuaded a leading English newspaper to appoint him as its correspondent in Berlin. Using a forged American passport, he arrived in the German capital via Sweden. For six days he went about his business without taking any pains to conceal his true identity. Inevitably, he was arrested. After four months of solitary confinement, he was moved to a civilian internment camp from which he eventually managed to escape.

During the years between the wars, Geoffrey Pike endured a life that was composed mostly of poverty—occasionally making a few pounds by writing advertising copy for Shell. However, by his own account, he was also an educationalist, a philosopher, an occasional broadcaster and a 'financier'.

At some point in his life of contemplation, he had worked out that seventy per cent of Europe is snowbound for five months of the year. In March 1942, he turned this fact to reasonably good purpose by composing a 54-page memorandum for what he called Operation 'Plough'. According to his idea, a specially trained force of no more than 1,000 men could pin down 250,000 German soldiers by its expertise in winter warfare. It would demolish hydro-electric plants in Norway (on which Germany depended for its production of iron ore), carry out raids on enemy garrisons, and generally make a nuisance of itself.

Such tactics would require considerable mobility, and the scientific side of Mr Pike's talents had the answer to this. It was to be a light-weight tracked vehicle named 'the Weasel' (later known as M29) that could be carried to its destinations by Lancaster bombers.

The plan for Operation 'Plough' was submitted to Mountbatten, who liked it and was prepared to take a generous view of Pyke's unmilitary appearance and sometimes offensive personality. He co-opted him on to his staff as Civilian Director of Programmes, Combined Operations.

Since snow was to be the natural element for the new force, it seemed probable that it would best be handled by Americans and Canadians. Mountbatten passed Operation 'Plough' on to the US Army's Chief of Staff, General George Marshall, who approved of it, and the 1st US-Canadian Special Force was born. For its emblem, it chose the crossed arrows of the Indian scouts.

The North Americans (as they were often called) and their Commanding Officer, Lieutenant Colonel Robert T. Frederick, demanded a great deal from their personnel. Whoever wished to serve in their ranks had to be skilled in demolitions, rock-climbing, skiing, amphibious assaults and must also have undergone basic airborne instruction. Operation 'Plough' itself was never carried out—not least because the Lancasters, which were the only means of transporting the Weasel, could not be spared from the bombing offensive. Nevertheless, members of the 1st Special Service Force distinguished themselves against the Japanese occupants of the Aleutian Islands (a necklace of land between Alaska and Siberia), and in North Africa, Italy and the South of France. For a while, they became known as 'The Devil's Brigade'—a nickname that owed its origin to a letter found on a dead German soldier. It referred to 'The black devils' (who) are all around us every time we come into the line and we never hear them.'

As a senior American officer put it, 'The main problem with the men was keeping them from getting killed. Their courage and aggressiveness verged on the edge of foolhardiness at times. Utter disregard for their own lives was common.' This attitude was reflected in statistics. Between December, 1943, and September, 1944, the force suffered no fewer than 2,300 casualties—a fact that becomes even more impressive when one remembers that, at any one time, its establishment was never more than 2,400 men.

After World War II, the British Commando responsibility was taken over by the Royal Marines, and the army units were disbanded. A Royal Marine Commando fought with much bravery in the Korean War, and so did units of US Rangers. But they, too, were disappearing. Trained for airborne duties, a Ranger company was attached to each division. Before the Korean conflict was over, however, the Pentagon had other thoughts. These men, the pundits decided, could serve to best effect if they were scattered among other units—where, hopefully, their ideas and expertise would infect less élitist soldiers. The training of Rangers continued—though individually, and not as units in their own right.

The 1st Special Service Force had gone into liquidation during January, 1945, when those who had survived its forays in Italy were transferred to the 474th Infantry Regiment. In June, 1952, however, the idea was revived and the 10th Special Forces Group was raised at Fort Bragg, North Carolina. It became the nucleus of the Special Warfare Center (now known as the John. F. Kennedy Center for Military Assistance). President Kennedy was particularly interested in its potential as a counter-insurgency force; and it was he who, in the autumn of 1961, authorised its troops to wear the Green Beret (the British Commandos were the first to wear green berets, but the words were not prefixed by capital letters). The unit's motto became 'Free the Oppressed'.

As in its previous existence, the standards required were exceptionally high. All the men were volunteers. Each had to undergo a period of special training lasting anything from forty-four to fifty-two weeks. A man had to be skilled in guerilla warfare tactics, able to function efficiently under adverse conditions for long periods, and capable, if circumstances required it, of acting independently.

As America became more and more involved in the war between North and South Vietnam, so did the Special Service Force's contribution increase. Initially, it was sent to assist the Montagnard tribesmen who inhabited the high plateau country around Plei Ku—over 200 miles to the north-west of Saigon. This was partly due to the fact that minority groups such as the Montagnards were important targets for Communist propaganda, and partly because of a plan to develop a paramilitary force from such communities. The deal was that they should be provided with weapons and training in return for declaring themselves for South Vietnam and participating in village self-defence programmes.

During the Vietnam War, the Green Berets became involved in missions such as this—and in combat reconnaissance patrols. Whether they freed the oppressed is, perhaps, a difficult question to answer. But they showed the courage that was expected of them; the ability to serve for periods of one year in remote camps far removed from the comforts and pleasures of Saigon; and the readiness, such as might be expected of professionals, to accept repeated tours of duty in combat zones.

But perhaps the most spectacular mission of the Special Service Force began at home base—at Fort Bragg. It involved many people in the United States from the president downwards. It was sensational in its conception—and in its failure.

11 The Empty Prison

From time to time, statesmen have sat around tables at Geneva and debated the treatment of prisoners of war. The outcome of each series of discussions became known as a 'Geneva Convention'. Its purpose was to lay down humanitarian rules to mitigate the barbarism of war; to establish rights for captives and to make sure that they were observed. In 1929, for example, it was agreed that a newly taken POW need tell his interrogators no more than his name, his rank, and his number. Officers could not be compelled to work, and certain minimum standards of care and maintenance for the prisoners were established.

Since Germany and Italy, Britain and the United States had been signatories to this document, it followed that men who fell into their hands were, on the whole, treated according to the rules (captured commandos were not—they were executed by the Gestapo). Japan and Russia, on the other hand, had not contributed signatures. It was an omission for which POWs in their hands paid a high price.

More concessions to the rights of a prisoner of war were established by the Convention of 1949. North Vietnam did not sign it—not least because, in 1949, the country did not exist. It was still part of French Indo-China. The American personnel who were taken prisoner during the Vietnam War endured the very worst excesses of brutality. Many were tortured; many kept in solitary confinement, sometimes for years; the standards of accommodation were abysmal; the diet seldom went beyond the provision of thin cabbage soup and a small piece of bread or some rice. Under such conditions, it is not surprising that many fell ill. Malaria, dysentery, internal parasites, and tuberculosis were among the ailments. Some died from them.

About twenty-three miles to the west of Hanoi, and not far from the Red River, is the small city of Son Tay. The POW camp on its outskirts had been named 'Camp Hope' by its inmates; the three buildings in which they were accommodated were dubbed 'The Opium Den', The Beer House' and 'The Cat House'. In a world where the standards were a long way less then tolerable, it had to be considered better than average. Solitary confinement, for instance, was a punishment and not the norm. Indeed, there were cells in which as many as three men were housed. This, for those who had existed for months, for years, in the dark and silent world of solitude, was a considerable improvement. Nevertheless, there were some very sick men at Son Tay and the number was likely to increase. No matter that it was better than some other places: the inhabitants of Camp Hope wanted to go home. It is, perhaps, remarkable that the human spirit can endure so much. People can suffer abominably and yet not only retain a sense of humour, but also devise ways of outwitting their oppressors. At Son Tay, the captive population discovered that the walls encasing the cells were not thick, and that it was possible to tap out messages (using a code, of course) from one to another.

This was a working camp. The inhabitants had to smash bricks into rubble to provide foundations for a new interrogation centre. They were taken in small parties to Mount Ba Vi, about eight miles to the north-east, to chop timber, and there were other duties. The means of communication that served so well in the cells could be applied to toil in the open air. Given the code, you could converse while smashing bricks or thumping an axe into timber—despite the fact that use of the voice was forbidden.

Prisoners at Son Ray were allowed to wash their clothes and to lay them out in the camp's small compound to dry. This took the art of communication a stage further. If the garments were laid out in certain patterns, it should not be beyond the wit of man to convey a message. There were, after all, frequent reconnaissance flights by US aircraft across the skies of North Vietnam. When the pictures were studied, anyone with reasonable intelligence and imagination must surely come to the conclusion that somebody down below had been trying to say something.

By the end of April, 1970, the pattern of the washing was becoming articulate, An Air Force Technical Sergeant named Norval Clineball, employed at the USAF's 1127th Field Activities Group in Fort Belvoir, Virginia, was dealing with intelligence material concerning American prisoners of war. There were, he believed, two prison camps to the west of Hanoi—one at a place named Ap Lo, thirty-one miles from the capital; the other at Son Tay. But, after studying a series of aerial photographs, Technical Sergeant Clineball decided that he knew rather more than this. Reading the messages contained in these wretched rags of laundered garments, he came to the conclusion that the inmates of Camp Hope were trying to tell him that fifty-five men were interned there. Six of them, for reasons that were not clear, needed to be rescued urgently.

Clineball discussed the matter with his chief, Colonel George J. Iles; and, between them, they concocted a rescue operation. It was so outrageously daring, so improbably in so many particulars, that, if it were done promptly, it might just conceivably achieve its purpose.

The trouble is that, when you are dealing with an entity so large as the United States of America, and when you are confronted by a war that is a hopeless jumble of combat and politics, these things take time. All manner of people are apt to become involved; all kinds of permission and approval have to be applied for and granted. Since the notion of Clineball and Iles would have required the co-operation of the Air Force and USN task force—and since, at the time, there were all manner of political straws drifting on the wind and possibly being about to settle somewhere, it was not lightly to be undertaken.

Looked at again, the aerial pictures seemed to confirm Clineball's diagnosis. They showed prisoners outside the compound, working on some task or another. The articulate washing spelt out SAR—which was a request for a search and rescue mission. There was also a K that somebody had thoughtfully stamped out in the compound's dust. 'K' stood for 'come and get us'. By a happy coincidence, a recently captured member of the Viet Cong had admitted that he had seen prisoners in the area of Son Tay carrying supplies of water. Yes—he was fairly certain that they were Americans.

The Clineball—Iles report was studied by Brigadier General James R. Allen, Deputy Director for Plans and Policy under the Air Force Deputy Chief of Staff for Plans and Operations at the Pentagon. The General was inclined to agree with their findings—and with their conclusion. Such a raid, he believed, would not be impossible. The matter should now be referred to Brigadier General Donald D. Blackburn the SACSA (Special Assistant for Counter-insurgency and Special Activities). Blackburn liked the idea; he and Allen worked it out in rather greater detail, and it still seemed to be sound. There was little reason, they decided, why the six POWs should not be snatched from captivity and brought home in, at the most, a fortnight.

But there was a wider aspect to the matter. In Paris, during that spring of 1970, representatives of the warring nations were trying to agree terms for a peace settlement and getting nowhere. Indeed, the talks seemed likely to die from sheer lack of enthusiasm. As Blackburn rightly decided, the American prisoners were the strongest items of currency in the North Vietnam collection of bargaining points. Some while earlier, the North Vietnamese government had released a number of American captives who had not been particularly badly treated. No doubt, they had been chosen with care—to conceal the lot of a more average inmate of a North Vietnam cage.

But suppose, in this raid, *all* the inhabitants of the Son Tay Camp could be rescued; suppose that, in the same operation, those at Ap Lo could also be released; and imagine that, on their return, the raiders brought photographs of the conditions—this, surely, would attract the attention of the world. The men who were restored to freedom would no doubt testify to the inhuman conduct of their captors—with two very desirable results. The world would raise its humanitarian hands in appalled surprise that such things could happen (thereby reducing the value of the North Vietnam currency in this respect). What was even more to the point, such an exposé might compel them to revise their ideas—to treat those who remained captive more tolerably.

The raid would have to conform to the first principles of the best raiding traditions of World War II: a quick in-and-out job carried out by as few men as possible and taking the enemy completely by surprise. Its scope might be large; its success measured in huge headlines, but it was not an invasion—nor even an undertaking such as the Dieppe raid of 1942. Nevertheless, as the idea wafted upwards from one layer of officialdom to another, there seemed no end to the number of people who had to give it approval. If Brigadier Generals Blackburn and Allen imagined it was an errand of mercy that could be arranged quickly, they were to be disappointed. The Chairman of the Joint Chiefs of Staff in the Pentagon, General Earle G. Wheeler, would have to give his assent. General Wheeler did—though it amounted to little more than a courtesy, for he was about to retire. The procedure had to be repeated when, on 10 July, his place was taken by Admiral Thomas H Moorer. The admiral might be expected to show sympathy for, during the second World War, he had narrowly escaped captivity at the hands of the Japanese. More recently, a close friend had been shot down in North Vietnam and was now a prisoner—though not at Son Tay. Sure enough, he approved of the idea and agreed that, if fifty or sixty POWs could be brought home, it would indeed be a propaganda victory. Likewise, the CIA headquarters at Langley, Virginia, gave an encouraging nod, and so did the DIA (Defence Intelligence Agency) at Arlington Hall Station, Virginia.

The aerial photographs indicated that Camp Hope contained two elements. One was a walled compound about 140 feet by 125 feet, with three small buildings (presumably the cell blocks) on the edge of it. The other was the administration area, which included quarters for the camp's guards. The compound wall was judged to be seven feet high. There were three guard towers—two at either end of the western wall, and one beside the main gate. A small building at the foot of the third was correctly identified as the hut in which malefactors served their terms of solitary confinement.

Whatever plan was put into effect, it would have to be accomplished quickly. There was evidence to suggest that, apart, from the camp's guards, there were 12,000 North

Vietnamese troops in the area—that is to say, within a fifteen minute drive of the prison. Units of the 12th Infantry Regiment were known to be quartered in Son Tay itself and in a camp 10 km away; there was an army supply depot employing 1,000 men; and even nearer, an artillery school. Finally, there was an anti-aircraft unit about twenty minutes away to the south-west.

Camp Hope was reasonably isolated, and it was thought that only about forty-five soldiers were employed on guard duties. There was, however, another building complex 500 yards away. Marked as 'secondary school' on the maps, it might serve to deceive the raiders at night, for its lay-out was nearly identical to that of Camp Hope.

The plan that was eventually code-named Operation 'Kingpin' went through a number of modifications. Blackburn had been assisted in his deliberations by an Army Colonel named Ed Mayer who was in charge of the Special Operations division. Back on 1 June, the two officers had conceived the idea of picking up the six men whose needs, presumably, were the greatest. The rescue, they decided, should take place when the prisoners were felling timber at Mount Ba Vi. On closer consideration, however, this did not seem to be such a good idea. Apart from the uncomfortable possibility that the six might not be there, what might be the effect upon other operations if anything went wrong? Any ideas of rescuing Camp Hope's entire prison population would have to be written off—and, indeed, that of Ap Lo.

Early in the plan's conception, there had been an idea to plant an agent in the vicinity of the camp. Equipped with a small radio, he would send messages by the most simple of codes and one that could not possibly be monitored by the enemy. One bleep would signal 'come and get us'; two bleeps, 'come and get me—there have been no signs of a working party for a week'. But, here again, there were snags. Since July of 1968, there had been a two-year pause in the bombing of North Vietnam. An aircraft flying over the country, and dropping an intruder by parachute, would be bound to attract attention. Once on the ground, he would be extremely conspicuous from the colour of his skin and the shape of his eyes (the task could not possibly be entrusted to a South Vietnamese, whose loyalty might be less than perfect). There was also the question of obtaining approval for such a project. These things take time, and time was Blackburn's greatest enemy. Mount Ba Vi could be forgotten. The raid would have to take place at Camp Hope itself.

Carried out in darkness, and assuming that the security was sufficiently thorough (the North Vietnamese were known to have an extremely efficient intelligence network), the surprise factor might be sufficient for fifty men to accomplish it. Ideally, they would depart by helicopter from CIA stations on the frontier of North Laos. This would involve a flight of about 105 miles to the target. Over this distance, the aircraft would not need to be refuelled during the journey. Furthermore, it was close enough to the camp for two or three more choppers to be placed on stand-by in Laos. They could be used for whatever purpose the progress of the raid might suggest.

Three helicopters, it was estimated, would be required for the raid. A small machine, an UH-1 'Huey', would land in the compound and disembark an assault team that would be responsible for releasing the prisoners from their cells. A larger machine—an HH-3—would land outside the compound. Its occupants would rush to the wall, blast a hole in it and assist in the evacuation. The men in the third aircraft would be responsible for overcoming the guards. The whole thing could be carried out in twenty-six minutes.

To divert the enemy's attention—and especially its anti-aircraft facilities—the naval task force in the Gulf of Tongking would be asked to mount a raid on Haiphong, the port of Hanoi. When somebody pointed out that there was a bombing lull in progress, which might inhibit such a venture, it was suggested that the pilots might drop flares. After all, it didn't matter very much *what* the aircraft did—so long as they kept the North Vietnamese busy.

Brigadier General Blackburn would have liked to lead the raid himself—with Colonel Mayer acting as his deputy. He was promptly urged to forget any such notion. He was too valuable where he was; and in any case, the mere possibility of a man with so much knowledge falling into North Vietnamese hands was not to be considered. Reluctantly he agreed.

Whoever carried out the operation would be recruited from the Army Special Forces based at Fort Bragg in North Carolina. Among the residents of Fort Bragg at that time was a not especially amiable colonel—a man who was once described as 'the only guy I know who genuinely hates people'—named Arthur D. ('Bull') Simons. Aged fifty-two, Colonel Simons had served with the 6th Rangers when they spear-headed the invasion of the Philippines in 1945. At one time, he had suffered a slight stroke, but his subsequent record—service in Korea, Laos and Vietnam—suggested that this had been the merest lapse in a record of good health and above-average courage. What was more, and despite his somewhat crusty attitude, his men trusted his leadership. As Blackburn explained when the Army Vice Chief of Staff, General Bruce Palmer, dug up the memory of his stroke—exaggerating in into 'a massive heart attack'——'Simons is ten times better than anyone else'.

When Don Blackburn visited Simons at Fort Bragg, he found him in excellent health and eager to take on a 'very sensitive mission' that might be 'kind of rough'. For command of the assault party, Colonel Simons chose Captain Dick Meadows—who, as a master sergeant, had captured a North Vietnamese battery of Russian-made artillery and thereby earned himself the first battlefield commission of the Vietnam war. The third party would be entrusted to Lieutenant Colonel Elliott P. ('Bud') Sydnor.

At some point in his life, or so it was popularly thought, the blood had been extracted from Colonel Sydnor's veins and replaced by iced water. Whatever the circumstances, he was never seen to react emotionally. He simply carried out whatever task it might be with a calmness and single-mindedness from which nothing could deflect him. As a human phenomenon, he was considered to be 'fantastic'.

Those responsible for planning the operation had to keep in mind its prime purpose: to bring home the contents of a prisoner of war camp—men who had been enduring terrible conditions for (in several cases) nearly six years. To expect them to be reasonably fit would be madness; some of them would no doubt have to be carried to the helicopter. Consequently, the raiders must take a doctor with them. For this role, the former chief surgeon of Fort Bragg—now serving in

Washington—Lieutenant Colonel Joseph R. Cataldo, was chosen. He, too, could not possibly be described as 'ordinary'. The descriptions of 'earnest', 'intense', 'dedicated' and even 'hyper-aggressive' have all been applied to him. The fact remains that, when he was invited to accompany the mission, he quickly agreed.

The Air Force side of the operation was put under the command of a 49-year-old New Yorker named Brigadier General Leroy J. Manor, who was serving at the Elgin Air Force base in Florida. The pilots selected by General Manor were all of them exceptional—indeed, the credit titles in this respect read rather like those for a flying circus in which all the performers are stars. Lieutenant Colonel Warner A. Britton was Fort Elgin's operations and training officer for the Aerospace Rescue and Recovery Service (in other words he was responsible for fishing astronauts out of the ocean). Lieutenant Colonel John Allison was also employed on this work. Lieutenant Colonel Herbert E. Zehnder had set up a record, when he piloted an HH-3 helicopter non-stop across the Atlantic from New York to the Paris Air Show of 1967. Major Frederic 'Marty' Donohue was recruited later in the day. During the time lapse, he had increased his 6,000 hours of helicopter flying by taking an HH-33 from Elgin to Saigon—a flight that covered 8,739 miles and involved thirteen in-flight refuelling operations.

The fifteen officers and fifty enlisted men who were selected from the complement of Fort Bragg were told as little as possible. The actual location and purpose of the raid was not vouchsafed to them until the last possible moment. In the first instance, volunteers were invited for an assignment that might be considered 'moderately hazardous'. Anyone interested should report to the base's theatre late one morning in August. Some 500 turned up. Simons told them the barest essentials—explaining, however, that taking part in the unspecified mission would not entitle a man to extra pay. He then suggested that they should consider the matter over lunch and come back afterwards.

About 250 returned for the second session and, for the next three days, Simons interviewed them and Cataldo gave each a quick medical examination. To make sure that this process supplied no clues at all, Simons asked such misleading questions as whether they could ski, whether they became seasick when the weather turned bad, and whether they considered themselves capable of surviving in a desert without supplies of water. Eventually, the Colonel completed his examinations and the chosen fifty were detailed for special training.

Meanwhile, there was the question of equipment. The assault party, to be led by Dick Meadows, would be armed with CAR-15s, a weapon not unlike the Schmeisser machine pistol, but which had the advantage of a folding stock. In the cramped interior of a UH-1 helicopter, even the smallest saving of space was to be encouraged. The rest of the force would carry 5.56 mm M-16 automatic rifles, and there were to be two belt-fed 7.62 mm M-60 machine guns firing tracer to seal off the approaches to the camp. Such demands as these presented few problems; but there were other, more difficult, items on Simons's shopping list.

For example, he needed six 35 mm Pen-EE cameras to take pictures of the cells. This is an automatic camera, slightly smaller than the average 35 mm, manufactured by Olympus. One of its advantages for such an operation is that it takes half-frame pictures. In other words, a film with thirty-six exposures would, in the Pen-EE, yield seventy-two pictures. However, when Simons made his request, he was told that none were available at the time. Instead, he procured Kodak Instamatics.

Demolition charges were needed to blow a gap in the compound wall, for the destruction of a bridge over which reinforcements might be expected to travel, and for other uses. Non-electric blasting caps were preferred, but when the first consignment arrived, 22 per cent was found to be malfunctioning. Eventually 100 that seemed to be effective were collected.

Another essential was an effective night-sight. The need for it was emphasised during practice on the ranges. Even Simons's best shots, firing at fifty yards on to targets, were landing no more than about one-quarter of their rounds to any effect. This was not due to poor marksmanship; the men simply did not have the right equipment. But when Simons asked for a night-sight, he discovered that neither the Army nor the CIA had anything to offer. So he turned his attention to magazine advertisements. He discovered the 'Single Point Nite Sight', that could be purchased for $49.50. It was, apparently, a Swedish invention manufactured in the UK. He bought one to try it out, and the improvement was remarkable. At twenty-five yards, all the rounds were smacking into a 12-inch circle; at 50 yards, they were landing faultlessly on the silhouette of man's torso. He promptly followed up his initial order with a demand for a further forty-nine.

General Manor had recommended that Wednesday, 21 October, should be chosen for the raid. The men were now training hard, using dummy buildings and assisted by a model of the Son Tay compound that had been built by the CIA at a cost of $60,000.

As they refined the plan, however, another snag became apparent. The UH-1 helicopter, which was to land the assault force in the compound, was not big enough. It could carry ten men; but, Dick Meadows insisted, he must have fourteen. Nor did it have the range to make the trip without in-flight refuelling. An HH-3 would have to be used; but this was too big for the job. Eventually, the matter was solved by Zehnder's co-pilot, Major Herbert Kalen. He could, he suggested, crash-land the bigger aircraft in this somewhat constricted space. It would, however, be considerably the worse for its experience, and he would not be able to take off again. The other choppers could, presumably, include the assault force on their manifests for the return trip? He was assured that this could be done.

The raiders were now divided into three units. The first would be Meadows and his assault team of fourteen men. The second would be Sydnor and twenty men, whose job was to take control of the camp's surroundings and its security guard. The third was to be commanded by Simons and made up of twenty-two men. Among its tasks would be that of exploding a hole in the compound wall.

When Blackburn and his colleagues sold the project to the chairman of the Joint Chiefs of Staff, it was merely one step in a number of such transactions. Since a diversionary raid by the US Navy was required, the commander-in-chief, Pacific, Admiral John S. McCain, Jnr, had to be informed. As it happened, the Admiral's son was in the custody of North Vietnam and the raid at Son Tay would bring him no closer to liberty. Indeed, if there were any reprisals afterwards, he would be bound to suffer. But McCain liked the idea, and he agreed that Carrier Task Force 77, then stationed in Tongking Strait, should co-operate to the best of its ability. The task force's commander was no less obliging—though he was given no explanation for this apparently eccentric sortie in which his aircraft would illuminate enemy territory for an hour or so, and then go back to the ships.

Defence Secretary Melvin R. Laird heard details of the raid from General Manor. He was more ambiguous. He would, he said, have to 'defer approval'. He went on to talk about 'co-ordination with high authority'—which, presumably, meant the President. He did not explain to Manor that, at the time, a number of attempts by diplomacy were being made to secure the prisoners' freedom. The Secretary of State, Henry Kissinger, wanted them to be sure to make the raid a success. It would be a pity if it merely added to the number of Americans in captivity. Simons, who briefed him, explained that there had been 170 rehearsals for the operation, and that its chances were rated at between 95 and 97 per cent. That, said Mr. Kissinger, was fine—but President Nixon would have to be consulted. Unfortunately, he was out of town at the moment.

The outcome of it all was that Nixon gave his approval—though he caused the operation to be delayed. The objection to the existing date was that the 25th anniversary of the United Nations organisation was due to be celebrated on 24 October. Nixon himself was to address the Assembly, and anything of this nature might be an embarrassment—especially as he was about to assume his role of diplomat extraordinary, carrying the capitalist olive branch into the heartlands of Russia and China. Eventually, 21 November was selected as suitable in both diplomatic and meteorological terms.

One question that most of the top brass failed to ask was whether those responsible for Operation 'Kingpin' were certain that there were still any POWs in Camp Hope. When the monsoon cleared, and reconnaissance flights became possible again, there might have been some doubts. The remote-controlled drones, Buffalo Hunters, which made the low-level missions, were not going about their business very well. Out of eight flights, six succumbed to mechanical defects (or else to

anti-aircraft guns); in the remaining two, the planes banked
too soon. The result was that excellent pictures were taken of
the surroundings, but none of Camp Hope. Consequently, the
matter was entirely in the hands of Lockheed SR-71 pilots—
flying at three times the speed of sound at an altitude of 80,000
feet.

The photographs from their missions were not entirely
reassuring. They produced no evidence to suggest that Camp
Hope was still occupied by prisoners. Colonel Simons admitted
the possibility that they had been moved to some other camp.
But, he suggested, it might equally well mean that they were
being confined to their cells. In which case, the raid was all the
more urgent.

But now there was another problem. The CIA post on the
Laotian frontier had been taken by the Communists. The
helicopters would have to make the journey from the air base
at Takhli in Thailand—and this would necessitate in-flight
refuelling.

At last, the fifty men, their officers and the helicopter pilots
were able to leave on the operation that had taken so long to
prepare, and which had occupied the minds of so many people.
From Elgin, the Green Berets were flown in a C141 Lockheed
Starlifter to Takhli. At the Thai air base, they were quartered
in billets tucked away from prying eyes in a remote corner of
the camp. They were given six hours in which to recover from
the journey. Then, at 14.00 hrs. local time, Simons and Manor
gave them an introductory talk about the assignment. It may
seem strange that it had been possible to keep them in the dark
for so long. Nevertheless, when the C141 touched down at
Takhli, the men knew that they were somewhere in South-East
Asia, but nothing more.

That evening, they watched a film. At 3.00 am next morning,
Manor was awakened by an orderly carrying a signal from
President Nixon. Operation 'Kingpin' could go forward. It was
left to the Brigadier General to decide the exact time—having
an eye to the weather.

As it happened, the weather was doing little to help the
venture. A typhoon was raging somewhere in the neighbourhood of the Philippines. A low pressure front was moving in
the direction of North Vietnam from China. The only hope

was a belt of high pressure that might form over Hanoi.

November the 19th was occupied by such things as receiving last minute instructions on search and rescue procedures (each man was issued with a small square of silk that, very ingeniously, combined such essentials as a map, an amazingly thin compass, and such useful Laotian and Vietnamese phrases as 'which way is north?', 'I need water' and 'Can you find me a doctor'—the sort of thing that no traveller should ever be without).

At 6.00 pm, they were told the final details about the raid. When it was over, there was no cheering—just a deep silence that, to the experienced ears of Simons and Sydnor, could only indicate whole-hearted approval.

They lunched early on the following day. Afterwards, Cataldo gave each man a sleeping tablet—to be taken at once. At 5.00 pm, they were awakened for a meal at which they were encouraged to eat well. There would not be another for the next twelve hours. Just before 10.00 pm they embarked in the C-130 Hercules transport that was to take them on the first leg of the journey to Son Tay.

The helicopters were waiting for them on the airfield at Udorn, a small town near the frontier. The idea was that they should follow a C-130 tanker to a point somewhere near the centre of Northern Laos. Here, they would refuel. The tanker would then return to its base and the lead would be taken over by another version of this extremely versatile breed. This aircraft would find the path to Son Tay and, if need by, light up the sky with flares. The flight was expected to take about three hours. Colonel Simons strapped himself into his seat and composed himself for sleep. He was, he instructed, to be awakened when the target was twenty minutes away.

As they approached Son Tay, they could see the lights of Hanoi ahead—whilst, eastwards, the sky was bright with the flares that Carrier Task Force 77's pilots had dutifully, if somewhat bewilderedly, dropped from their A-7 attack aircraft (the 698 mph Corsair II). What with the naval contribution, the choppers, the C-130s and a fair number of fighters lurking invisibly in the night sky, there were no fewer than 105 US aircraft scattered about in North Vietnamese air space.

Marty Donohue was the first to land. The timing had to be exact. The guards were changed on the hour and on the half-hour; it was therefore assumed that they would be at their least wakeful at fifteen and forty-five minutes past the hour. But Donohue had judged it perfectly. He was exactly on schedule.

As he came down towards the target, a cannon in each of the HH-3's side doors opened up, pumping shot into the two guard towers on the west wall. The tower at the gate was spared for fear that there might be a POW in the cooler at its base. The trees were taller than the aerial photographs had suggested, but they presented no hazard. Once the towers had been cut to pieces by cannon fire, he brought the machine down to a comfortable landing in a nearby paddy field to await the arrival of the liberated prisoners.

Herb Zehnder came next. His was the not very enviable task of depositing Dick Meadows and his assault team in the compound. On the way down the helicopter's blades did a sharp job of pruning a number of trees, then it crashed on the small rectangle of North Vietnamese soil. Lieutenant George L. Petrie, the first man to alight, was literally thrown overboard by the shock of impact.

Captain Meadows lost no time. While his men went about their business, he spoke through a bullhorn. 'We're Americans', he called. 'Keep your heads down. We're Americans. This is a rescue. We're here to get you out...' And so on. But nobody appeared to pay the slightest attention. There was a good deal of small arms fire being exchanged on the far side of the wall. Here, there was nothing—and certainly no evidence of any prisoners.

And then there was an explosion as a large hole was blasted through the wall. This, Meadows assumed, must be Simons and his twenty-two-man support group. As the newcomers drew nearer, however, he was surprised to see that Sydnor was in charge. Colonel Simons had, it appeared, landed in the wrong place.

The confusion was due to the similar group of buildings, about half-a-mile away, marked 'secondary school' on the map. Warner Britton, the pilot had been so busy concentrating on coming down in one piece, that he mistook it for the prison camp. He soon returned to ferry the Colonel and his men to the correct target. In the meanwhile Simons's party lost no time in exploring their surroundings. Simons himself accounted for a very frightened Vietnamese guard who had obviously been caught completely by surprise. A few moments later, a crowd of men came running from the school buildings. The establishment, it seemed, was no longer catering for the needs of North Vietnam's brighter children—it was serving as a billet. But, for whom? The men were considerably taller than the average Vietnamese, and it seemed probable that they were Russian technicians. As the neighbourhood bristled with Soviet anti-aircraft equipment, they were probably there to advise on how to use it. Simons and his warriors slew an estimated 200 of them before Britton re-embarked the Green Berets and took them on the short journey to their intended scene of action.

Apart from the somewhat misjudged landing of Warner Britton, the raid was beautifully managed. No one could estimate how many of the enemy and their accomplices had been killed; the intruders suffered only one casualty—a sergeant who received a flesh wound in his thigh. Unfortunately, the operation did not achieve its objective. The better part of four months had passed since there had last been an American POW at Son Tay. They had all been moved to a much larger and, it had to be admitted, more comfortable establishment at Dong Hoi ('Camp Faith' to those who lodged there).

The irony of it was that, some days before the raid, the Defence Intelligence Agency had known that there were no prisoners at Son Tay. The source of information was impeccable; a member of the North Vietnam Enemy Proselyting Office (a somewhat grandiose title for the department responsible for the custody and mind-bending of captives). This official had struck up an acquaintance with a gentleman known as 'Alfred', who was serving on the International Control Commission in Hanoi. Moving warily at first, the two men had eventually agreed to trade information. At one of their more recent meetings 'Alfred' had sought the latest facts about the dispersal of American POWs. Soon afterwards, just as he was about to depart on a flight to Hong Kong, his North Vietnamese contact presented him with a packet of cigarettes—knowing very well that he did not smoke.

When the cigarettes were examined by DIA experts, they were found to contain a message in code (a very similar one to that used by the POW's themselves, when tapping out communication on walls). It informed the reader that, due to floods brought about by an unusually heavy monsoon, the captives had been moved to Dong Hoi back in July. The floods themselves, as it happened, might have been caused by a CIA operation known as 'Popeye', in which cloud-seeding units made up of silver and lead iodide were discharged into the atmosphere by aircraft, and which increased rainfall beyond that normally experienced in the area.

The operation, it seems, was doomed by a lack of communications that appeared to carry security to a point that verged on paranoia. As far as the POWs were concerned the raid came four months too late. And what, after all, were their captors to make of an operation in which a great many carrier-based aircraft lit up the sky for a while and then turned back without doing anything else? Or what was the point of fifty-odd highly trained and daring soldiers raiding an empty POW camp? After all, there was a perfectly good dam in the vicinity of the camp. Why did they not demolish that? At least it would have made some sort of sense. The ways of an oriental may well be inscrutable, but Westerners. . .

World War II, unlike World War I, was never described as the one to end them all—possibly because it had dawned upon even the most doughty propagandists that such a pious hope was out of the question. Repeatedly, mankind has shown itself incapable of settling disputes without the use of force.

No doubt the United States did well to use the word 'counter-insurgency' in connection with its Special Service forces. Likewise, it was sensible that one seminar attended by senior officers at the Command and General Staff College, Fort Leavenworth, should take as its theme 'Wars of Liberation'. Most wars are described as such with various degrees of inaccuracy—and frequently the supposed beneficiaries have no fervent wish to be 'liberated'. Another favourite word is 'insurgency'. In the opinion of the Pentagon, hostilities are liable to erupt within nations' frontiers and not necessarily across them. The result of insurgency may be a civil war—or, as the activities of the IRA in the British Isles demonstrate, an ordeal by terrorism. But, whatever it is, its effects cannot be entirely localised. Terrorism—like smallpox, cholera and rabies— is a matter for international concern.

During the past two decades, there have been a number of organisations conducting terrorist operations. They include the Baader-Meinhof gang, the Red Brigade, the Popular Front for the Liberation of Palestine (PFLP), the Black September movement and, of course, the IRA. In airports and conference rooms, streets and banks, and even at the Olympic Games, they have pursued their grim and bloody purpose, ready for martyrdom on behalf of causes that cannot be won by martyrs.

As the wretched history of their achievements shows, the enemy no longer wears a uniform nor practises its craft upon a parade ground. It is the young couple who arrive at the last minute to catch an airliner (and bypass the security check), the anonymous face in a crowd, the mentally sick youngster raised on bitterness and resentment, the baby-faced hoodlum in dark glasses.

They can seldom be brought to battle, but, when they are, special skills are needed. Raiders, it might be argued, are best dealt with by raiders, and several countries have created forces for this purpose. In Great Britain it is the Special Air Service (SAS), which can trace its origins back to the Commandos.

Number 62 Commando, under a Scots Guards officer named David Stirling, was formed in July, 1941, for operations behind the enemy lines in North Africa. In February, 1943, with a strength of ten officers and forty other ranks, it took to the sky and devoted itself to clandestine operations. More recently, it has served with remarkably good effect in Northern Ireland— and has, upon occasion, given the benefit of its expertise to similar organisations outside the UK.

After the slaughter of eleven Israeli athletes at the Munich Olympics in the summer of 1972, Israel decided that it, too, must have an anti-terrorist force—in this case Unit 101, otherwise known as the 'Wrath of God'. The Federal Republic of Western Germany was also inspired by the Munich fiasco to train a special force for such work—the *Grenzschutzgruppe* 9

(abbreviated to GSG9), which was a Commando unit attached
to the German Border police. In Italy, there is the Squadron
Anti-Commando, in Holland the Marines and in France the
National *Gendarmerie* Action Group. Some, such as the SAS are
entirely military organisations; others are composed of fighting
policemen.

The GSG9 showed its quality in October, 1977, when a
Lufthansa Boeing 737 was homeward bound from Palma,
Majorca, to Frankfurt, with eighty-six holidaymakers on board.
As it was crossing over the Mediterranean into French airspace,
it was hijacked by two men and two women belonging to the
PFLP. They demanded the release of eleven members of the
Baader-Meinhof gang—their allies in the dark corridor of
terrorism.

After making refuelling stops at Rome, Larnaca in Cyprus,
Dubai, and Aden (where the aircraft's captain, Captain Jurgen
Schumann was shot dead in front of the passengers), the Boeing
eventually came to rest at Mogadishu, the hijackers' leader—
'Captain Mahmoud', in real life a psychopath named Zuhair
Youssef Akache—may have expected a favourable reception.
He does not, however, appear to have realised that Russia had
recently withdrawn its support of Somalia in favour of another
client state, Ethiopia. The country's President Siyad was hoping
that West Germany would make good this deficiency. Consequently, when Chancellor Helmut Schmidt sought the
president's agreement to intervention by GSG9, he agreed.

The commandos were led by Lieutenant Colonel Ulrich
Wegener. As the result of an offer made by the British Prime
Minister, James Callaghan, two members of the SAS—Major
Alistair Morrison and Sergeant Barrie Davies—were attached.
The force was transported to Mogadishu in a Lufthansa Boeing
707. At 2.06 am local time on 18 October, the brief battle—if
such it can be called—began. The commandos used special
'stun grenades' which are harmless, but explode with a very
loud bang and a dazzling flash, immobilising opponents by
shock for about six seconds. They then forced their way into
the aircraft, killed three of the terrorists and seriously wounded
a girl member of the gang, who was fighting a rearguard action
from the plane's toilet. Some of the passengers suffered superfi-
cial leg wounds from terrorists' grenades. All of them survived.

Colonel Wegener had alread had experience of this type of operation. He had spent six weeks being tutored by the FBI in the United States, and he had also attended a course at the Israeli paratroop school. At the latter, he did so well that (or so it is said) he had been invited to take part in an anti-hijack raid that took place in 1976. The scene of action on this occasion was Entebbe.

12 The Airlift

On the morning of 27 June, 1976, a number of passengers were waiting at Athens airport, to embark on Air France's flight number 139 from Tel Aviv to Paris. Since the ground staff had called a lightning strike that day, formalities were kept to a minimum. There were, for example, no security checks.

One hundred and three of the aircraft's passengers were Jews, many of them from Israel. Among those who joined the flight at Athens were two Germans—Wilfried Böse and his girl friend, Brigitte Kohlman—and two Palestinians. Böse, who had long hair, was wearing a red shirt and a pair of grey trousers; Fräulein Kohlman wore a pale blue blouse, a dark denim skirt and flat-heeled shoes. They were travelling under the pseudonyms of 'Mr Garcia' and 'Mrs Ortego'. The names of the Palestinians were Fayez Abdul-Rahim Jaber and Abedel Latif. All four had travelled to Athens from Kuwait on board a Singapore Airways plane.

At noon, the French aircraft climbed into the clear summer sky and presently levelled off at its cruising altitude. Ten minutes later, the travellers in the economy class heard a scream from up front. The young German in the red shirt and one of the Palestinians (somebody noticed that he had a large moustache—he was probably Jaber) immediately ran along the aisle towards the first-class compartment. A couple of minutes later, two stewardesses appeared. They were obviously very frightened, but they managed to calm down the passengers who had now become alarmed. There was nothing, they insisted, to worry about—though their faces were less reassuring. Nor were they helped when, second later, the inter-com clicked

into life. Instead of the customary soothing remarks of the
aircraft's captain, they heard the harsh rather excited voice of
Brigitte Kohlman announcing that they were now under the
control of 'the Che Guevara Group'—working, it seemed, in
collaboration with the 'Gaza Unit' of the 'Popular Front for
the Liberation of Palestine'. They had been hijacked.

Hijacked airliners are the outcasts of the sky. The reactions
of most airport authorities, especially those in the Middle East,
are to deny the pilots the use of their runways. They render
them useless by littering them with bulldozers and other items
of hardware; at night, they switch off the landing lights.

There is usually one exception to the rule, however: Libya.
The country's President, Colonel Moammer Gaddafi, is known
to sympathise with terrorists—to give them money, supply them
with arms and to provide them with sanctuary. It was, then,
not surprising that flight number 139 should touch down at
Benghazi to refuel. The aircraft remained on the ground for
the better part of seven hours. A woman who was feeling unwell
was allowed to disembark; the others were confined on board.
The doors, one of the hijackers explained, had been booby-
trapped—and, near the exit, a drum filled with high explosive
had a fuse poking ominously out of its top.

At 5.15 pm, the terrorists collected the passengers' passports,
placing them neatly into plastic bags. Two hours later, a cold
supper was served. At about this time, Wilfred Böse made
another announcement over the inter-com. It was strangely
polite. He regretted the inconvenience and discomfort that the
events of the past few hours had entailed. They would, he
promised, take off again as soon as possible. It was in the best
tradition of flight-deck announcements.

But, by now, the attitudes of the two Germans had been
brought into sharper focus. Böse was usually politely reassuring;
Kohlman was more brutal. For at least one Israeli, she awakened
memories of the World War II concentration camp guards.
She was unlovely to look at—her complexion marred by acne
scars and her eyes bloodshot. Somebody afterwards described
her as 'an animal'. Another passenger used the adjective 'vile'.
She was inclined to shout, to become impatient and quite
possibly violent at any hesitation to obey her instructions.
Nevertheless, Bóse was judged to be the more dangerous of the

two. Nobody doubted that his urbane manner concealed the worst intentions—whereas with Brigitte Kohlmann, you at least knew where you were.

Night had long fallen before the aircraft resumed its journey. It was impossible to tell where they were going. Damascus and Beirut were among several conjectures until, at 3.15 am, Böse made another of his announcements. Within a few minutes, he said, the aircraft would be landing at Entebbe.

They remained on board for another nine hours after the plane had landed. From time to time Böse resumed his reassuring broadcasts. Uganda's dictator, Idi Amin, had, he told them, hurried back from Mauritius, where he had been making his final appearance as chairman of the Organisation of African Unity. He was now at the airport—acting as an intermediary in the negotiations. Everything, the young Germans stressed, was being conducted 'properly'.

At last, just after mid-day, the passengers were allowed to disembark and move into the terminal building. That afternoon, Amin visited them. Several of them noticed with irony that his uniform was embellished with the wings of an Israeli paratrooper. After a polite round of applause from his audience, he explained that it was due to his personal kindness that the aircraft had been permitted to land on Ugandan territory. His compatriots referred to him as 'Big Daddy'; his involuntary guests might care to think of him in a similar light. It would have been more convincing if he had resisted the temptations to appear with a Palestinian bodyguard in which each man was armed and uniformed.

So far as the negotiations were concerned, Amin said, 'Israel has already rejected the terrorists' demands, though the other nations involved are prepared to accept them.' He did not, however, state what the terms were. Indeed, the information was not passed on until 3.30 pm the following afternoon, when one of the hijackers—probably Böse—spelt it out. Fifty-three interned terrorists had to be released from captivity—forty of them in Israel, six in West Germany, five in Kenya, and one each in Switzerland and France. The transaction had to be completed by mid-day on 1 July.

The situation became clearer, and more ominous at 7.10 that evening, when everybody holding an Israeli passport was ordered to leave the main hall of the terminal and to assemble in a lounge adjacent to it. Since the PFLP was involved, and since by far the greater number of the captive terrorists were in Israeli gaols, they could no longer be any doubt about who were the hostages. If the negotiations failed, it seemed probable that they would be murdered. They could only hope that the Israeli government would not be too intransigent.

Meals were served from time to time; the hostages were issued with blankets; and Amin put in another appearance. One of the terrorist guards explained that the demands had not yet been accepted; but, no—there was no intention to kill them. The Israelis had been segregated simply because the main hall had become too crowded. The mood of these people varied. On one occasion, when a man asked for a cushion to make his young child more comfortable, he was struck violently with the butt of a revolver. At others, the gang seemed to be more relaxed, and would discuss the situation calmly. But at all times they carried their guns (Russian Kalashnikov sub-machine guns) with the actions cocked. A pile of cardboard boxes at one end of the room was pointed out. Each, it was explained, was packed with high explosive. If it were touched, it would automatically detonate.

The hijacking of Flight Number 139 had been an expensive and, it had to be admitted, well-planned operation. The instigator was Dr Wadi Hadad, the ruthless head of operations in the PFLP hierarchy. The action itself was scripted by an unpleasant young Latin American named Ilich Pamirez Sanchez—more commonly known as 'Carlos' and sometimes as 'the Jackal'.

Carlos was twenty-eight at the time, and his record of violence was impressive. He had been responsible for the kidnapping and subsequent murder of the Israeli athletes at the 1972 Olympics, the abduction of the OPEC ministers from their conference room in Vienna at the end of 1975, and for several individual assassinations. Although he was not one to flinch from duty in the front line (if it can be so called), he did not take part in the affair of flight number 139—for one thing his features were so well known from press photographs that he would surely have been identified, even at a Greek airport where the guards and security men were enjoying a day of idleness in support of a pay-claim. Also, this particular operation was not suited to his style.

Ever since the age of fourteen, he had industriously worked his way up to the top ranks of world terrorism. No doubt he was proud of his accomplishment—possibly, vain. He was prepared to deal with leading athletes and men of ministerial rank. Lesser fry, such as a planeload of bewildered and rather frightened tourists were beneath him. Nevertheless, at Dr Hadad's behest, Carlos had scripted the present drama; and, on the evidence of 1 July, it seemed as if he had done a very reasonable job. Not only had the execution been effective; the planning behind it showed a nice sense of politics and their more recent history.

Hadad had originally suggested that it should be an exclusively PFLP operation. Carlos had disagreed. To plant four Palestinians on board the aircraft would be to invite suspicion. It should, he insisted, be conducted on more international lines. Two members of the PFLP might certainly be included. The remaining couple—for four people had become the standard hijacking unit—should be recruited from the Baader-Meinhof gang in Germany.

The geography of the operation required particular attention. Kuwait would serve well as a point of departure for the very sensible reason that, while the Kuwaitis were enjoying the profits from their oil fields, most of the administrative duties were performed by Palestinians (they accounted for 200,000 of the country's 800,000 population). Whilst by no means all of them were militants, most could at least be considered sympathetic to the PFLP cause.

Athens was attractive in view of the airport's labour unrest and the promise of a strike. To achieve their purpose, the hijackers would have to board an aircraft in which the majority of passengers were Israelis. The obvious choice was an El Al flight, but this was quickly dismissed as too dangerous. The Israeli airline was known to employ extremely efficient in-flight guards. The conditions on the Air France service between Tel Aviv and Paris via Athens were more relaxed.

Good luck and careful planning put the spotlight on Air France's flight 139 on 27 June. With the connivance of the authorities at Kuwait and the unwitting co-operation of the strikers at Athens, the German-Palestinian team was able to pass through all barriers—not only with its identities unquestioned, but also with its full complement of weapons, explosives and ammunition. So far, so good. The next question was where the hijacked aircraft could be accommodated while negotiations were taking place.

Benghazi's credentials for the role of refuelling point were impeccable, but the journey could not end there. In this respect, Entebbe in Uganda was more promising. The key to the matter was its president, Field Marshal Doctor Idi Amin Dada, self-appointed holder of the Victoria Cross, Distinguished Service Order *et als*. Carlos obviously had taken pains to study Ugandan history and, what was more, he quite clearly knew his Idi Amin. The president's term of office as chairman of the Organisation of African Unity was drawing to a close. What better way in which to conclude it than by a great diplomatic gesture; by acting as mediator in a dispute that was creating anxiety among much greater nations? Amin the butcher (for such he was already known to be) would be replaced by Amin the great humanitarian, the diplomat completely extraordinary.

The relationship between Amin's Uganda and Israel had been a strange one. It had been no idle conceit that prompted the president to wear Israeli paratrooper wings when he visited the hostages. He had been presented with them during a visit to Tel Aviv not long after he had come to power. In those days, or so it seemed, the two nations were inseparable. Israel helped Uganda to build up its army from an ill-trained battalion amounting to no more than 800 men; it provided planes for the Ugandan Air Force and it taught pilots how to fly them. On one occasion, an Israeli officer had actually saved Amin's life by warning him of an assassination plot.

Until 1972, Israel could do no wrong in the eyes of the African dictator, but then everything turned sour. In February, 1972, Amin decided to invade the neighbouring state of Tanzania. Israel, he hoped—indeed, he assumed—would assist him. As it happened, Israel was not prepared to do anything of the kind. The weapons and the knowledge had been provided for defensive purposes. President Amin's plan was out of the question.

Love can so easily turn into hate, and this is what happened. Suddenly the State of Israel became hideous to Amin. More or less overnight, all the Israelis residing in Uganda had to remove themselves. Diplomatic relations were broken off; Amin considered matters carefully and reminded himself that, after all, he was a Moslem. It was his duty to champion the Palestinian cause. It was sensible to cultivate Libya's Gaddafi— with whom he now discovered ideological common ground, and from whom he might hope to acquire arms and money. Gaddafi welcomed him into his militantly anti-Israeli fold, and must have listened with smiling approval when, in September, 1972, Amin informed the United Nations Secretary General that:

> Hitler was right about the Jews, because the Israelis are not working in the interests of the people of the world, and that is why they burned the Israelis alive with gas on the soil of Germany.

Hadad and his Venezuelan side-kick, Carlos, were no doubt safe in assuming that Entebbe would provide a resting place for the homeless aircraft. They may even have surmised that, should their demands be turned down. Amin would not be too scrupulous to turn a blind eye on the massacre of 103 Israeli passengers.

To begin with, certainly, events seemed to be moving in their favour. The foursome who had taken over the aircraft and brought it to Entebbe at gunpoint were ready for a rest. Hijacking an aircraft is, after all, a tiring pursuit. In his role of negotiator and with sufficient regard for world opinion, Amin could not allow his own troops to relieve them. In any case, it was not necessary. Five senior members of the PFLP terrorist movement had already arrived in Uganda. When the Air France plane touched down, they were waiting on the tarmac to receive it—suitably armed with sub-machine guns and explosives. As if to show that he approved of their presence, Amin publicly shook hands with them.

Most of the negotiations took place over the telephone between the dictator and an Israeli colonel named Bar-Lev, who had headed a military mission to Uganda in the days of compatibility, and who had struck up a friendship with Amin. Needless to say, they were monitored by Israeli experts, who translated them into an evaluation of Amin's state of mind. It cannot have been easy; for, as with any other unstable person, his mood swung from one extreme to the other in a manner that was both violent and unpredictable.   July 1 came and went. There was still no agreement, but at least the two sides in the conflict were still talking. Indeed, in Israel, the attitude of Prime Minister Yitzhak Rabin and his government seemed to be softening—possibly in response to the innummerable letters they had received from the hostages' relatives, demanding their release at no matter what price.

Anyone who believed that this was likely would have done well to recall an incident that had occurred in 1972, when a hijacked Sabena airliner landed on the tarmac at Lod. On this occasion, the terrorists had insisted upon the release of 319 prisoners. Talks carried out under supervision of the Red Cross went on for twenty-four hours without seeming to achieve any purpose. Then, in a beautifully conducted operation, an Israeli assault squad forced its way into the aircraft, shot down the two male hijackers and captured their female accomplices. One passenger was killed in the fighting—the others escaped unharmed. It was, it seemed, unwise to assume that, whatever discussions were heard to take place in Tel Aviv, there was nothing else happening in the background.

Meanwhile the telephone was kept busy; and, for so long as it was being used, there was hope. On the evening of 3 July, two-and-a-half days after the original deadline had expired. Amin returned to his house less than one mile from the airport. He went to bed, and by midnight was fast asleep. It was, perhaps, a mistake; for the night of 3–4 July was of above-average interest.

For Israeli Prime Minister Yitzhak Rabin and his cabinet, the preceding days had been filled with an agonising decision. The question was whether to capitulate to the terrorists' demands, or whether to attempt a rescue operation. Methodically, the facts were set out and studied. Entebbe Airport was more than 2,000 miles from Israel. Since Amin's change of heart in 1972, and encouraged by the oil-rich Gaddafi, one African state after another had declared its hostility to Israel. Now there was only one that might be considered friendly: Kenya. If any raid were to be carried out, Kenya's assent was vital.

Uganda had come a long way since Israeli experts had raised its armed forces from the slough of inefficiency. According to a sufficiently accurate estimate, they now consisted of 21,000 well-armed and well-trained soldiers equipped with 267 armoured troop carriers, SAM ground-to-air missiles, howitzers and mortars. In addition to this, the Ugandan Air Force had well over fifty combat planes, including thirty MiG-9s and the more recent MiG-17s. It was thought that about half of the army was concentrated between Entebbe and Kampala (twenty-one miles away). Twenty-one of the fighter planes were at Entebbe airport, which was ringed by a force of crack infantrymen supported by Russian-manufactured tanks.

Rabin and his army chief-of-staff, Lieutenant General Gur, listed the points for and against a rescue operation. Against it were such consideration as the 2,500 miles that separated Entebbe from Sharm el Sheikh, the southernmost airfield in Israel; the fact that long tracts of hostile territory, bristling with SAM missiles and radar devices lay in between; the fact that Entebbe airport was heavily guarded; and the fact that it would be impossible to fly there and back without refuelling.

What, then, could be written down on the credit side? Again, there were four points. Israel now had the sympathy of anti-terrorist forces throughout the world, and they were ready to contribute information. Despite its fall from favour, Israel still had a good intelligence network in Africa. Kenya had not unreasonably taken affront at Amin's continued threats from across the frontier, and might, just possibly, be considered an ally. Finally, there was a more abstract consideration, but one that, in a situation such as this, was priceless. Once again, the Jews were under attack. They had suffered in the concentration camps; they had been compelled to fight for a homeland; they had been slung out of Uganda; they had been oppressed in Russia; and now the dismal train of events had taken another turn. They were ready, indeed eager, to fight back.

On the Wednesday following the hijacking (30 June), General Gur was already explaining the feasibility of a raid providing he had speed and surprise. Indeed, he was anticipating his government's decision by discussing a possible venture with a few carefully selected officers. If the negotiations could be dragged on beyond the deadline, such any operation would have to take place after midday on Saturday 3 July and before 2.30 am on the Sunday morning.

This was a matter of air traffic. From noon on the Saturday, there were no incoming or out-going flights at Entebbe until, in the dark hours of the Sunday morning, a solitary VC10 came in to refuel. After all, it would be senseless to attempt to land troops, however skilled they and the pilots might be, if the sky was cluttered with the comings and goings of scheduled airliners.

But, before anything else could happen, the attitude of Kenya had to be ascertained. When El Al flight number LY535 took off for Nairobi on this same Wednesday, there were fifty 'businessmen' on board. Each was a member of the Israeli secret service. The number was, perhaps, unnecessarily large, for the bulk of the work was done by a handful of them. These men established themselves at the house of an Israeli merchant—where, presently, they were visited by the chief of Nairobi police, Lionel Bryn Davies, and by a gentleman named Bruce McKenzie who had once served in the British SAS and was now a close friend of President Kenyatta. Later, the leader of Kenyatta's élite General Service Unit, Geoffrey Karithil, put in an appearance. Between them, they were able to assure the visitors that there could be objection to Israeli Air Force planes flying through Kenyan air space—and that President Kenyatta would affect not to notice if any of them should be put down at Nairobi to refuel.

Meanwhile, General Gur was developing his ideas. In 1971, the Israeli Air Force had acquired a number of Hercules transports which had been affectionately nicknamed 'Hippos'. Four of them would be required, plus an escort of Phantoms for part of the journey. Two Boeing 707s would also be used; one to serve as a flying hospital, the other to be employed as an airborne command post in which the Israeli Air Force chief, Benny Peled, would have his headquarters. The route of the raiders would be southwards along the international air lane that bisects the Red Sea, until they reached a point off-shore from Djibouti. Here they would change course to the south-

west, overflying Ethiopia and passing into Kenyan air space.
The two 707s would land at Nairobi to refuel. The flying
hospital would remain there; the aerial headquarters would
resume its journey to Entebbe.

The Hercules aircraft would make the trip non-stop—helping
themselves to Ugandan fuel once the mission had been
completed, and they were ready to take off.

The raid, assuming that it took place, was to be code-named
'Thunderbolt'. But who was to take part in it? So far as pilots
were concerned, Peled insisted that no preference should be
given to seniority. He would be guided by the duty roster—as
if it were no more than a routine exercise. Such was his
confidence in his officers, that he considered any member of
the IAF was competent for an operation that was bound to tax
his skill to the limits.

To lead the army's contingent, General Gur selected Brigadier General Dan Shomron. Born in a kibbutz in 1937, he had
enlisted in the army as a paratrooper. He fought in the Sinai
War of 1956; in the Six Day War, he led the first troops to
reach the Suez Canal. He was tough, immensely able, and an
expert in commando-style tactics.

As second-in-command with special responsibilities, a young
lieutenant-colonel named Yonatan Netanyahu was chosen.
Netanyahu had been born in the United States. At the age of
eighteen, he was conscripted into the Israeli army, and his
subsequent career somehow managed to combine the roles of
Israeli commando fighter and philosophy student at Harvard.
He was, perhaps, in the great tradition of soldier-poets. During
the Six Day War, he played an important part in capturing
the Golan Heights from the Syrians. He was decorated for his
valour, but he paid for it with a severe wound in the arm. As
a result, he was discharged from the forces with a 30 per cent
disability pension. He returned to America and continued his
studies at Harvard. He also underwent surgery there that eased
the incessant pain in his damaged limb, but did little to restore
its efficiency. In physical terms, he was still 30 per cent disabled.

But nothing could keep Yonatan Netanyahu away from
Israel. He returned from the United States, persuaded the
authorities to overlook his injured arm, and was earmarked for
commando duties. With his intelligence, his almost fanatical

love of his country, and his extreme courage (at the age of seventeen, he wrote, 'Death does not frighten me, it arouses my curiosity. I do not fear it because I attribute little value to a life without a purpose. And if it is necessary for me to lay down my life in the attainment of the goal I set for it, I will do so willingly')—with these qualities, he was a natural leader for hazardous and unorthodox operations.

The plan conceived for the rescue operation was divided into several elements. Initially, it was necessary to seize the airport's control tower, and for this purpose the architects of 'Thunderbolt' decided to use subterfuge. A white Mercedes was commandeered from a civilian in Tel Aviv, and repainted black to match one of the vehicles in Amin's personal fleet. One of the more burly members of of the assault group was to be made up to resemble the dictator; with a bit of luck, the guards on duty would present their arms rather than fire them.

Netanyahu was made responsible for the control tower and for freeing the hostages. Another unit was to lay an ambush against any Ugandan troops that might be rushed from the direction of Kampala and, especially, from the garrison at Idi Amin's residence. Yet another was to attack the airport perimeter—demolish the MiG fighters and put the radar installation out of action. Finally, a dozen men were assigned to guard the 'Hippos' as they waited on the runways. All told, about fifty commandos would be involved. The terrorists were to be shot on sight; casualties among the Ugandan soldiers were to be kept to a minimum. Ideally, there would be none at all.

On Friday 2 July, 'Thunderbolt' was rehearsed in every detail, though there was still no certainty that it would take place. It was easy enough for the service chiefs to work out the design for an operation and to set it up; the difficult part fell to Rabin and his ministers. They were, after all, being asked to sanction what amounted to an act of war. And what if it failed? The hostages of flight 139 would undoubtedly be slaughtered. For ever afterwards, Rabin and his government would be haunted by the question of whether, ultimately, discussions might have prevailed, and those 103 lives saved.

Always aware of those few hours during which the sky above Entebbe airport would be free from traffic, the military was understandably becoming impatient. The Hercules aircraft were standing by; the 707s and the Phantoms. The cream of Israel's experts in irregular warfare had been brought up to a pitch where they were ready for anything. To abandon the idea would be a most shocking anti-climax.

At about 3.30 pm on the afternoon of 3 July, Peled and Shomron decided to take matters a stage further. The fleet of aircraft took off, but they were not finally committed; they could turn back. There was no need. Fifteen minutes later, just as they were passing over the southern point of Israel, Rabin delivered his verdict. The word was, 'Go!'

It was not an easy flight. All the transport aircraft were painted with civilian registration numbers; the two 707s were decorated in El Al livery. They flew in a loose formation, sometimes out of sight of one another, with only the blobs on the radar screens to indicate their positions. The fighters kept well away at a higher altitude, using jamming devices to play havoc with ground detection apparatus. Nevertheless, the sudden increase in traffic along the Red Sea air lane was bound to attract attention. Quite early in the journey, the pilots had to descend to a few hundred feet above the water to escape a group of Arab surveillance ships fitted with sophisticated Russian electronic hardware.

But everything was going wonderfully well. The 707s landed at Nairobi without hindrance—without indeed seeming to arouse more than passing interest the minds of the Kenyan authorities. Lake Victoria was obscured by a canopy of thick mist; beyond it, the sky was clear and they could discern the lights of Entebbe. There were one or two flashes of lightning accompanied by a good deal of turbulence. Otherwise conditions could be rated as good.

It would be foolish to pretend that four Hercules transports can be set down at an airport, even at dead of night, with rousing some small attention. Nevertheless, it was imperative that the landings should be executed calmly, smoothly, in the most orthodox manner possible. That way, a few precious minutes were saved before the sleepy custodians of Entebbe Airport suddenly awakened to the fact that these were no routine arrivals. To help with the illusion there was no jamming on of brakes, no sudden and violent reversing of engines to slow down the taxiing aircraft. The pilots relied on natural forces and a certain amount of luck to pull them up in the correct places.

Netanyahu, the black Mercedes, and a squad of men—their faces suitably blackened to mislead the sentries and wearing Ugandan-type jackets—hastened to the control tower where, as they had hoped, the guards saluted. It was their final duty. Less than a second or so later, they were lying dead—shot down by automatic pistols fitted with silencers. The young colonel and his commandos wiped the make-up off their faces and threw away the jackets before moving on to their next task. Nevertheless, something must have warned the Ugandan crew in the tower that all was not quite as it should have been. Suddenly, just as the Mercedes was being driven away, somebody pulled a switch, and the runways were thrown into darkness.

As it happened, it assisted the raiders. The last of the 'Hippos' had landed safely; but now the defences were waking up. One aircraft in particular—the Hercules that, once the raid had been completed, would be the the last to leave—was in danger of being caught in the cross-fire of a pair of machine-guns. By switching off the lights, the air-traffic controllers had wiped out visual contact between the defending troops and the invaders. The Ugandan gunners could only direct their shots to where they *thought*, or hoped, the targets might be.

The action at Entebbe lasted for less than an hour. It was a masterpiece of speed combined with a thorough understanding of what had to be done, and of the airport's lay-out. Shomron set up his headquarters close to the passenger building. Having shot the control-tower sentries, Yonatan Netanyahu and his assault force hurried to the terminal and forced their way inside. The terrorist Böse was standing with his back to a window. Taken completely by surprise, he swung round and slowly raised his gun. He was killed before he could do anything else. Brigitte Kohlman, now known by the hostages as 'the Nazi bitch,' had a grenade in one hand. In the other, she held a Kalashnikov—which she was pointing at her captives. She died when somebody emptied a sub-machine gun magazine into her. Two other terrorists were discovered elsewhere in the building, hiding under a bed. They, too, were dispatched and so was a close personal friend of Wadi Hadad, Jayel Naji el-

Arjam. All told, seven terrorists died that night. Three more were probably taken back to Israel for cross-examination (though the Israeli authorities have denied it).

At first the hostages were told to lie down on the floor. Then, once the terrorists had been shot down, they had to be moved to a Hercules that was waiting outside the building. It was not easy. Some, for example, were in the toilets when the shooting began. They imagined that the deadline had finally expired and that the massacre had begun. They had to be convinced that it was safe to emerge.

There was no let-up in the speed of the operation. On the perimeter, the demolition squads were accounting for the MiGs and the radar installation. Before the aircraft were sent up in flames, and the radar blown to small pieces, certain key components were extracted for transport to Israel and detailed study. There was, after all, some useful intelligence to be gained, an invaluable opportunity to study the products of the Soviet armourers.

At the airport's gates, the opposition turned out to be less than they had anticipated. Instead of the armoured column that they feared might move up from the direction of Kampala, there was only a platoon of Ugandans travelling in light trucks. They were quickly put out of action.

By now, light rain was falling. Shomron's men were two minutes ahead of their schedule; and, fifty-three minutes after the first aircraft had landed, the Hercules carrying the hostages rolled off the runway and back into the sky.

In another 'Hippo', where two operating tables had been set up, surgeons were working on the wounded. So far, there were no fatalities. By now heavy fire was coming from the control tower where, earlier on, the guards had fallen for the 'Amin' ruse. Colonel Netanyahu and his assault party hurried off to deal with it, and they were soon attacking it with machine-gun fire and bazookas. It was at this point that one of the two tragedies of the Entebbe affair occurred. During the exchange of fire with the Ugandan in the tower, and seconds before the bazooka shells smashed it into fragments, Netanyahu was hit in the back. He was carried to a Hercules, but he died shortly afterwards. He was the only member of the raiding party to be killed.

The other victim of Entebbe was a 75-year-old lady named Mrs Dora Bloch. While she was under guard in the airport terminal, she had choked on a morsel of food. The Ugandans had removed her to hospital. Since she held dual British-Israeli nationality, she was visited by Mr Peter Chandley of the British Embassy on the day following the rescue operation. She seemed to be comfortable; she was asleep and a nurse told him that her condition had improved.

One hour later, Mr Chandley returned to the hospital to bring her some food. Her bed was empty. When he asked where she was, somebody told him that she had driven back to the airport on the previous night. This, of course, was ridiculous. He looked into the matter and discovered that, shortly after his earlier visit, Mrs Bloch had been taken from her bed by four of Amin's bully boys, dragged screaming along a corridor, and (it had to be assumed) been murdered. When Mr Chandley reported the results of his investigation, he was dismissed as a liar by Amin and expelled from Uganda.

Taking off in a fully laden Hercules on a shortish runway without any airport lights for guidance is not the easiest of tasks. In one instances, a co-pilot had to lean out of a flight-deck window to guide his captain along the white line, lit by a thin moon, that marked the centre of the tarmac. The operation itself necessitated a complicated balancing act between the engines and the ailerons, which is strictly not for beginners.

When the 'Hippos' landed at Entebbe, each had enough fuel for ninety minutes' flight in its tanks. The original plan had been to refuel from Ugandan stocks; but, by the time everything was ready for departure, the situation had become too violent. Nairobi was fifty minutes' flying time away. It would be better to wait until then.

Operation 'Thunderbolt' was on its way home. The hostages had been rescued; the raiders had suffered amazingly few casualties; all the components, even the black Mercedes (later restored to its original white at the insistence of its owner) were intact. The impossible, or something very close to it, had been achieved. Israel's honour was secure; the prestige of 'big Daddy' Amin had taken another tumble. Speed and the unexpected had triumphed again.

The breed of men who used to go ashore on hostile coasts under the cover of darkness lived on—though they now came out of the sky. The enemy had changed; the circumstances were greatly different. But the raiders of today are cast in the same mould as their military forefathers. They are, indeed, not so very far removed from the Egyptian soldiers who, under Captain Thute, occupied Jaffa in the 15th century BC.

Bibliography

Bowen, A., *The Naval Monument*, 1836
Brown, Anthony Cave, *Bodyguard of Lives*, 1976
Churchill, Winston S., *Their Finest Hour*, 1949
Churchill, Winston S., *The Grand Alliance*, 1950
Churchill, Winston S., *The Hinge of Fate*, 1951
Cochrane, Thomas, 10th Earl of Dundonald, *The Autobiography of a Seaman*—Vol 1, 1860
Coles, Harry L., *The War of 1812*, 1965
Collier, Richard, *Duce—the Rise and Fall of Benito Mussolini*, 1971
Davie, Michael (Editor), *The Diaries of Evelyn Waugh*, 1976
Dobson, Christopher and Payne, Ronald, *The Carlos Complex*, 1977
Gunther, Harold W., and Shalla, James R., *'E' Company, 2nd Ranger Battalion*, c1946
Heilbrunn, Otto, *Warfare in the Enemy's Rear*, 1963
Hillegas, H. C., *With the Boer Forces*, 1900
Humble, Richard, *Before the Dreadnought*, 1976
Jackson, H. M. Lieutenant-Colonel, *Rogers Rangers*
James, William, *James Naval Occurrences*, 1817
James, William, *The Naval History of Great Britain*, 1902
Kelly, Francis J. Colonel, *U.S. Army Special Forces 1961–71*, 1973
Ladd, James, *Commandos and Rangers of World War II*, 1978
Lund, Paul and Ludlam, Harry, *The War of the Landing Craft*, 1976
Marryat, Florence, *The Life and Letters of Captain Marryat*, 1896
Marryat, Frederick, *Frank Mildmay—or the Naval Officer*, 1872
McElwee, *The Art of War*, 1974
Millar, George, *The Bruneval Raid*, 1974

Mosby, John, *The Memoirs of Colonel John S. Mosby*, 1917

Napier, Sir Charles, *The History of the Baltic Campaign of 1854*, 1857

Pienaar, Phil, *With Styn and de Bret*, 1902

Pitt, Barrie, *Zeebrugge*, 1958

Robertson, Terence, *Dieppe—the Shame and the Glory*, 1963

Ryan, Cornelius, *The Longest Day*, 1960

Saunders, Hilary St. George, *The Green Beret*, 1949

Schellenberg, Walter, *The Schellenberg Memoirs*, 1956

Schemmer, Benjamin, *The Raid*, 1976

Simmons, Edwin H. Brigadier-General, *The United States Marines 1775–1975*

Skorzeny, Otto, *Skorzeny's Special Mission*, 1957

Stevens, E. H., (Editor) *The Trial of von Falkenhorst*, 1949

Stevenson, William, *90 minutes at Entebbe*, 1976

Thomas, Donald, *Cochrane—Britannia's Last Sea-King*, 1978

Updegraph, Charles L. Jnr, *U.S. Marine Corps Special Units of World War II*, 1972

Warner, Oliver, *The Sea and the Sword*, 1965

Warner, Philip, *The Zeebrugge Raid*, 1978

Young, Peter, *Commando*, 1970

Index